P9-BBV-924

NOTE FROM THE PUBLISHER

Often when we have a new author with a new concept, we ask for a foreword by a respected authority in the field. We feel this book is important enough to receive a different type of treatment, since the authorities in this field are really all of us, people like you and me, in all walks of life—communicating in business and in relationships. We have given a sampling of respected leaders advance copies. Here's what they say:

"Likability, believability, and trust, the path to making contact with the emotions, is Bert Decker's practical formula for successful communications. When I follow Bert's advice, I connect with my audience."

—Phillip J. Quigley, President, Pacific Bell

"I wish that every teacher I've had, every lecturer, every presenter, had read and heeded the lessons of the First (emotional) Brain. It's refreshing to see the latest findings of brain and behavioral science brought to such practical, everyday use. If you have anything to say, anything to teach, anyone to convince, you owe it to yourself and others to energize your communications by learning how to make an emotional connection—the message of *You've Got To Be Believed To Be Heard*."

—Dr. David S. Sobel, Regional Director,
Patient Education, Kaiser Permanente

"This is a fantastic book. Bert Decker has taken a very critical characteristic of success and made it fun and exciting. From my experience as Chief Executive of four different companies I've seen that effective communication is the common denominator for great successes. *You've Got To Be Believed To Be Heard* places communication in a very imaginative and clever manner that is thought provoking for our universal need to become effective managers. This book should be added to the 'must' reading list."

—Charles A. Lynch, Chairman, Market Value Partners
(former chairman of DHL, Levolor, and Saga Food)

"I have probably bought 1,000 of the 1,001 books on speaking. *You've Got To Be Believed To Be Heard* is THE book. It contains a big idea that everyone should know about, whether they speak professionally, as I do, or not."

—Patricia Fripp, CPAE, Past President,
National Speakers Association

"Bert Decker gives you so much more than just a 'format' for your next speech or interview. He builds in you a capability and confidence to communicate with others effectively every day, in every situation."

—Paul Hazen, President, Wells Fargo Bank

"Using fundamental brian mechanisms, Bert Decker shows that effective communication involves our personality in all its manifestations. Anyone, businessman or professional, should read it."

—John W. Harbison, M.D. Chairman,
Department of Neurology, Medical College of Virginia

"Bert Decker's use of the latest research in Neuroscience will help all who read his book. It gives an excellent scientific explanation of what effective communicators have known intuitively for generations."

—Dr. Leonard M. Shlain, Surgeon, Pacific Presbyterian Hospital, San Francisco; Author, *Art and Physics*

"Cocktail parties to conference rooms, nabobs to neighbors, Bert's book steamrolls those impenetrable barriers to communication. By tackling this complex subject and reducing it to enjoyable, easy-to-read, informative vignettes, he proves his point— he communicates! This book is going to help a lot of people."

—Ben Sottile, Chairman, CEO, Gibson Greetings, Inc.

"*You've Got To Be Believed To Be Heard* is an exciting book—I read it cover to cover on a flight between New York and San Francisco. Couldn't put it down. Bert Decker communicates as well in print as he does in person. His ideas are relevant and immediately useful. The relationship between First Brain intuition and establishing trust is a concept that alone is worth the price of the book."

—Steve Heiman, Author, *Strategic Selling*, Chairman, Miller-Heiman

"I recommend it without qualification. I found the book immensely confirming and immensely helpful. I read it in two sittings, which is most unusual for me. I do not tend to get caught up in books generally, for so few have much new information. In addition, so few are really a joy to read. It leaves my mind changed from just reading it. I especially enjoyed the First Brain/New Brain concept. I learned a great deal from that."

—Harville Hendrix, Author, *Getting the Love You Want: A Guide for Couples*

"When you finish reading this book, your only regret will be that you didn't have the opportunity to read it earlier in your career. But it is never too late to learn to communicate effectively."

—James A. Vohs, Chairman/CEO, Kaiser Permanente

"There are people (like me) who started reading speech texts and learned we might as well be shouting at the deaf. Making as much intelligible sound as one hand clapping. Conveying as much emotion as a signpost. Some of us were exposed to the Decker Method of communicating and discovered we not only had something to say; people were ready to receive the messages. *You've Got To Be Believed To Be Heard* understands that the world is too busy to allow boring people to succeed. Fortunately, the book speaks emphatically to those who would be heard."

—Reg Murphy, Publisher, *The Baltimore Sun*

"Communicate he said, and communicate he did! Bert Decker opens everyone's eyes to the need to be believable in everyday communications."

—Robert E. Wall, President, Advanced Interventional Systems, Inc.

"Bert Decker has done it! He's explained speaking—in writing—in such an engaging 'way with words' that even the most speech-phobic individual will want to try it."

—Dr. Ellyn Bader, Ph.D., Clinical Psychologist, Coauthor,
In Search of the Mythical Mate, Director, The Couples Institute

"To really make it happen in communication you have to connect emotionally. Bert not only shows us how, he connects with his audience in this fast paced book—a must for every one in developing and utilizing their interpersonal skills for their business and personal lives."

—Jack P. Edwards, President/CEO, Itel Rail Corporation

"At a time when American companies desperately need to communicate well and energize their people while producing leaders at all levels, Bert Decker provides an empowering guidebook for communicating well to succeed in business. . . . A perfect blend of wisdom and practical experience."

—Charles Garfield, Author of *Peak Performance*
and *Second to None*

"The concept of the First Brain and its role as the gatekeeper—making initial decisions as to whether people can be trusted—opened for me a whole new way to understand how people established and maintain relationships. Decker has helped to identify these processes in a way that will lead to greater clarity and effectiveness as I work with people."

—Dr. James P. Osterhaus, Clinical Psychologist, Director,
CPC Counseling Center, Author, *Counseling Families*

"All of the Sprouse-Reitz associates who experienced Decker Communications' training have been empowered, and *You've Got To Be Believed To Be Heard* will bring the same self-confidence and effectiveness to thousands more. It is full of new insights and important information."

—Robert A. Sprouse II, Chairman, Sprouse-Reitz Stores, Inc.

"If you want to learn to lead, you must read this book. Bert hits it spot on the mark. If you read this book and put it into practice, you are certain to develop a more solid foundation for your leadership aspirations."

—James M. Kouzes, Coauthor, *The Leadership Challenge*,
President, TPG/Learning Systems

"Communication is the sure way to motivate an audience or an individual to action. And Bert Decker really communicates in his very 'with it' book, *You've Got To Be Believed To Be Heard*. The sentences are alive and vital. He lifts the mind and thereby upgrades performance. I prophesy it will be a winner for it says something and says it powerfully."

—Dr. Norman Vincent Peale

"It will take you more than a minute to read *You've Got To Be Believed To Be Heard*, but it is worth every second. Bert Decker makes communicating come alive in a way that will help you connect with others in a meaningful way. A must read!"

—Ken Blanchard, Ph.D., Coauthor, *The One Minute Manager*

"Full of insights and great ideas—Bert activated my First Brain. Even the most seasoned speaker will find some gems in this book. He creates a new concept with the First Brain that is really useful. Drives his points home with great examples— principles through illustration. A very good read."

—Roger von Oech, Author, *A Whack On The Side Of The Head*

"Nothing assures success in life as much as the ability to speak well in public. Nothing. And nobody has packed as much useful information about the art of public speaking into one book as Bert Decker. If you want to get ahead, read Decker's masterpiece, *You've Got To Be Believed To Be Heard*. It's a great book. I enjoyed it and learned a lot."

—Al Ries, Author, *Positioning*, Chairman, Trout & Ries

"Bert Decker is to communicating what Tom Peters is to management. Whether connecting with an audience of one or one of thousands, *You've Got To Be Believed To Be Heard* must be your partner. Bert's book is the definitive work on mastering communications. Buy it, own it, write in it . . . and don't loan it out!"

—Judith Briles, Author, *The Confidence Factor* and *Woman to Woman*

"Great book! Lots of practical, easy to use and invaluable information, tips and techniques that will enable anyone to maximize their communication skills. Everyone should have a copy on their desk."

—Robert J. Kriegel, Author, *If It Ain't Broke . . . Break It!*

YOU'VE GOT TO
BE BELIEVED
TO BE HEARD

YOU'VE GOT TO BE BELIEVED TO BE HEARD

Bert Decker
with James Denney

ST. MARTIN'S PRESS
NEW YORK

"Threads" by James A. Autry, from *For Love & Profit*. Copyright © 1991 by William Morrow and Company. Reprinted by permission of William Morrow and Company.

YOU'VE GOT TO BE BELIEVED TO BE HEARD. Copyright © 1992 by Bert Decker. All rights reserved. Printed in the United States of America. No part of this book may be used or reproduced in any manner whatsoever without written permission except in the case of brief quotations embodied in critical articles or reviews. For information, address St. Martin's Press, 175 Fifth Avenue, New York, N.Y. 10010

Production Editor: David Stanford Burr

Illustrations by Ben Barbante

Cover Photo by Peggy Parks

Book Design Erich Hobbing

Queries can be directed to:
800–547–0050

Decker Communications, Inc.
44 Montgomery Street
San Francisco, CA 94104
415–391–5544.

Library of Congress Cataloging-in-Publication Data

Decker, Bert.
    You've got to be believed to be heard : reach the first brain to
communicate in business and in life / Bert Decker.
        p.   cm.
      ISBN 0-312-06935-9/HC   ISBN 0-312-09949-5/PB
      1. Oral communication.   2. Business communication.   I. Title.
P95.D4   1992
302.2'242—dc20

91-37859
CIP

10 9 8 7 6 5 4

This book is dedicated to my dad, Milt Decker,
and my late wife, Deborah Cain Decker.

I only wish they both could be here now to share in its completion, because
they both had so much to do with its creation.

Contents

Preface

The reason that an author's appreciation of specific individuals comes at the front of a book is because the book wouldn't have happened without them. At least that's the way it is for my book.

And there is no question that the biggest thanks of all are to my family. To my lovely and loving wife, Dru Scott, and my very special children, Allison, Sam, and Ben. They are the ones who have sacrificed the most in giving up the time and attention that is required by the birthing of a book. I also appreciate their encouragement and understanding. Instead of being complainers, they have been my cheerleaders.

I had a bonus as well. In addition to being my wife, Dru is also a best-selling author and a dynamic speaker—successful long before I met her. I have learned much from her in our mutual work, and in our relationship I have learned much about how to be a better human being.

All the people at Decker Communications, Inc., have been extremely helpful, but special thanks are due my great friend and great manager, Dan Toth. As president and chief operating officer of our company, he runs it so I can write and speak. And he runs it well.

I am indebted to Terry Lee, my trusted, loyal, and talented cohort who has always provided both support and encouragement, and has been there from the beginning. And to my training and speaking partner, Fred Verhey, who has been there almost from the beginning, I am indebted as well.

To those in the publishing world who first had faith: Mark Joly, my agent at Scott Meredith Literary Agency who believed in this book and sold it, and to George Witte, my editor at St. Martin's Press, who bought the concept and the book, and helped mold it. It is a continuing pleasure to work with these men.

Perhaps most important to the core of the book are the thanks due to the input and feedback over the past decade from the two dozen people on the Decker training staff. It is in this cauldron of our training programs that the refinement of these ideas has been hammered out, and I am grateful to have been blessed with such warm, generous, and smart people to work with. And just as important to the framing, forming, and molding of the ideas have been the many thousands of participants in my programs, speeches, and consultings. Without you, there would be no book of substance—just empty theories.

Some special thanks: To Chuck Schwab, who has been as good a mentor as one could hope for. His advice in starting and running a company has been invaluable. I have learned a lot from him, and his support and encouragement have been most generous and helpful. And the critical "big idea" in this book would not exist in its present form without Harville Hendrix. At the beginning of his book, *Getting the Love You Want*, he makes a brief reference to the impact of the "Old Brain" in choosing one's mate. This was a major catalyst for the First Brain concept in my book. I am deeply indebted for that singular inspiration.

Finally, a massive thanks to Jim Denney, the man who helped impart whatever color and life the words give this book. Jim was more than a collaborator, although he did that. He was and is a writer of great humor and intellect. To work with him was more than a pleasure, it was an experience. We did the entire editing (on our incompatible IBM and Macintosh computers) using CompuServe, and I always looked forward to receiving his messages and asides, as well as his edited copy. He did a truly great job. One regret in finishing this book is that I won't have Jim Denney's messages on CompuServe to look forward to every day. At least until the next book.

Bert Decker
Danville, California
August 1, 1991

Introduction

One of those rare communication events occurred at the end of the 1991 Gulf War. General H. Norman Schwarzkopf gave a press briefing so powerful and memorable it was replayed *in its entirety* by several of the major networks. That briefing turned a military leader into a hot media star! Was it a fluke—just one more example of Andy Warhol's fifteen minutes of instant and fleeting fame? I don't think so.

Immediately after he returned from the Gulf, Schwarzkopf's ability to communicate was tested. He addressed a joint session of Congress, to repeated ovations. At his West Point commencement speech he was "by turn, funny, profane and blunt as he threw away a prepared speech, abandoned the lectern and stalked back and forth across the stage of Eisenhower Hall telling the new generation what he thought and what he believed." He made personal appearances all over; standing arm-in-arm with Mickey Mouse in Orlando, Florida; serving as Grand Marshal of the Mother of All Parades in New York City; riding in the pace car at the Indy 500 on Memorial Day. Schwarzkopf has been offered over $5 million for his memoirs, a record for nonfiction, and is already one of the highest-paid public speakers in the country at $60,000 a crack!

Why? Is it only because he won a war? Hardly. Sure, he's a great general, but there have been many other leaders who have had nowhere near the impact of this man. Why?

Because he knows how to *communicate*. Effectively. Powerfully. Persuasively. He is above all believable. He reaches us on an emotional level. He reaches that part of our mind that reacts to feeling and emotion and openness and enthusiasm—that part of our mind that I call the First Brain. He makes *personal contact* with his listeners, and in the best American tradition he is rapidly parlaying his ability to communicate into wealth and success.

And he does all this without even having to look the part of a battle-hardened general! In the film version of his life, General Douglas MacArthur was portrayed by Gregory Peck. Who will play Schwarzkopf? Jonathan Winters? Willard Scott? Clearly, a dashing physique and leading-man good looks have not been factors in Norman Schwarzkopf's success. And he is not unique in this regard.

John Madden is a comfortably homely and overweight ex-coach in the National Football League—yet he makes multimegabucks as a sportscaster and advertising spokesman. By contrast Bill Walsh is an ex-coach who also happens to be legendary, photogenic, and a certified football genius with three Super Bowls to his credit—yet his earnings from sportscasting and endorsements amount to small change compared to Madden. Why?

Because Madden reaches our First Brain; Walsh doesn't.

What is the single most important factor that determined who won and who lost in almost all, if not all, of the presidential elections since Kennedy-Nixon in 1960?

Those who won reached our First Brain. Those who lost didn't.

Now the most important question for you: How can you get that promotion or better-paying job, make that critical sale, find that richer relationship, that greater sense of accomplishment and satisfaction in life?

By discovering the power of the First Brain.

This book is about a discovery that puts enormous power in your hands—the power to become more effective in every arena of your life, the power to achieve what you want in life. It is this discovery that I call the First Brain.

"First Brain" is the secret of believability, essential to effective, persuasive communication. The First Brain is the secret to attaining mastery of the direction of your personal and professional life. The First Brain is our emotional brain. It is real. It is physical. And it is powerful. Neglect it, ignore it, fail to realize and harness its power—and most likely you will fail to communicate effectively. Understand it, and you will connect in your communications. You will have *emotional contact* with your listeners.

This book is about a new model of communications. Today is no longer an era when oratory and rhetoric flourish, when the stentorian impact of a Winston Churchill thrives. There are no Churchills today—there are the Norman Schwarzkopfs. And as we'll see, there is a reason. We need a different model of communicator—and you can learn to be one, simply by putting the principles of this book into practice.

In this book you will learn how to use the power of the First Brain to reach and persuade an audience of one—or an audience of thousands.

You will also learn how to master your own First Brain to overcome the fear of speaking under pressure—an anxiety we all face to some degree. (And I do mean *all* of us.)

Speaking before groups is my life, my bread-and-butter—but I know what the fear of "public speaking" feels like. I've learned how to overcome that fear and use those driving emotions in a positive way. I guarantee that you can learn it, too.

I'm going to show you what I have learned—partly through trial and error, but mostly through experience and intensive research—about how to effectively and confidently reach, persuade, and motivate with the spoken word. For the past twenty-five years, I have literally immersed myself in the world of spoken communications. Every week I find myself in dozens of speaking situations, addressing audiences ranging from small-group seminars to several thousand conventioneers. My company has offices in cities across the U.S., with seventy-five people training tens of thousands of executives and professionals on how to have greater personal impact in all their communicating situations, from one-on-one meetings to business presentations to formal speeches.

This is the crucible in which my ideas have been framed, formed, molded, tested, and refined. In these pages, I will share these practical ideas with you, and *prove* to you that they *work*. With real-life examples I will show you how they have worked not only for me, but for the more than fifty thousand business and professional people who have been trained in the Decker Method™.

Most importantly, I will show you how they can work for *you*.

When you've finished this book, you will have the tools for success that some of the top political, professional, and business leaders in the nation have paid thousands of dollars to obtain. No longer will you have to rely on a tortuous process of trial and error to learn what works and what doesn't. Now you can have the advantage of knowing your strengths and weaknesses, of knowing how to really reach people with your message. By applying the discoveries in this book, you will gain the edge you need to get what you want out of your career and your personal life.

By the end of this book, I strongly believe you'll "think First Brain" in every communicating situation you're in. But don't worry about having to wade through a lot of technical jargon or scientific ideas. This is not a "brain book." It's a practical book and reader-friendly in every way. It's a book you can put to immediate use to make yourself more effective in every aspect of your life.

The New Communicators begin the story. Read on to see how your story can be like theirs.

"When the conduct of men is designed to be influenced,
persuasion, kind, unassuming persuasion, should ever be adopted.
It is an old and a true maxim that a drop of honey
catches more flies than a gallon of gall. So with men.
If you would win a man to your cause, first convince him
that you are his sincere friend. Therein is a drop of honey that
catches his heart, which, say what he will, is the great
high road to his reason, and which, once gained,
you will find but little trouble in convincing his judgment
of the justice of your cause,
if indeed that cause really be a just one. On the contrary,
assume to dictate to his judgment, or to command his action . . .
and he will retreat within himself, close all the avenues
to his head and his heart . . .
Such is man, and so must he be understood
by those who would lead him . . . "

ABRAHAM LINCOLN, 1842

"In my library are about a thousand volumes
of biography—a rough calculation indicates
that more of these deal with men who have
talked themselves upward than with all the
scientists, writers, saints and doers combined.
Talkers have always ruled.
They will continue to rule.
The smart thing is to join them."

BRUCE BARTON (1886–1967)

Scholar, editor, author, congressman, sales executive, businessman, and founder of the
ad agency Batten, Barton, Durstine and Osborne.

Part I

THE EMOTIONAL CONNECTION

1

The New
Communicators

SNATCHING DEFEAT FROM THE JAWS OF VICTORY

The knowledge you need in order to communicate persuasively and effectively is actually very simple. Yet some of the best and the brightest didn't have it.

Take, for example, Governor Michael Dukakis's 1988 race for the White House. Now there was a defeat! Dukakis was a very bright and capable candidate, surrounded by bright and capable advisors. But he didn't have the elementary secret to communicating effectively and persuasively—and he blew his shot at the number one CEO job in the world. (Walter Mondale did almost the same thing four years earlier.)

A bright and gifted congresswoman named Pat Schroeder didn't have this knowledge either—and her bid for the White House ended before it even began.

It eluded sports megastar Bill Walsh—and he lost the opportunity to make millions in product endorsements.

Do you know who Katherine Ortega is? Probably not (even though you probably see her name every day), because she missed it too.

As I write, Dan Rather continues to carry on without it, singlehandedly dooming the "CBS Evening News" to the ratings cellar. If Rather isn't out of his anchorman job by the time you read this, he probably will be soon.

Do you think I'm exaggerating? Dramatizing yes; exaggerating no. I'm not about to call a noted politician, a famous sports star, or a network news anchor a "failure," but I am saying that they lack a key piece of the communications puzzle. And they suffer for it.

The fact is, all the aforementioned professionals missed the opportunity to multiply their success many times over because they didn't know the secret of the New Communicators—a secret so simple that once it is grasped, anyone can take advantage of it.

I can hear somebody out there saying, "But I'm not in the public eye." Not so! Unless you are a cave-dwelling hermit, you *are* in the public eye. Your face may not be a fixture on the evening news, but you can't deny you meet other people eyeball-to-eyeball on a daily basis.

We are *all* in the public eye. We may not be in the White House or earn millions in product endorsements or anchor a network news show. But we all have a lot at stake. Your next job. Or that promotion. Or that big sale. Or that raise. Or your relationship with your kids. Or your marriage.

Clearly, the ability to communicate is the single most important skill determining your success in life.

So why did Dukakis, Schroeder, Walsh, Rather, and Co. miss the boat? Simply because they failed to understand that *communicating is a contact sport*. They failed to make emotional contact with their audience. They failed to reach the hearts as well as the minds of their listeners. More specifically, they failed to reach the "heart of the mind"—what I call the First Brain—the emotional part of the mind. (As we'll see later, there really is a "heart" in the head.) Let's look at the specific cases.

The $60,000,000 Mistake

The people in the Dukakis campaign spent $60,000,000 trying to get their man elected—and they lost. Why? Following the triumphant conclusion of a rousing and harmonious convention, Dukakis was seventeen points ahead of George Bush in the polls. The Dukakis TV ads were slick, well-produced, and forceful.

Just before the Bush-Dukakis debates in the fall of 1988, polls showed the country considered Democrat Dukakis more knowledgeable than Republican Bush. This perception was later summed up by *Time's* Washington correspondent David Beckwith, who observed that Bush does not possess "a keen intellect," that he "has never been known for imaginative ideas, probing insights, or creative brilliance." By contrast, a *Time* profile of Dukakis extolled his "intelligence," his "smartness," his "keenness of mind."

After the debates, political professionals polled both radio and TV audiences to find out who won. They found that radio listeners gave the debate to Dukakis. Dukakis won on debating points. He won among those who only *heard* what he had to say.

"THE MAN WHO SEALS OFF EMOTION"

During the thick of the 1988 presidential primary, *Newsweek* did a profile on Democratic front-runner Michael Dukakis. The magazine found him to be "the Mr. Spock of politics, a totally rational alien. . . . He is often put down as a colorless drone—an 'earnest nerd,' 'poetic as a slide rule,' a 'word processor,' of a politician. If he were a car, somebody said, he would be a Honda Civic, economical, reliable, completely unexciting."

A similar Dukakis profile in *Time* was headlined, "THE MAN WHO SEALS OFF EMOTION" where " . . . the Duke's political handlers plead with him, 'Let some feeling out, Michael, please!'

"Dukakis has learned well how to bury his feelings. In early campaigns his manager, Francis Meaney, used to stand close behind him and remind Dukakis to tell voters he needed them. The candidate was always too impersonal. . . . Would he be able, as President, to give up some of that distance and reach out and grab what he will really need from other people? Is there something beneath that metallic surface to persuade others that at heart his instincts are generous and truly human? Can Dukakis, a man who seals off his emotional responses, establish an emotional connection that moves the country? . . .

"Americans crave that kind of connection with the person of the President."

But the overwhelming majority of the Bush-Dukakis audience was watching on television, not just listening to the radio. And the television audience rated Bush the victor. According to the *Los Angeles Times* the poll was 47 to 26 percent, and CBS showed 48 to 25 percent. By the fateful second Tuesday in November, Bush had beaten Dukakis 54 to 46 percent.

What's more, the Bush-Dukakis debates were a virtual replay of the Reagan-Mondale debates of the previous election. In both cases, the debates were considered decisive to the election results. In both cases, the Democratic candidate was considered the more knowledgeable, better prepared, and perhaps even smarter debater. In both cases, the

Democratic candidate "won" the debate, according to those who heard it on radio, but soundly lost the debate with TV viewers—and the electorate.

Why? As a society, we claim to respect intelligence, knowledge, and expertise—all of which should have given Dukakis and Mondale an edge, according to the polls. And it had nothing to do with party affiliation, for in sheer numbers of registered voters, the Democrats had yet another edge.

What happened was that Bush and Reagan understood what Dukakis and Mondale totally missed: Communicating is a contact sport.

Speaking of Sports . . .

Bill Walsh is not only one of the most successful National Football League coaches of all time, but he has been called a "football genius." He won three Super Bowls with the San Francisco 49ers, a team that he built from scratch. A technically precise, flawlessly gifted leader, Walsh is also handsome and photogenic. A brilliant mind, with experience, good looks, and phenomenal success in the trenches—the perfect

Bill Walsh (AP/Wide World Photos)

combination for a second career as a sportscaster on TV, right? Actually, no. Walsh is cerebral all right, but he rarely smiles, shows little emotion, and has a nasal voice. He has limited advertising endorsements, and NBC is now wondering what to do with his contract. I recently overheard a football fan, a 49er fanatic no less, say, "He's got to get back in football and out of the public eye." If only Bill Walsh knew that communicating—like football—is a contact sport.

Jack Nicklaus won his first U.S. amateur golf championship in 1959, and his first Masters tournament in 1963. He's still going strong in the 1990s. More than a golfing champion, he is a sports legend. "The Golden Bear," as he is called, has great natural ability and power as a golfer. But as a communicator he's more of a tamed tabby—with a high voice that undermines his expected authority. He's a great golfer, and because of his talent on the course he is certainly *seen* in some TV endorsements. But he's not *heard* very much. He's successful and well respected, but because of his voice his personal exposure and endorsement dollars are not what they could be.

If the most successful and handsome stars of sports can't sell your product, then who do you turn to? Would you hire, say, a lumbering side of beef, a guy with a face that would make a freight train take a dirt road? Would you hire a guy who's hard to schedule because he travels everywhere by bus or train and refuses to fly? Would you hire a guy who quit as coach of the Oakland Raiders? (A good coach, but no superstar.) Would you hire John Madden to sell your product?

As I'm sure you're aware, Miller Lite beer did hire John Madden, and the result was one of the most successful, effective, and long-running series of commercials ever.

Madden didn't plan a career as a communicator and product pitchman. Upon retiring from football coaching in 1979, he figured he'd go into real estate with a friend. His first day on the job, he spent a few hours in line at the town hall in Pleasanton, California, waiting to get a sewer permit for a shopping mall. That was his first and last day in real estate.

While Madden was wondering what to do next, two things happened: He was approached by CBS executives, who wanted to team Madden with Pat Summerall in the broadcast booth, and he was approached by the agency in charge of the Miller Lite commercials. He accepted both jobs, and now earns around a million a year from CBS, plus enough from Miller Lite to feed and house a family of ten until the next Ice Age. He was offered—and turned down—the origi-

John Madden (AP/Wide World Photos)

nal role of Coach on "Cheers," as well as the role John Candy played opposite Steve Martin in *Planes, Trains and Automobiles.* (Ironically, Madden fears planes. So CBS Sports gives free rein to his travel on the custom-made Greyhound bus—the $500,000 Madden-cruiser.)

Today, John Madden is a superstar—not because of his coaching ability, but because he is a New Communicator. He's honest, natural, likable, and believable. His fame rests not so much on his sports career as on his career in Miller Lite commercials. Today, though he has endorsed products ranging from Toyotas to antihistamines to motor oil, it is still the beer that made John Madden famous—and vice versa. Today, people recognize him on the street and shout, "Less filling!"— to which he enthusiastically responds, "Tastes great!" Here's a coach who knows a contact sport when he sees one—and I don't mean football.

And of course there's the phenomenon of Michael Jordan. Sure, he's an amazing basketball player, but is that the only reason that he *heads the list* of sports-endorsement income leaders? Not likely. In 1991

Michael Jordan not only won as most valuable player when his Chicago Bulls won the NBA championship, but with his smile and winning manner he won the hearts of the American public. He connects with people. And that translates to $11 million in 1992 endorsements to top the megastars in *all* sports.

Michael Jordan and John Madden are proof that being at the top of your profession is not necessarily what gets you the recognition, applause, and big money you're looking for. That sure counts, but it's also essential to be liked, believed, and trusted. It's a matter of making emotional contact.

The Posture of a Candidate

September 28, 1987 was supposed to be Kickoff Day for Patricia Schroeder's campaign for President of the United States. Over 2,000 supporters had gathered around a platform outside the Denver Civic Center to hear Schroeder's announcement. She had already traveled 75,000 miles, visited 29 states, and delivered scores of stump speeches. But instead of announcing her formal candidacy (she had already had an informal candidacy for four months), she told the crowd, "I learned a lot about America and a lot about Pat Schroeder. And that's why I will not be a candidate for President."

The crowd groaned in disappointment. Schroeder wept in defeat.

Why did Pat Schroeder stumble in her brief run for the White House? She was highly visible, articulate, and intelligent (Phi Beta Kappa and magna cum laude from the University of Minnesota, as well as a Harvard Law grad). Yet her campaign was a resounding dud. Why?

The essential reason can be found in a *Washington Post* article. A month before Schroeder's campaign demise the *Post* quoted Lucy Mattix, a Raleigh, North Carolina, political activist, as saying she was "very impressed with (Schroeder's) grasp of defense issues and her willingness to take on the powers that be. But I think she needs some work on her presentation. She slumps . . . and her voice jumps around. She is not very presidential."

In other words, Schroeder is smart, she's politically aggressive, but in her voice, her manner, and her bearing, she fails to make emotional contact with her audience. She misses the connection to the power that persuades.

"A Silver Foot in His Mouth"

Ever hear of Katherine Ortega? Probably not. But I'll bet you a dollar you're carrying around a dollar with her signature in your wallet. She was the Treasurer of the United States during the Reagan years, and her signature is on every Federal Reserve Note printed during her term.

The Republican Party chose Katherine Ortega to give the keynote address at the 1984 Republican convention. It was a mistake for the Republicans and a tragedy for Ortega—not because of what she did, but what she didn't do.

She didn't communicate. She read words on paper. She spoke in a monotone. She nervously looked down at her notes. She bored the audience. She flopped. Within a very short time, both Ortega and her speech were forgotten.

Compare her story with that of Ann Richards, the state treasurer of Texas. In 1988, the Democrats gave Richards the same assignment the Republicans had given Ortega in '84—keynote speaker for the party's convention.

When Richards got on the platform, she didn't read a speech. She made contact—sizzling, emotional contact—with an audience of millions, both on the convention floor and via television. She was funny, folksy, feisty, and confident as she peppered the opposition party with a volley of stinging barbs (including the famous assault on George Bush as being "born with a silver foot in his mouth"). The press and the public loved her, so much so that they elected her governor of Texas. She became a national figure largely because of one speech. Because she communicates, she makes contact. She plugs into the power that persuades.

Would You Rather Have Rather?

Remember Walter Cronkite? Candid, reassuring old Walter is like a favorite uncle (or grandfather) to most of us. The polls continue to find him the most trusted man in America. He wept on camera the day JFK was shot. He could tell you the world is ending tomorrow, and somehow you'd feel everything will still turn out all right.

After Cronkite retired, CBS picked feisty, astringent Dan Rather of "60 Minutes" to take his place. Certainly, Rather had the experience, visibility, and credentials to deliver the news. In highly charged confrontations with Presidents, and in the combative "60 Minutes" arena, Rather had proved he could make the airwaves crackle with electricity. But the moment he sat down in the anchor chair, something was missing. Viewers sensed it, and quickly defected to ABC and NBC. The ratings for "The CBS Evening News with Dan Rather" plummeted.

The CBS brass panicked. Something was wrong with their star newsman, and they didn't know what it was or how to fix it. They tried softening his image by dressing him in fuzzy sweaters. They added snazzy computer graphics and built a new set around him. They took away his desk and had him read the news standing up. In short, they changed everything but what really needed to be changed: Dan Rather himself.

What's wrong with Dan Rather? Just this: There's very little emotional connection between Rather and the viewer. He looks affected, distant, and aloof. His upper lip stiffens when he talks, giving him

Dan Rather (AP/Wide World Photos)

the appearance of holding something back. These are not things a viewer would ordinarily perceive at the conscious level—but we're talking about a dimension of communication that takes place at an unconscious level. We're talking about trust, believability, and likability—the emotional connection.

"A COMBUSTIBLE CHARACTER IN THE COOLEST OF MEDIUMS"

Time magazine offered its appraisal of Dan Rather: "Combative and high-strung, Dan Rather remains more reporter than anchorman. . . . Rather has never seemed completely comfortable in the anchor chair. A courtly and painstakingly polite man in person, he seems stiff and tense on camera. Even his attempts at spontaneity and good humor look programmed. One week he tried ending his broadcast with the sign-off 'Courage'; widespread derision forced him to drop it after three nights. Walter Cronkite, Rather's predecessor, was calm and reassuring, an avuncular figure to the nation. Rather seems tightly coiled and uneasy, an eccentric cousin capable of almost anything . . .

"Once he took possession of Uncle Walter's chair, Rather experienced a rough ride. Ratings began to dip, and CBS's image makers began tinkering with Rather's dress and demeanor. Early on, they put him in sweaters in an effort to soften his intensity. For a while, Rather tried hard to be warm and homespun, his writing full of purple prose and corny puns. (Before the start of the Reykjavík summit, he announced, 'Ready, set, Gorbachev.') Later he reverted, with equal strain, to a straitlaced, sober, almost glum delivery . . ."

During the 1988 presidential primary campaign, Rather engaged in a live, hot-tempered exchange with candidate George Bush, ending when Rather abruptly cut off the Vice-President in mid-reply. Said *Time*, "The tightly coiled anchorman, a combustible character in the coolest of mediums, seemed almost to spring out of his chair, unsettling his audience with high-voltage intensity."

The magazine went on to contrast the Bush-Rather exchange with an interview of Soviet leader Mikhail Gorbachev by NBC's Tom Brokaw, terming the latter encounter ". . . deferential, dignified, comforting. . . .

"Says Rather, 'I . . . didn't grow up as a reporter believing that my job was necessarily to be popular.' That attitude may not be a prescription for success as a network anchor. . . ."

Indeed.

We trusted and liked Walter Cronkite, but not so much Dan Rather. Rather makes us wonder, "What's his angle? What's his agenda?" The upper echelons at CBS still don't seem to grasp what it is that enhances or diminishes trust in their on-screen talent. That's why CBS continues to run a third-rated (and, in terms of effective communication, third-rate) news operation.

Who should be anchoring the news at CBS? I'd Rather have ABC's Ted Koppel. Dan Rather is an Old Communicator—affected, distant, and austere. He makes his listeners uneasy. But Ted Koppel is a New Communicator—natural, unfeigned, genial, and viewer-friendly.

Even if you are not running for national office or anchoring the network news, the same principles that work for people like Reagan, Bush, Richards, Koppel, Madden, and other New Communicators can work for you. Once you've learned how to make an emotional connection with your listener, you'll be better able to get that new job or promotion, close that sale, and relate more effectively to your spouse and kids. By becoming a New Communicator, you'll be able to get what you really want out of your life and your career.

A WORKABLE STRATEGY FOR SUCCESS

If you want to influence, persuade, or motivate people, you have to make emotional contact with them. This is true whether you are:

- The President of the United States, delivering the State of the Union Address
- A teenager asking Dad for the car
- The board chairman addressing the annual stockholders meeting
- A Bible teacher talking to a small class at church
- A salesperson calling on a client
- A manager at the weekly staff meeting
- A wife talking to her husband about their vacation plans
- A trainer teaching time management or
- An author on the "Oprah" show

These are all situations in which success or failure hinges on effective communication—and effective communication hinges on our ability to make emotional contact with the listener.

Already you know more about effective communication than some of the brightest minds in business, sports, and politics. Really. You know that effective communication is more than just saying words. You know that in order to get your message across effectively and persuasively, you have to make emotional contact with your listener. You know that communicating truly is a contact sport that requires you to plug into the power of the First Brain—the emotional part of the mind. And there are many, many who just don't know.

2

Emotion Versus Fact

A LIVING, BREATHING RÉSUMÉ

Christine Figari is a trainer who has been with Decker Communications, Inc., for over eight years. She first called me on the phone when the company was only a couple of years old and quite a bit leaner than it is today. "We're really not hiring new trainers right now but go ahead and send your résumé," I said. "We're always looking for good people."

I was working in my office the next day when my receptionist, Bobbie, brought her résumé in. "I told her you wouldn't be able to talk to her without an appointment," said Bobbie, "but she insists on seeing you in person." I quickly scanned the résumé and saw it was good, but nothing spectacular. I thought this was a little pushy, but figured I ought to at least be friendly, so I walked down the hall. I found Christine to be much more impressive than her résumé.

What really struck me was her certainty—a lot of energy in her voice and her manner, great posture, an authentic smile. She radiated confidence and competence. I learned more of what I needed to know about Chris within the first thirty seconds after we shook hands than from her entire résumé.

We ended up talking for half an hour. Two months later, she was hired.

That's the power of a living, breathing résumé versus the ink-on-paper variety. Chris understood she wasn't just looking for a job. She was selling herself—her skills, her competence, her confidence, her personality. She understood these are qualities you just can't convey on a piece of paper.

Communication Is Selling

So what are you selling? After all, we're all selling something.

Does that rub you the wrong way? Are you like so many who object to that word *selling*? I hope not. Because every time you and I communicate, we are selling. Some of us sell products. Some of us sell ideas. Some sell a viewpoint. And we all sell ourselves. In every arena of our careers and private lives—management, sales, training, education, politics, church, clubs, home, or cocktail parties—we are engaged in selling something.

In this context, the idea of selling can be used interchangeably with the idea of persuasion and reaching agreement. Once we see communication as a form of selling, it suddenly hits home that we had better get serious about communicating *effectively* if we want to be successful, to have some influence—or simply to have others hear and understand us.

So, if communication is selling, then what we want is for our listeners to "buy in," to agree. We want to influence our listeners to make a decision in our favor. And what will our listeners base that decision on? Primarily, on how they feel about us, on information received at an emotional level, on whether we've made emotional contact.

If the first thing to understand about communication is that we are all selling something, then the second and even more crucial thing to understand is this:

> ## People Buy on Emotion and Justify with Fact.

You may resist this statement. You may want to shout, "No! No! No! I am a rational, cognitive human being! I make calm, considered, well-thought-out decisions! I do not buy on emotion!"

But I can prove this statement. And I'll show you why it's really the key to effective communication. By the time you've finished this book, I hope you'll have this principle scrawled across your time manager, emblazoned on your desk blotter at work, taped to the dashboard of your car, and posted on your refrigerator at home. Contrary to our academic training, people do buy on emotion and justify with fact. Once we've accepted this basic fact of communication, we can use it to become more effective and persuasive in our own communication.

Here's the proof. Think back to a major decision you made. A big purchase such as a car or house. Your choice of college. Your first job. The person you married. These are major life-affecting decisions, and we all like to think we make such decisions in a fairly (if not completely) rational way.

SUB-, UN-, OR PRECONSCIOUS?

Any attempt to divide and subdivide the mind by the use of semantics is doomed to imprecision. The little that we do know with certainty about the mind tells us that its processes cannot be parsed into neat categories.

Although terms such as subconscious, unconscious, and preconscious have acquired clinical definitions among psychiatrists and psychologists, most laypeople use these words rather carelessly and interchangeably. Moreover, the words subconscious and unconscious have acquired connotations from Freud, Jung, and their respective disciples that could easily confuse the issue. So I've chosen to use the word preconscious, which seems to be appropriately free of such baggage.

Preconscious means: "Not present in consciousness but capable of being recalled without encountering any inner resistance or repression."

This is a good description of the level of consciousness we are describing when we talk about making emotional contact when we communicate. Our listeners are probably not consciously aware of the nonverbal cues we give which, taken together, shape either a positive or negative impression of us as speakers. But they are probably preconsciously aware.

Ask a listener, "What was it you liked or disliked about that speaker?" and he or she might pause for a moment to mentally "rewind the tape" and play back some visual and auditory impressions. Then the listener would likely reply, "He seemed unsure of himself. He didn't have much confidence in himself or his message. I felt anxious and nervous just listening to him." Or, "She seemed so warm and spontaneous. Very relaxed and confident. She held my interest the whole time."

We rarely pause to consciously inspect the state and activity of our preconscious mind. But it is there, all the same, recording impressions, making judgments, and powerfully affecting the communication process.

But let me ask you this: When you were making that big decision, did you take out a yellow legal pad, write "Pro" and "Con" at the top, and make a list of all the reasons for deciding yes or no? Not likely. And if you actually did that, did you then make your choice purely on the basis of the weight of those answers? And what then were the primary, scale-tipping reasons for your decision?

I'm not saying you didn't do research or give the decision a lot of thought. I am saying that most of our major decisions are overwhelmingly influenced at the emotional level, the preconscious level. We in effect decide (or "buy") at that level and then use our intellect to justify our decisions.

When Christine Figari arrived in person at my office—a "living résumé" rather than a dead piece of paper—she established emotional contact with me as a prospective employer, and she closed the sale. As an employer, I "bought" Chris on an emotional basis. I liked her, I was impressed with her, and I knew that the clients of our company, whom she would be training, would like her and be impressed with her, too. I'm not sure that I would have "bought" Chris on the factual basis of her résumé alone.

Let me describe a few situations from everyday life to further show you what I mean when I say that people buy on emotion and justify with fact.

Tom Loves Kaye

Tom and Kaye are getting married. (A true story with names changed.) Tom's a stockbroker, a facts-and-figures, data-oriented kind of guy. Sure, he's in love with Kaye, but he's figured this whole thing out rationally—or so he thinks! Look at his reasons for marrying her: First, she's smart. Then there are her eyes, deep blue with flecks of violet. Of course they get along well and are from the same neighborhood. And then there are those lips with just a hint of a pout. On top of that, Kaye makes an incredible ratatouille Provençale. And she's got a great sense of humor (meaning, she laughs at his jokes).

Okay, so Tom's Republican and Kaye votes Independent. And yes, he's an Episcopalian and she's a not anything. He likes staying home, reading books, working with computers, listening to golden oldies.

She hates typing but likes windsurfing, rock-climbing, and New Age/ fusion. But according to Tom, they've really got a lot in common.

Right.

Jana Loves Her House

Or take another example. Jana, a single woman in her early thirties, is thinking about buying a house. It fits her personality perfectly: cute, a lot of charm, though a little drafty. Jana calmly, unemotionally draws up a ledger of pros and cons:

PRO	CON
It's cute	Wrong neighborhood
It's got charm	Leaky plumbing
L. R. paneling matches my coffee table	Wiring is shot
It's quaint	I can't afford the payments

Okay, she reasons, so the neighborhood's a little run-down. And the place needs some fixing here and there. And the mortgage payments will eat up two-thirds of my take-home pay. No problem. I'll just take peanut butter sandwiches to work instead of eating out. And I'll sell my car and take the bus to work. Maybe I can get a weekend job. With that, Jana arrives at the perfectly rational, unemotional decision that she can afford her dream house.

Right.

Does any of this sound familiar? If you think about it, and if you're honest with yourself, you have to admit that most of your decisions are often made on the basis of "This is what I want to do." Then you think up all the reasons why what you want to do is really the logical thing to do. We all buy on emotion and justify with fact. All of us. I see it in myself all the time.

Driving It Home

The car I'm driving right now was bought on emotion.

I like big cars. So when my wife, Dru Scott, and I walked onto the lot, my gaze was immediately arrested by this roomy, classy, all-white Lincoln Town Car. We took it for a test drive, then brought it back to the lot. I wanted that car, but I didn't want to be impulsive. (I'm naturally impulsive, but trying to curb it.)

"What do you think?" the salesman asked eagerly. He knew the hook was set. He was just waiting to reel me in.

"This is my first look," I said, shaking my head. "I need to look at a few other models first. Besides, it's really more than I'd planned to spend."

The salesman's face sagged. We got in my old car and started to drive off. Before we had gone half a block, Dru turned and with an understanding smile said, "You really like that car, don't you?"

That's all I needed. I grinned, spun the wheel, whipped back into the lot and *bought* that big, beautiful car, just like that. I still like that car. It was a good decision. But it was an *emotional* decision.

The fact that we buy on emotion is a *natural* fact, neither good nor bad. Sometimes buying on emotion gets us into trouble—the kind of trouble Tom and Jana are headed for. And then, sometimes we get lucky, as I did when I bought that car. An emotional decision isn't necessarily the wrong decision.

There's no shame in admitting we're emotional creatures, and that emotion has a powerful driving influence on everything we do, think, and choose. In fact, it's foolish not to admit it. The truth is, if you want to reach, persuade or motivate people, you have to make emotional contact with them.

America Votes on Emotion

John F. Kennedy was a political leader who knew how to make emotional contact with his audience. A few weeks before the debates, Kennedy trailed Nixon in the polls, 53 to 47 percent. By election day, Kennedy not only caught up with, but nosed ahead of Nixon. Historians attribute Kennedy's narrow 1960 victory over Richard Nixon to their televised debates—a view shared by Kennedy himself, who said, "It was TV more than anything else that turned the tide." It was generally agreed that Richard Nixon (like Mondale and Dukakis in later debates) "won" the debates on radio. He won on debating points. Yet it was Kennedy who emerged victorious among TV viewers.

When Nixon arrived at the Chicago television studio for the first debate, he was haggard and drawn-looking because of intense campaigning combined with a recent hospitalization for a knee injury from which he had not yet fully recovered. He had lost twenty pounds and was not feeling well. He had spent five hours stuffing his head with answers to potential questions.

During the debate, he sweated profusely under the studio lights, streaking the pallid "Lazy Shave" makeup that was supposed to hide the deep five o'clock shadow on his jowls. Even though Nixon's discussion of the issues was cogent, and his grasp of events and factual detail was authoritative, all the viewers could recall of the debates was the image of a candidate who perspired under pressure, whose eyes darted during questioning, who seemed to lack confidence and poise.

In the debates and on the campaign stump, Nixon tried to appeal on the basis of facts, records, and statistics. As one historian observes, "Nixon constantly emphasized his superiority over Kennedy in experience, expressing it in the form of statistics. He had had 173 meetings with Ike, he said, and 217 with the National Security Council, over which he had presided 26 times. He had attended 163 cabinet meetings, presiding over 19. He had visited 54 countries, with extended discussions with 35 presidents, 9 prime ministers, 2 emperors, and the Shah of Iran."

Statistics are cold and cerebral. And so, the nation concluded, was Richard Nixon. America wanted emotional contact with its leader. JFK was happy to oblige.

Kennedy arrived for the first debate looking calm, assured, and dashing. In contrast to Nixon's "Lazy Shave" pallor, Kennedy was tanned from a recent campaign swing through California. On-screen, he was animated and totally in control. Whereas Nixon radiated edginess and anxiety, Kennedy communicated in a natural, relaxed style that Cold War-weary voters found reassuring.

In those early days of television, almost as many people heard the debate on radio or read it in newsprint as saw it on TV, so the impact of TV was not as great as it might be in our video-saturated world of the 1990s. Kennedy, who was trailing in the polls before the debate, just squeaked by Nixon with a scant 112,000-vote margin out of more than 68,800,000 votes cast. Had the video technology of the 1980s and '90s been around in 1960, I think it's safe to say that Kennedy would have buried Nixon in a landslide.

Kennedy won because—either consciously or intuitively—he understood how to make *emotional contact* with his audience. Election results have comparatively little to do with a candidate's intelligence, managerial skill, position papers, or party affiliation. Sure, they count,

DISSECTING THE NIXON DEBACLE

On September 26, 1960, the CBS television network preempted "The Andy Griffith Show" in order to present the first of four televised debates between Richard Nixon and John F. Kennedy. Carried live from Chicago, the first debate was seen by an audience of 70 million people. For Old Communicator Nixon, it was an unmitigated disaster. While his opponent skillfully used the new visual medium of television to make emotional contact with the audience, Nixon found himself impaled by its penetrating rays.

Dissecting the Nixon debacle in her book *Richard Nixon: The Shaping of His Character*, Fawn Brodie commented, "Those who missed the television and heard Nixon and Kennedy only on radio thought Nixon had clearly bested his opponent. But many television viewers who saw the Nixon pallor, the trickle of sweat pouring down his chin, the struggle to overcome his discomfiture at the Vanocur question [regarding an embarrassing remark about Nixon by President Eisenhower], remembered very little else. Nixon's running mate, Henry Cabot Lodge, watching the debate on TV in Texas, blurted out . . . when the debate was over, 'That son-of-a-bitch just lost us the election!' "

Nixon's on-screen appearance was so alarming, Brodie noted, that "Hannah Nixon [Nixon's mother] called Rose Woods in dismay to ask if her son was ill, and a disturbed Pat Nixon immediately took a plane from Washington to Chicago." Barry Goldwater called the debates "a disaster," and *The New Republic* concluded, "The debates ruined Nixon."

Nixon mistakenly thought the audience would build, debate by debate. Instead, the audience fell by 20 million after the first disastrous outing. It's inconclusive but intriguing to speculate that the reason those 20 million viewers tuned out was that they had already made up their minds after Nixon's initial performance.

Eight years later a "New Nixon" emerged, reshaped and reanimated by Roger Ailes, the man who later coached the debate and campaign performances of New Communicators Ronald Reagan and George Bush. The "New Nixon" learned to smile. He played to the crowds and to the unblinking eye of TV. The "New Nixon" was visual and energetic, employing such visual ploys as standing on the hood of a limousine and flashing V for victory. The "New Nixon" showed us a lighter side, appearing on Rowan and Martin's "Laugh-In" to pose the burning question, "Sock it to me?"

The "New Nixon" of course won the presidency in 1968 and 1972. Then the habits of the Old Communicator crept back in as Nixon "stonewalled" the Congress, the press, and the public during the Watergate scandal. The rest is history.

they're important, but you have to have something else first: *human contact* with the decision maker—the voter. Election results are more profoundly influenced by the question, "Which candidate do I trust?" than any other issue. This is an emotional question. When America chooses its leaders, it buys on emotion and justifies with fact.

My $450,000 Mistake

I didn't understand this concept twenty years ago, and it cost me dearly. I was a producer-director of documentary and political films. When the National Park Service put a major $450,000 film contract out for bids, my film company went after it with a vengeance. We had a good record with past work with the Park Service, and this was a *big* contract. After writing the proposal, we knew it was good. The ideas were innovative. Our credentials were solid. This should be a winner. And sure enough, out of the hundreds of proposals submitted, we were among the three finalists.

My friend Carl Degen was on the five-person committee that would make the decision. He had told me our written proposal was tied for the lead. The committee then flew me and the two other producers to Washington, DC, for the interview of finalists. I remember sitting at a table with the committee for an hour, talking about our film concepts, and answering questions. Then I went back to the hotel and waited through the afternoon for the committee's decision.

Finally, the phone rang. It was Carl. "Sorry, Bert, I hate to be the one to tell you that you lost."

"But why?" I said, disbelieving. "The proposal was great! Carl, you even told me we were in the lead with the written concepts! What went wrong?"

There was a long hesitation, then Carl said, "Bert, you looked nervous."

I remember thinking, That's not right! It shouldn't matter if a guy is nervous in an interview, so long as he can deliver quality goods, on time and on budget. Besides, it was a high pressure situation—he could be expected to be nervous. "Unfair!" I said then.

But now I would just say, "Of course!" On paper, at the "facts" level, our proposal and our company looked great. But in person, I blew it. My words were okay, but I sent out a message that registered on an emotional level. It was a *silent* message—perhaps consisting of poor eye communication, fidgety gestures, and the like—but those silent cues *screamed* that I lacked self-confidence. My visible nervousness undermined my message and the committee's trust in me. It was a $450,000 lesson, but an important one. For that was when I found out that people buy on emotion and justify with fact.

3

Your Personal Impact

"HE SAID I NEEDED HELP"

In 1982 Charles Schwab sold the discount brokerage firm that bears his name to Bank of America. The price tag: $50 million. Schwab was living the American dream. Starting from scratch, he built a thriving corporation out of his own ingenuity and hard work. When he sold it he was living on top of the world—or he should have been.

Instead, Schwab felt like he had to start a whole new phase of his career.

Why?

"As a kid I was good at a lot of things, but I could never remember in sequence. I think a lot of it goes back to the fact that I was dyslexic. I only found out I was dyslexic a few years ago, because when I was younger, no one knew how to diagnose dyslexia. No one knew what my problem was. I just knew there were things I couldn't do that other kids could do with ease, such as memorizing a passage of poetry. In those days they taught public speaking in a rote, memorized way. So I had no confidence in that area and was unable to get up and speak in front of people."

Schwab was never a poor student. As a child he exhibited the mental acuity and talent that would one day propel him into the ranks of America's top executives. But because of an undiagnosed problem that hampered his ability to decode and use language, he was slow in sequential thinking and reading while good in the abstract. But abstract wasn't (and isn't) rewarded in our school system. So the young

Charles Schwab shunned any speaking because he felt inadequate in front of the class.

His own experience has given him empathy for others with dyslexia. "My son is dyslexic and my sister is dyslexic," he says. "I set up a foundation for the parents of dyslexic kids, because these kids need parents who are trained to understand, accept and deal with the problem. And the parents need their own support, too."

Schwab, who overcame his early limitations and became one of the most successful businessmen in America, recalls with irony the day shortly after he sold his company for $50 million.

"Soon after the company was sold," he remembers, "one of my most trusted officers—he'd been with me since the beginning—came up to me and said, 'Chuck, you need help.' I was amazed and frankly a little upset. Here we had just reached our dream, were on a new plateau with the backing to expand our business, and I was being criticized by one of my most trusted.

Charles Schwab

"But he was right. If we were to succeed at this new level—this higher profile—I did need help in becoming more of a 'public' figure. We used still photos extensively and effectively in our advertising campaigns, but I had always shied away from any engagements that required me to communicate. To speak. He was just saying that I had to change."

And Charles Schwab did change—he did do something about his communicating (as we'll see later). Today you often find him in front of an audience, looking relaxed and confident. He doesn't pretend to enjoy it, but he knows he's effective as a speaker. Watch him in his television commercials for Charles Schwab and Co. He's believable, likable, and persuasive—the ideal spokesman for his company. Charles Schwab was not always a natural communicator. But today he's a New Communicator, one of the most effective speakers on the American business scene, because he made a decision to do something about his personal impact.

Are You a Public Speaker?

How do you answer this question in your own mind? It's a question I frequently ask when I speak professionally before large groups: "How many of you are public speakers?" Even in a room of 1,000 people, I rarely see more than a dozen or so hands go up. So I say, "How many of you are private speakers—or would like to be?" A lot of laughs on that one.

The point is clear: we are *all* public speakers. There's no such thing as a "private speaker" (except a person who talks to himself).

Every person who talks to another person is a public speaker. You and I are continually in the public eye, selling our products, our ideas, ourselves—all the time.

As you can see, "public speaking" means a lot more than merely "giving speeches." We're talking about your *personal* impact. We're talking about your ability to connect emotionally with others whenever you have something to say.

A Giant of a Public Speaker

His favorite TV show is "America's Funniest Home Videos." He owes a good number of his 240-plus pounds to his hankering for mint-chocolate-chip ice cream. He has a good-natured, moon-shaped face, and a portly build that invites comparisons to comedian Jonathan Winters and NBC's jovial weatherman Willard Scott. Even his name sounds kind of funny: Norman Schwarzkopf.

But Saddam Hussein knows there's nothing funny about the chief strategist of Operation Desert Storm. He's a black-hearted dictator's baddest nightmare. He looks so harmless! Yet he's strong, tough, and powerful. General George Patton said, "War is simple, direct and ruthless. It takes a man who is simple, direct and ruthless."

To look at him, you would never mistake him for a Patton, a Nimitz, or a MacArthur. He just doesn't look the part of a hard-bitten blood-'n'-guts general who leads men and women and wins wars. And

Norman Schwarzkopf (AP/Wide World Photos)

now the persona of General H. Norman Schwarzkopf has become a symbol of American achievement and the American spirit at its best.

Why? Well, because he won the war, of course. But also because he is a public speaker—*and always has been*. It just took the media spotlight to show the world what his troops, family, and friends already knew. He *communicates*, powerfully and persuasively. He reaches the emotions of our First Brain. He succeeds in connecting with people.

Schwarzkopf's giant skills as a public speaker first exploded on our TV screens during his famous strategy briefing at the conclusion of the Gulf War in February 1991. This press conference (where he revealed the now-famous "Hail Mary" surprise plan) was so memorable it soon became a hot-selling videocassette.

In May 1991, Schwarzkopf made an encore appearance before an electrified, emotionally charged joint session of Congress. His speech was interrupted dozens of times by standing ovations. He spoke for only 16½ minutes—and he spent over a third of that time waiting for applause to subside.

With passion, he spoke of the pride of the American soldier: "We're the United States military, and we're damn proud of it!" There was a catch in his throat as he paid tribute to the fallen. His eyes glistened, his voice choked, and he cast a sentimental smile toward his wife and children in the gallery as he said, "We also want to thank the families . . . It was your love that truly gave us strength in our darkest hours." His expression flashed with hot, righteous indignation as he excoriated "the prophets of doom, the naysayers, and the flag burners."

Schwarzkopf climaxed his address with a rolling refrain, "Thank you, America! . . . Thank you, America! . . . Thank you to the great people of the United States of America!" It was a star-quality speech by a man who is not a great orator in the classic sense. It was a grizzly-bear performance by a man with a teddy-bear face.

The Gulf War made Schwarzkopf a hero. Yet it is his ability to communicate that is rapidly making him a very rich hero. Schwarzkopf, who entered military life wanting little more than a chance to serve his country, is well on his way to becoming a thriving capitalist, whether he likes it or not. Because he knows how to communicate. And for millions he will now be not only a hero, but the very model of a New Communicator.

Some people seem to intuitively grasp what it means to be a New Communicator. The rest of us have to learn it and work at it. But all of us can become more effective communicators, even New Communi-

---

MORE THAN A GENERAL

"Returning to West Point, General Norman Schwarzkopf is an old soldier not fading away. In a commencement speech he told the cadets that West Point is teaching them how to be the military leaders of the 21st century. Duty, honor, country. 'Believe it,' said The Bear. 'Believe it.'

Late that evening, as Schwarzkopf and his wife, Brenda, sat talking with their hosts, Lt. Gen. Dave Palmer, superintendent of West Point and also Class of '56, and his wife, Lu, cadets began arriving, abandoning their books and their beds. First a trickle, then a river. More than 1,000 filled the street, then the yard, then the flower beds and up on the porch of Thayer House as the military police and the general's own security people first gave ground and then gave up. 'Schwarzkopf, Schwarzkopf, Schwarzkopf,' they chanted.

Palmer said, 'They were really fired up by his speech. I thought it was the usual football-rally type crowd, but when Norm and I went outside we were moved; we couldn't move an inch in the crush.' It took Palmer and Schwarzkopf 10 minutes to work their way out to the street and climb onto the roof of an MP car where all the cadets could get a good look at the old soldier. It was long past 1 A.M. when they dispersed to grab some sleep before reveille at 5:30 A.M."

U.S. News & World Report, May 27, 1991

---

cators, once we understand how the communication process works. Just as Charles Schwab, Norman Schwarzkopf, and thousands of other people have done, you can have the kind of personal impact that truly persuades and motivates.

THREE FUNDAMENTAL TRUTHS

Personal impact is *power*—power to achieve whatever you want in your life and your career. The secret of attaining personal impact is based on three fundamental truths I've discovered in my quarter-century of work in the communication field.

Truth Number 1

The spoken word is almost the polar opposite of the written word.

Truth Number 2

In the spoken medium, what you say must be believed to have impact.

Truth Number 3

Believability is overwhelmingly determined at a preconscious level.

Truth Number 1: Writing Versus Speaking

I can't emphasize this too strongly: The spoken word and the written word are not just different ways of communicating. Speaking and writing are polar *opposites* when it comes to communicating.

Written communication is linear, single-channel input. We take in written communication word by word, line by line.

Spoken communication, by contrast, is multichannel input. In spoken communication, the message we receive is not merely a row of words, but also a kaleidoscopic array of nonverbal cues.

The Information Channel

If all you want to do is transfer information, don't say it, put it in writing. Written communication is much more effective than speaking for exchanging facts, data, and details. You can read five times faster than a person can speak. You can go back and reread for a clearer understanding. You can concentrate on content and ignore the nuances. You can skim it, file it for later reference, or fax it if you want. Written communication is the "information channel," and it definitely has its place.

But if your goal is to influence, to persuade, to get your point across, then you've got to say it—and *say it with impact.*

The Action Channel

Writing is like a monaural recording: the message comes through on only one channel. Speaking, however, is like a multichannel super-stereo in which there are not just two but dozens of channels simultaneously feeding information into our brains. The speaker's posture, expression, energy level, eye contact, inflection, intonation, volume, and actions are just a few of the many cues that accompany and modify the words of the message.

Written communication goes directly to the cerebral cortex, the highly developed reasoning and analytical portion of the brain. Spoken communication carries energy, feeling, passion, and goes right to the emotional centers of the brain—what I call the First Brain (more to come on this critically important mechanism). It is this emotional side that we have to reach if we want to motivate and persuade people because, as we've already seen, people buy on emotion.

I would guess that about 80 percent of the average person's communication falls into the category of *speaking to persuade*. This is action-oriented communication. It takes place not only in speeches on a platform, but in presentations, in meetings, in across-the-desk discussions, in informal chats over lunch, and on the golf course. It takes place at church, at home, at the car dealership, in small claims court, at a yard sale.

Once we've grasped the crucial fact that writing and speaking are completely different ways of communicating, then it becomes clear that the job of selling ourselves, our ideas, and our products should not just be in writing. To convince and motivate, we must say it with impact.

If you want the boss to give you a raise, don't send him a memo. Go to his office, look him in the eye, and *persuade* him that you're worth it. *Show* him you're worth it.

If you want to sell that client on your product, don't write her a letter. Get into her office and *persuade* her that she's got to have that product.

If you're looking for a job, don't mail out résumés like so much junk mail. Get into that employer's office and *persuade* him you're the only person for the job.

A Whole New Way of Thinking

Most of us are like Tony, a bank computer analyst I trained in Effective Communicating™, our basic two-day program. Tony was a bright guy with a very logical mind, a wizard with computers, and an effective writer. He had just been promoted to manager, and his company had told him to take the training. He did it—grudgingly.

Tony resisted almost every exercise we did during the first morning. He didn't like speaking extemporaneously. He didn't like being video-taped. More than once, he asked, "What are we doing this for?" We usually win people over very quickly in the course, but Tony was a special case. Out of a dozen participants, he was the only holdout.

Just before lunch during the first day, I talked to the group about speaking versus writing. I immediately saw a look of skepticism on Tony's face. "I'm sorry, Bert," he said, "but I just can't buy this. Writing and speaking are just two ways of doing the same thing. Words on paper or words in the air, what's the difference? To me, communicating is very simple. You can either say it or you can write it, but once it's been heard or read by someone else, it's communicated, period."

"Tony," I said, "a favor. Stay with us, go through the exercises, listen to everything we say. When it's all over, if you still feel the same way, you get your money back."

After lunch we did impromptu exercises. We videotaped the partici-pants as they tried new communicating skills. Then, in private coach-ing sessions, I reviewed each participant's taped performance with him or her. When Tony's turn came, we went into the coaching room, turned on the videotape, and compared Tony's morning performance with his afternoon performance. Tony was amazed at what he saw. Even with his skepticism cranked full blast, even with all his foot-dragging and questioning, he had made visible progress. In the after-noon tapings, he looked much more relaxed, confident, and natural. He saw that he could get up before a group of people, make an emotional connection with them, and actually be persuasive, likable, believable, and completely himself. "Incredible," he said. "I'm amazed at the difference."

In the afternoon, Tony stood up before the group and said, "I want to say something to all of you. You know I've been resistant to everything we've been doing here today. I still don't want to believe that speaking is any different from writing, but I can't deny it any-more. I've seen the proof on video. What makes this hard for me is that I've got to change my whole way of thinking."

Tony put his finger on it: We have to change our whole way of thinking about communicating. It means changing some very stub-born and deeply grooved habits. It means dumping old mental programming and inserting new. It means shedding comfortable but self-defeating behavior patterns. And completely revising our thinking is one of the hardest things for a human being to do.

"Faced with the choice between changing one's mind and proving there is no need to do so, almost everyone gets busy on the proof."

JOHN KENNETH GALBRAITH

I'm confident that you—unlike my friend Tony—won't need to be dragged kicking and screaming to this inescapable conclusion: writing and speaking are almost totally different ways of communicating. The facts are clear: If all you want to do is transfer information, put it in writing. But if you need to motivate, persuade, and influence people, *say it with impact.*

Truth Number 2: You've Got to Be Believed to Be Heard

In the spoken medium (and that's all I'm "talking" about here) what you say must be believed in order to have impact. No message, regardless of how eloquently stated, brilliantly defended, and painstakingly documented it may be, is able to penetrate a wall of distrust, apprehension, or indifference. If you want your listener to be persuaded and motivated, he or she must believe your message. And for your message to be believed, you must be believable.

The New Communicators on the scene today are people who have an intuitive grasp of what it takes to be believable. A partial list, below, will give you an idea of who I'm talking about.

Politics	Business	Media	Sports
George Bush	Lee Iacocca	Jane Pauley	John Madden
Mario Cuomo	Charles Schwab	Oprah Winfrey	Mary Lou Retton
Ronald Reagan	Steve Jobs	Ted Koppel	Magic Johnson
Ann Richards	John Amerman	Phil Donahue	Bob Costas

All these people have three things in common: They communicate effectively, sometimes brilliantly. They are believable. And they are successful.

Truth Number 3: Belief Is Determined at a Preconscious Level

Where does believability come from?

You can't build believability out of a mountain of facts and figures. You can't even build it out of stacks of elegantly crafted words. Authoritative credentials—a title or a Ph.D.—may buy you some credibility, but only enough to get your foot in the door. You still have to be believable to "close the sale."

And believability is an emotional quality. It's built on an emotional level.

The National Meeting

Let's say you're attending a national sales meeting. You're in an auditorium with 500 other people from your company. The first speaker is introduced to a round of applause. He steps to the podium, adjusts his glasses, fumbles with a sheaf of pages, and begins reading his speech. His eyes are downcast. His voice is high and tremulous with tension. After a seeming eternity, he reaches the end of page one. The microphone picks up the nervous rattle of the paper as he turns to page two.

You groan inwardly and tune out. You flip to the back of your printed agenda and check the speaker's credentials. "And I was looking forward to hearing this guy," you say to yourself. "It says here he's an expert, but he sure doesn't seem too confident of his material."

(The speaker really is an expert in his field. Too bad he appears to lack conviction and enthusiasm. Just this morning, he was talking about this very same subject to a colleague. He was full of excitement, he was expressive, he was confident. One-on-one, he's natural and believable. Put him on behind a lectern, and he's a cure for insomnia. At most, maybe five percent of his content gets through.)

The next speaker is introduced. She uses overhead graphics with bold colors and forceful images. She has a strong, distinctive voice, with a wide dynamic range. Instead of planting herself behind the lectern, she moves freely about the platform, making eye contact around the room. She has an interesting smile and open gestures. She's talking about financial projections (you thought this was going to be a yawner) yet you find yourself listening. You even find yourself feeling enthusiastic about financial projections, and laughing at the speaker's wry asides.

Coffee-break time. You chat with some of your associates. Sue introduces you to a new sales rep. You shake his hand—oops, limp and clammy—and the guy looks so grim. How did he ever get hired? (You're not conscious of it, but he is actually sending out additional subconscious cues through his posture, eye contact, voice, and other signals, all of which add up to a negative impression. He sends these same cues when he calls on accounts. In a few months, he'll be history.)

And so it goes. Throughout this sales meeting, you've been bombarded with literally thousands of stimuli—the sights, sounds, and personal energy of speakers, colleagues, superiors, subordinates, friends, and new acquaintances. And they have received a similar array of verbal and nonverbal cues from you. An enormous amount of communication is taking place as these thousands of multichannel impressions are carried to your brain. Most of these impressions register at a preconscious level. As a result of these impressions, your brain forms a continuous stream of emotional judgments and assessments: Do I trust this person? Is he or she honest? Evasive? Friendly? Threatening? Interesting? Boring? Warm? Cold? Anxious? Confident? Insecure? Hiding something?

The emotional judgment that is formed in your preconscious mind about the speaker determines whether you will tune in to his or her message—or tune out.

If you don't believe in someone on an emotional level, little if any of what they have to say will get through. It will be screened out by your distrust, your anxiety, your irritation, or your indifference. Even if the facts and content are great by themselves, they are forever locked out because the person delivering them lacks believability.

Like a Drunken Sailor

On March 24, 1989, the hull of the oil tanker *Exxon Valdez* grated against the shoals of Prince William Sound in Alaska. The ship rumbled to a stop and began hemorrhaging black crude. Thus began the worst environmental disaster in U.S. history—a disaster that would see Exxon pay out most of its $5 billion annual earnings on a $3 billion cleanup bill.

But the damage to the environment was only half the story. Like a tanker steered by a drunken sailor, Exxon proceeded to sail full-steam-ahead into one of the worst public relations disasters in modern memory. Led by chairman and CEO Lawrence G. Rawl, Exxon did everything wrong.

You probably remember the images of Rawl on television news. When he first appeared before the media—after a full week of silent stonewalling—he appeared grim, closed, stolid, nonhuman. His message was defensive, even defiant. He blamed the government for his own company's slow cleanup response and attempted to minimize the scope of the spill. In successive meetings with the press, Rawl continued to chisel out his company's hardline position with flinty resolve.

In the public mind, Rawl and Exxon were interchangeable. The persona Exxon displayed to the public was Rawl's—grim, closed, nonhuman, defensive, defiant. For all practical purposes, Exxon was Rawl. When 10,000 Exxon credit customers dipped their credit cards in oil, sealed them in Baggies, and mailed them back to Exxon, they didn't do so only because a ship accidentally ran aground in Alaska. They did so because the public face of Exxon symbolized everything

Lawrence Rawl (AP/Wide World Photos)

supposedly evil about big business: arrogance, irresponsibility, and greed.

In private, Lawrence Rawl may be a warm and genial guy. And it's possible that Exxon is not really arrogant, irresponsible, greedy, and evil. But just try telling that to the American people, the American press, and the 1,000-plus angry shareholders who demanded Rawl's resignation at the May 1989 stockholders' meeting. The perception of Exxon as an "ecopathic" corporate villain has been indelibly stamped on the public mind, largely due to Rawl's own personal impact.

Rawl survived the stockholders' challenge to his leadership. Exxon survived the initial $3 billion cleanup tab, and continues to survive the negative personal impact of Lawrence Rawl. But for how long? And at what cost? The legal suits continue, as Exxon's settlement with Alaska was thrown out by Judge Russel Holland because he thought it wasn't enough. Was that partly because of the attitude of Exxon? We have no way of knowing, but we do know that the anger against Exxon continues too. "Exxon can blame itself for its public image as arrogant and insensitive. When the plea bargain was unveiled, Chairman Lawrence G. Rawl said: 'The settlement will have no noticeable effect on our financial results.' Presumably, the chairman was seeking to reassure investors, but he wound up further infuriating the public with his apparent lack of remorse."

Could Exxon have done more than merely survive the Alaska tragedy? What would the public perception of Exxon be today if the company had been represented by a man like Lee Iacocca?

The Ten-Figure Turnaround

You probably know Lee Iacocca's story. In November 1978, just a few weeks after being sacked by Henry Ford II as president of the nation's number two automaker, Iacocca signed on as captain of a sinking ship called Chrysler. The day he came aboard, Chrysler posted a third quarter loss of nearly $160 million. Two headlines emblazoned the front page of the *Detroit Free Press*—CHRYSLER LOSSES WORST EVER and LEE IACOCCA JOINS CHRYSLER.

The Chrysler organization was in chaos and would take more than two years to turn around. Chrysler ended the first half of '79 with $260 million worth of red ink, plus an inventory of more than 100,000 unsold cars. The second half of '79 was even worse. After the fall of the Shah, Iran's revolutionary government prodded OPEC into driving up oil prices, which in turn depressed automobile sales even further.

Lee Iacocca (AP/Wide World Photos)

While already $4.75 billion in hock, Chrysler turned to the federal government for $1.5 billion in federal loan guarantees. The public was not enthused about the deal. Many business and government leaders were stridently opposed. "Let market forces decide if Chrysler lives or dies," they cried. "No bailout!"

But President Carter signed the loan guarantees into law in January 1980—and Chrysler proceeded to rack up a record $1.7 billion loss for the year.

The following year, 1981, Chrysler lost "only" $476 million. In 1982 came the *real* good news: Chrysler ended the year $170 million in the black.

In 1983, sales leaped more than 50 percent, pushing profits to $925 million for the year, a company record. Chrysler was back for good, and rumors of "Iacocca for President" swept the country. Chrysler offered 26 million shares of stock at $16 ⅝. Those shares more than doubled in value within a month.

On July 13, 1983, Iacocca presented Chrysler's creditors with a check for $813,487,500, representing complete repayment of the outstanding balance of the federally guaranteed loan. It was repaid *seven years ahead of schedule.*

The following year, sales rose another 37.4 percent, handing Chrysler a huge $2.4 billion profit. That year Iacocca's salary, bonus, and stock options totaled roughly $13 million.

One Man?

Now, am I actually going to attribute this amazing multibillion dollar turnaround to the personal impact of one man?

You bet I am!

It was Lee Iacocca who personally went to Capitol Hill and convinced a skeptical Congress to okay the $1.5 billion loan guarantee package— against overwhelming odds. In *The Iacocca Management Technique*, Maynard M. Gordon observed that Iacocca "set about masterminding the drive to win congressional approval and put his magnetic personality solidly behind the effort." *That's personal impact!*

Iacocca personally handled the job of approaching bankers and insurance company executives to get crucial loan extensions and other concessions. Again, *personal impact!* He visited every Chrysler plant and talked with the workers, many of whom were hostile after suffering huge austerity-measure wage cuts. He inspired the Chrysler troops to pull together and put their company back on its feet. *Personal impact!* Iacocca spoke and pressed the flesh at dealer meetings, conventions, and regional and national dealer associations. During the dark years from 1979 to 1981, he almost single-handedly headed off the threat of mass defections by dealers to Japanese franchises. *Personal impact!*

But most important of all, the Chrysler turnaround coincides precisely with the personal appearance of Lee Iacocca in the company's ads in 1981. Early Iacocca appearances consisted of a brief standup delivery of such lines as, "If you buy a car without considering Chrysler, that'll be too bad—for both of us." Later commercials featured candid footage of Iacocca in his own element, talking to colleagues and employees at Chrysler, communicating the company message of quality and value with spontaneous sincerity. *Personal impact!*

Had it not been for the personal impact of Lee Iacocca, Chrysler would have gone into bankruptcy by 1980, leaving billions in unpaid loans and bills, throwing thousands out of work and sending shockwaves through the economy. If you had to put a price tag on the personal impact and believability of Lee Iacocca, it would easily run into ten (or more) figures.

What if Lee Iacocca and Lawrence G. Rawl had changed places. If Rawl had taken the helm of Chrysler in 1978 would the company have even recovered, much less thrived? I doubt it. And if Iacocca had taken charge of the *Valdez* oil spill would it have been the unbelievably costly communications disaster that is still going on? I doubt that too.

Millions and even billions of dollars ride on the personal impact of those at the top rungs of the world's corporate ladders. Your fortune is every bit as significant to you as those megabucks are to them, and you can attain it the same way—with personal impact.

THE NEW COMMUNICATOR AS CORPORATE PITCHMAN

When Lee Iacocca began appearing in Chrysler ads in 1981, many people considered it an act of desperation, doomed to fail. Some pointed to the ineffective ads for Eastern Airlines featuring then Eastern chairman and former astronaut Frank Borman. What these people failed to realize was that Borman was not a New Communicator.

Iacocca was—and is.

In *The Iacocca Management Technique*, auto industry watcher Maynard Gordon noted how Lee Iacocca's personal impact and believability conjured up the Chrysler miracle:

"Chrysler sales rose steadily as more and more Iacocca spots appeared on prime-time dramas, during major athletic events, and between segments of the morning news shows. Chrysler surveys showed that new-car buyers who had ducked Chrysler products for years or had never visited a Chrysler showroom became 'converts' as a result of the 'credibility' [or believability]—an almost undefinable quality—embodied in Iacocca's assertion, 'If You Can Find a Better Car, Buy One.'

"The messages were upbeat and blunt, pitching the products and the company, rapping the competition, daring the viewers or readers to visit Chrysler dealerships and compare them against GM or Ford. . . . A surprisingly large number of Chrysler product buyers . . . said it was belief in Iacocca's message and sincerity that motivated their purchase. He backed up the ads in person, not through a Ricardo

(*cont. on page 42*)

Montalban or Ed McMahon. . . . *It's safe to say, looking back over eighty years of American automotive history, that no other senior executive could have accomplished the Iacocca feat of resurrecting the sales volume of a line of cars that such a preponderant majority of Americans had written off as defunct.*" [Emphasis added.]

In the early "New Chrysler" ads that appeared in 1981 and '82, Iacocca delivered only the tag lines such as, "I'm not asking you to buy one of our cars on faith. I'm asking you to compare." Soon Iacocca was writing his own copy, which enabled him to deliver his lines with genuine conviction. It was his idea to point his finger confidently at the viewer and declare, "If you can find a better car—*buy it*," one of the most effective Chrysler slogans ever. Then came his famous "Made in America" commercial, which began on this startlingly honest and straightforward note: "There was a time when 'Made in America' meant something. It meant you made the best. Unfortunately, a lot of Americans don't believe that anymore. And maybe with good reason."

Iacocca proved that the ability to communicate effectively is a multi-billion dollar make-or-break factor. As Maynard Gordon concludes, "No other senior auto executive at the time could communicate . . . with Iacocca's flair for color and candor. . . . The Iacocca persona was, and still is, an irresistible force propelling Chrysler."

Part II

USING ALL
OF YOUR MIND

4

The Gatekeeper

WHO WINS—THE GIRL NEXT DOOR OR THE PROM QUEEN?

In the fall of 1989, the all-seeing, all-knowing executives of NBC looked at their long-running morning show, *Today*, and decided it needed some tinkering. So they moved attractive young Deborah Norville from the news-reading job on *News at Sunrise* to a cohost slot at the *Today* desk. It wasn't that the *Today* show was faltering. In fact, it continued to be the top-rated broadcasting powerhouse it had been since the early days of television.

So why add Norville to the lineup? It was a classic case of "It ain't broke—so we fixed it." Did they ever.

It's not hard to understand why Norville got the promotion. Her sleek blond luster is justly matched by her intelligence and journalistic credibility.

But somehow, during Norville's move, Jane Pauley got lost in the reshuffle. She was made to feel like a fifth wheel. So in December 1989, a misty-eyed Jane Pauley said good-bye to *Today*. When she left, she took with her the perky, quirky chemistry that made the show work.

We didn't need to worry about Jane. She came back. The one with the uncertain future wasn't Jane Pauley but the *Today* show itself.

Immediately after Pauley's departure, the show began to skid out of control. With Jane, the show had enjoyed a 4.4 rating and a 21 share. But during the first quarter of 1990, those numbers dropped

Jane Pauley (AP/Wide World Photos)

to a 3.8 rating and an 18 share—a shocking 14 percent decline. The most dismal numbers came at the worst possible time—the February ratings "sweeps" when the show's advertising rates are determined. The show sagged *22 percent* below its pre-Norville levels.

Industry analysts called it a "meltdown." Heads rolled, beginning with executive producer Dick Ebersol's. Angry affiliates stormed the network ramparts, clamoring for blood. Profits evaporated. Those lost ratings meant a slump of about $100,000 per day in ad revenue—or around $25 million per year.

What was it about Jane Pauley that made her worth $25 million annually to NBC's bottom line? What does Jane Pauley have that Deborah Norville doesn't?

In a word, warmth. An open smile with just a touch of wry wit behind it. An honest sense of humor. A delightful sparkle. A bit of girl-next-doorishness. Jane Pauley is a natural New Communicator.

Compared to all that, the best Deborah Norville has to offer is not bad—a sexy brand of competence and the cool, unapproachable beauty of a prom queen. But NBC seriously miscalculated in thinking the average viewer—male or female—would prefer to wake up and have breakfast with the prom queen rather than the girl next door.

And then NBC finally saw the light, or stumbled into it, with Katie Couric. As Norville's temporary replacement during her pregnancy leave, Couric caught on with the public in a way that reminds us of Pauley's original start—and the *Today* show ratings began climbing again. Why?

USA Today calls Couric "the people's choice." She has a fresh, irreverent manner that connects. *Today* anchor Bryant Gumbel says, "I can see most people relating to her almost like a little sister." And Couric, who peppers her conversations and interviews with humor, says of herself, "I didn't think I had the right stuff. I didn't think I was glamorous enough and that is probably still true." ABC's George Watson says that she has that "girl-next-door quality. If you want to wake up to someone who has energy, enthusiasm and intellect, Katie's hard to beat." As Deborah Norville could tell her, glamor is not the key ingredient.

With Couric winning the permanent job as co-anchor of *Today*, she would agree that beauty and competence are not enough. They help, but to communicate effectively, we must make a personal connection.

MAKING FRIENDS WITH THE GATEKEEPER

It should be obvious by now that effective communication is a lot more than simply transferring information from me to you, or vice versa. There is a gate between us through which communication must pass. The gate is tended by a Gatekeeper, standing guard before the House of the Intellect. The Gatekeeper's name is *First Brain*.

Will the Gatekeeper open or close the gate of communication? Will our message get through, or will it be blocked?

Whenever we communicate, our listener's Gatekeeper is right there on guard, figuratively asking, "Friend or foe?" The Gatekeeper has complete power to grant or deny access to our listener's higher analytical and decision-making processes. A New Communicator is a person who knows how to befriend the Gatekeeper, who knows how to become "First Brain friendly," so that his or her message can get through effectively and persuasively.

First Brain Power

Contrary to what you've probably been taught, effective communication is only partly concerned with our intellectual human brain, what I call the "New Brain." Before we can communicate effectively with our listener's New Brain, we must consider a hidden and generally unrecognized part of ourselves. I call it the "First Brain." Though it is hidden from our consciousness, it is real, it is physical, and it is extremely powerful.

If the brass hats at NBC had understood how the First Brain works, Jane Pauley would still be hosting *Today*, and NBC would be millions richer.

If the CBS brass had understood how the First Brain works, Dan Rather would be out of there and their third-rated evening news show would probably be a first-rated show, hosted by Ted Koppel—or perhaps Jane Pauley.

If Michael Dukakis had understood how the First Brain works, he might have gone to the White House.

If Lawrence Rawl had understood how the First Brain works, he might have reversed the public, press, and political perception of Exxon. Instead of looking like the epitome of corporate evil, Exxon might have gained a reputation as a company that shoulders its responsibility and fixes its mistakes.

Just a few pages from now, you will know what all of these people failed to understand. You will know how the First Brain works. And you'll know how to succeed where some of the brightest minds in business, politics, and the media have failed.

The First Brain Revealed

You may be surprised to learn that your brain is not really one brain but several. You've probably heard about the differences between "left brain" thinking and "right brain" thinking, but that's not what we're talking about here. The truth is that many people emphasize only the left/right brain distinction (see box: "A Brain Myth"). Though there are differences between them, the "left brain" and "right brain" are actually just two halves of the highly developed cerebral cortex—what I call the New Brain.

But there's a more important "brain" to be aware of, and knowing how this "brain" works can profoundly affect the way you communicate with others. This "brain" is a much more forceful and fundamental part of you than either the left or right brain. I call it the First Brain.

The First Brain is the nonreasoning, nonrational part of our brain. Simply put, it is the seat of human emotion, composed of the brainstem and the limbic system. It's the most primitive part of the brain, consisting of components that existed between 200 million and 500 million years ago. .

The New Brain is the cerebral cortex—that large, intricately folded, hemispherical mass that surrounds the more basic First Brain. The New Brain is the seat of conscious thought, memory, language, creativity, and decision-making. I call it the New Brain because it is so recent compared to the First Brain, a mere three or four million years old.

When people communicate by the spoken word, they almost invariably aim their message at the New Brain and completely overlook the First Brain. That's why even such competent, intelligent people as Dan Rather, Michael Dukakis, Pat Schroeder, Deborah Norville, Bill Walsh, Walter Mondale, and Lawrence Rawl fail to effectively get their message across to their audiences.

This is not to say that the New Brain is unimportant. On the contrary, our goal is to get our message across to the New Brain, because that's the decision-making part of our mind. *But to reach the New Brain, our message must first pass through the First Brain, the emotional*

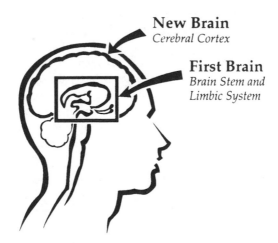

New Brain
Cerebral Cortex

First Brain
*Brain Stem and
Limbic System*

(For a more detailed look at the First Brain, see Endnotes: "The Brain within a Brain.")

part of the brain. If we leave the First Brain out of the equation, our message will be distorted or diminished—or it may not get through at all.

A BRAIN MYTH

"Everybody knows" all human thought is neatly divided between the two hemispheres of our brain—our left and right brains. The linear thought processes of language, logic, and mathematics occur in the left brain. The conceptual thought processes of art, music, creativity, and inspiration occur on the right.

The problem with what "everybody knows" is that much of it just ain't so.

Though left brain/right brain lateralization is a well-established fact, documented by the "brain-mapping" research of Nobel-winner Roger Sperry, most people have a grossly distorted and oversimplified view of what this really means. The left and right brains are often misconstrued to be totally separate systems. Though separated from each other by a deep vertical cleft, the left and right hemispheres of the brain are kept in constant communication and coordination via the corpus callosum—a thick cablelike structure containing thousands of information channels.

Supposed "left brain" functions such as language actually involve both hemispheres. Researchers have found that the language in a good story or novel tends to excite as much or more brain activity in the right hemisphere as in the left. Researchers have also found that if the "speech centers" in the left brain are injured, the right brain is frequently able to take over some of the language functions of the left brain.

While there are definite differences between the functions of the left brain and the right brain, these distinctions pale into insignificance compared with the all-important contrast between the New Brain and the First Brain. The task of a New Communicator is not to just reach the right brain or the left brain. These are just two halves of the New Brain. The New Communicator's real task is to reach the First Brain first.

The reason the First Brain is so important to effective communication is precisely because it is the seat of emotion, and emotional response. It is clear that the most important language in effective communicating is almost an unspoken language, *the language of trust.* In Chapter 1, we discovered that in order to communicate effectively, we must make *emotional contact* with the listener. In Chapter 2, we learned that *people buy on emotion and justify with fact*. In Chapter 3, we learned that in the spoken medium, we must be *believed* in order to have impact, and that believability is overwhelmingly determined at a *preconscious* level.

Everything we've talked about in the first three chapters—emotional contact, emotional impact, believability, and trust—takes place in the preconscious realm of the First Brain. Though the goal of effective communication is to get our message across to the cerebral, rational processes of the New Brain, we can't do this without getting through the First Brain first. It's the listener's First Brain which makes the decision whether or not to trust and believe the speaker. It's the First Brain which decides whether a person represents comfort and nurture—or anxiety and menace.

The key to understanding the First Brain is realizing that its essential purpose is survival. The two basic parts of the First Brain are sometimes called the reptilian or mammalian brains, for that is almost all that those creatures have. And for them, the purpose of the First Brain is primary and essential—they must immediately "feel" and react to danger. For that is what the First Brain basically does—quickly analyzes all incoming data in light of the question, "Is this situation safe?"

Now we human beings have a highly specialized, complex, sophisticated and astounding New Brain that *thinks*. But, surprisingly enough, the role of our First Brain remains essentially the same. Even in an ordinary, civilized, social conversation between two human beings in the 1990s, our First Brains are still only interested in one question: "Is it safe?"

If you want to get your message across, you must reach and connect with the First Brain. You must persuade your listener's First Brain that you are trustworthy—that you are likable—that you represent warmth, comfort, and safety.

How the First Brain Works

Now, at this point, you may be thinking, "All this stuff about the brain—isn't that too complicated for me to understand?" Sure, the human brain is a very complex organ, and we are only beginning to fathom it. But there have been important and exciting new discoveries in brain research in recent years. And applying these exciting fresh

First Brain and New Brain Compared

First Brain	New Brain
♥ Instinctual and Primitive	♦ Intellectual and Advanced
♥ 300 to 500 million years old	♦ 3 to 4 million years old
♥ Emotional	♦ Rational
♥ Preconscious/Unconscious	♦ Conscious
♥ Source of instinctive survival responses: hunger, thirst, danger, sex, and parental care	♦ Source of thought, memory, language, creativity, planning, and decision making
♥ Common to many animals	♦ Uniquely human

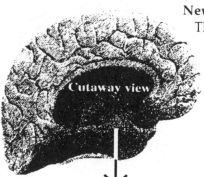

New Brain:
The folds of the cerebrum consist of a very thin 1/8-inch thick layer of brain cells called the Cerebral Cortex. All conscious thought takes place within this thin layer of brain cells.

Cutaway view

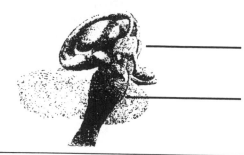

First Brain:

Limbic System, the emotional center

Brain Stem, providing immediate instinctual response

revelations of what we *do* know to the communications process is really very simple to explain and understand. *Most important of all, the First Brain concept is a powerful and transforming new truth.* Isn't it worth understanding a few simple facts about our complex human brain in order to gain the power to achieve what you want in life?

The profound role of the First Brain in the communications process has been virtually ignored by communications experts and theorists— until now. With the unveiling of the First Brain concept, we suddenly have more at our disposal than a grab bag of "public speaking" techniques. We now have *knowledge*—an understanding of why certain behaviors work and others don't. And that knowledge is the power to make us more effective and persuasive every time we speak.

Now we know that all the hundreds of sights and sounds we give off as communicators—all the visual and auditory cues we project— must first pass through the figurative switching station of the listener's First Brain. This emotion-powered switching station inside our listener's head determines if we are believable, likable, and worth listening to. Everything we say, all the stimuli we communicate, is filtered and modified by the listener's First Brain before it is sent on to his or her New Brain—the cerebral cortex—to be analyzed and acted upon.

"Much evidence now indicates that the limbic area [First Brain] is the main switch in determining what sensory inputs will go to the neocortex, and what decisions will be accepted from it . . ."

LESLIE A. HART

from *How the Brain Works*

If we are energetic, enthusiastic, and believable, our words will actually be given more impact and energy by the listener's First Brain before they are switched to the New Brain. But if we appear boring, anxious, or insincere, our words may not even reach their destination. Instead, our message will be discolored or even tuned out at the switching station by our lack of believability. If we lack believability, we risk failure in all the areas of our lives that really matter to us.

To be persuasive and successful, we must be believed, and belief is overwhelmingly determined by the preconscious mechanism of the First Brain.

First Brain Friendly

How, then, do we make friends with the Gatekeeper—the First Brain—so that our message can get through the gate? How do we become "First Brain friendly?"

By being natural. By learning to use energy, enthusiasm, motion, expression—all the multichannel, nonverbal cues that enable us to make emotional contact with the listener. By becoming freer—less inhibited—more naturally ourselves.

Jane Pauley succeeds where Deborah Norville fails because Jane Pauley is intuitively "First Brain friendly." She's warm and genuine, not afraid to let down her guard, and even risk a quip that's a little bit "corny." After watching her for a few weeks, you feel you know her, that she's a friend, that she would invite you over for a chat over coffee. Norville is gracious, attractive, but unapproachable.

Ted Koppel succeeds where Dan Rather fails because Koppel is "First Brain friendly." Koppel is open, witty, relaxed, whereas Rather is affected, cold, and tight as a wound spring. The First Brain welcomes Koppel, but considers Rather a stranger, a source of anxiety, someone to distrust.

Charles Schwab, George Bush, Norman Schwarzkopf, Ronald Reagan, Lee Iacocca, and John Madden all succeed where so many others fail because—either intuitively or intentionally—they have learned how to become "First Brain friendly." They know how to befriend the Gatekeeper within their listeners—and thus they know how to persuade and to achieve their goals.

To become a New Communicator, you must understand that the Gatekeeper can either lock the door and block your message, or fling the door wide open to receive your message. And you must recognize that it all depends on you.

In the rest of this book you're going to learn how to use your natural self to reach the First Brain of your listeners. And you will learn how to control your own First Brain to overcome your own fear of communicating and speaking when the pressure is on. Most important of all, you'll learn how to use your newfound understanding of the preconscious mind to achieve your personal and business goals.

So, from now on, *think First Brain.*

5

Getting to Trust

TRUST

Webster's says it is "the absolute certainty in the trustworthiness of another" and "absolute confidence in the truthfulness of another." Where do you find the word *truth* in the dictionary? Right after the word trust.

MAKING EMOTIONAL CONTACT WITH A NATION

"No speaker is more compelling than one who believes what he is saying. As the camera pulled in tight on the President's face during last Tuesday's State of the Union address, the millions of people tuning in saw a President who was finally projecting the vision that all the high-priced media handlers had been unable to supply for him. With images drawn from World War II, when as a young Navy pilot he flew 58 combat missions, Bush spoke convincingly of a cause that is just, moral and right; of the dangers of appeasement: of the need for sacrifice so that 'the strong are neither tempted nor able to intimidate the weak.' "

Time magazine, February 11, 1991

Believability

In our communication with others, *trust* and *believability* are virtually synonymous. Interchangeable. You can't have one without the other.

Can you think of even one person you trust but do not believe? Or vice versa?

To communicate persuasively and effectively, you must win the trust of your listeners. And to win their trust, you must be believable. How do you do it?

First of all, *belief is a First Brain function.* Belief is acceptance on faith. Some people will believe you on first impression. Most need at least a little convincing. They need to see you, hear you, and interact with you before they can invest belief in you. Either way, belief is emotionally based. It bypasses the intellect. It comes from the nuances of behavior, not from facts or logic. It is perceived and felt rather than analyzed.

The Language of Trust

The First Brain houses the labyrinth of our emotional makeup— and I do not use the word labyrinth merely as a metaphor. Look at the picture of the limbic system, a major component of the First Brain (Endnotes, Chapter 4), and you can see that it is physically fashioned in the intricate, convoluted shape of a labyrinth. The hidden urges and needs that drive human behavior—and that often seem so murky and labyrinthine to the logical side of our minds—arise from the depths of the First Brain.

The First Brain does not understand words. It speaks an altogether different language: the language of behavior. Whereas our New Brain spends most of its time sifting words, symbols, concepts, and data, the First Brain hunts for meaning in thousands of nuances of human behavior that the New Brain never even registers. Does the voice quaver—or does it project authority? Do the hands gesture nervously—or forcefully? Do the eyes flicker hesitantly—or gaze unflinchingly? Is the posture diffident—or confident?

This is the language of the First Brain. It is the Language of Trust. And it is learned early.

Yet They Shall Come as Children

Watch a child during its first six months of life. Study the child closely—the wide eyes that take in every movement, that glance at every sound. Observe how that child responds to a gentle touch, a murmured reassurance, a smile—especially a smile! That child has no language, no preconceptions, no categories with which to make logical sense of his or her world.

Very little of what a baby perceives is imprinted on his or her New Brain. Most of the sights and sounds that are imprinted on a baby are traced in the neurons (brain cells) of the First Brain.

You can communicate with a baby, but not with words. To communicate with a baby, you use facial expression, energy, sound, touch, and motion. The baby responds with the same set of nonverbal cues. This is the language of First Brain communication.

The First Brain is being imprinted even before birth, while the baby is still in the womb. The First Brain experiences the warmth and comfort of the womb. It receives the sounds of the mother's steadily pulsing heart, her gentle respiration, her musical laughter, her complaints, her sighs. The First Brain of an unborn child is learning at a primitive level—about contentment, warmth, safety, and trust. It will soon learn about discomfort, the cold sensation of a draft on naked skin, the wonder of life outside the womb, the uncertain anxiety of a strange face.

During a layover at Kennedy International Airport in New York, I struck up a conversation with a young woman who was traveling with two children, one a four-year-old boy, the other a babe in arms, a little girl. Thinking of these concepts, I struck up a conversation.

"Beautiful baby," I said cleverly. "She must be about six months old."

The mother smiled. "Yes," she replied proudly. "This is Susie." Susie cooed contentedly. "And this is Timmy." Timmy shied away. Something in his First Brain told him to be wary of strangers.

"Tell me," I said, "who was the first person Susie recognized beside yourself?"

"Well," she said, "Susie made goo-goo sounds at Timmy when she was about a week old. I think she recognized him as early as that."

"When did she recognize her Dad?"

"She smiled at him when she was about a month old. She's only begun recognizing friends and relatives in the last couple of months. And she doesn't warm up to strangers at all." Susie is a typical baby. Her First Brain is functioning right on cue. In the first few weeks of her life, she was already using her First Brain programming, learning whom to trust and why.

Susie knows she can trust Mother (her primary caregiver), she can trust another Little Person (her four-year-old brother Timmy), and, in time, she can even trust Daddy and friends of the family. She knows that a smile means attention and fun, and that a soothing touch means nurture and warmth. Over the next year she may also learn that a nervous person who exudes a lack of confidence is more likely to accidentally hurt a baby than Mother is. She may also learn that a person who doesn't smile is likely to lack warmth, and may act unpleasantly.

The point is that most of the learning we experience in the first few weeks and months of life is First Brain learning. It is our First Brain, not our New Brain, that receives most of the imprinting in those early stages of life, and those deeply etched imprints stay with us forever. One of those imprints is a program for determining whom we trust, and why. We learn early that the people we should trust are those who smile, who radiate warmth and confidence, whose touch conveys strength, empathy, and composure. These are the qualities that attracted us and reassured us when we were small and helpless—and these same qualities are no less important to us now that we are grown.

To communicate effectively, we must relearn the language of trust, the language of emotional contact . . .

The language of the First Brain.

You're Being Grokked

Did you ever interview someone for a position in your company and immediately *know* they were the person for the job? But you didn't know why. Did you ever hear a radio sportscaster or talk show host and immediately turn him off because he turned you off? But you didn't know why. Did you ever catch the eye of another person and just *know* you have fallen completely and instantly in love? But you didn't know why.

Then you know what it means to "grok."

If you're a science fiction fan, you probably know the word *grok* and need no further explanation. It's one of those onomatopoeic words that sounds exactly like it means. The word was invented by Robert Heinlein in his classic novel *Stranger in a Strange Land*.

Heinlein's protagonist, Valentine Michael Smith, had the ability to grok—that is, the ability to instantly grasp the entire inner reality of people and situations. Smith, of course, was an alien, a "man from Mars," so his grokking is a science-fictional ability that doesn't exist in the real world. After all, it's logically impossible to immediately know and understand another person almost as soon as you meet them, isn't it?

Or is it?

The fact is, we *all* can grok, and we are *all* being grokked. Of course, none of us are aliens, so we are not able to grok as fully and deeply as Valentine Michael Smith groks. But we are better grokkers than we realize.

Whenever you meet someone or encounter a situation, your First Brain receives literally thousands of cues that are registered at the preconscious level. Our intuition comes from this. You form an almost immediate impression of that person or situation—you have an intuition "about" that person—an impression that is detailed and often richly colored with emotion. The more you learn to plug into and trust your own ability to intuit, the more useful it becomes.

First Brain Intuition

Our Western cultural tendency is to approach communication as if it is all New Brain content, facts, arguments, logic, and reason. The fact is, an equal or greater part of all human communication consists of First Brain intuition.

Lee Iacocca is a naturally effective communicator because he appeals to the First Brain in all of us. He doesn't consciously work at making First Brain contact. He just does it. A lot of people have this natural gift without understanding how it works.

In his autobiography, Lee Iacocca reflected on how perplexed he was by the "Iacocca for President" ground swell that began appearing in the press and on bumper stickers following his engineering of the Chrysler turnaround. "There was a story in *Time* about possible presidential candidates in 1984, and again my name was mentioned. The magazine said I could run for President because I have 'an expressive face.' Another example of persuasive political logic?"

Iacocca didn't consciously understand the power of First Brain intuition. He didn't understand that his "expressive face" (which is one factor of many making up Iacocca's personal impact) is what we are all looking for. We instinctively believe and trust someone whose face is an outward display of inner feelings; we distrust the person who wears a mask. For good or ill, the power of television has indeed transformed our First Brain intuitive ability into "persuasive political logic" when choosing our leaders (despite Iacocca's New Brain resistance to the idea). The candidate who speaks the language of the First Brain, the Language of Trust, is the candidate most likely to be believed, and elected. And that language communicates very rapidly— it is often grokked at a glance.

A Glimpse of the Truth

I met Bev Moore when I was an undergraduate at Yale and I was dating a girl in her dorm at Smith College. I really fell for her—she had sparkle and spunk and an athletic vitality packed into a slight frame—not to mention blond hair, blue eyes, and an upturned nose. We saw a lot of movies together, skied on weekends, and laughed a lot. I was in love, and so was she.

One weekend, after we had been dating for about eight months, Bev took the train from Northampton to New Haven to visit me. It was a lousy weekend. I don't know what put us in the mood we were in. Certainly the weather didn't help—a cold, gray, threatening kind of sky. We had shared a lot of great weekends in the past, but this one was just as gray and foreboding as the clouds overhead.

Saturday we went to the football game at the Yale Bowl. Yale lost in an upset. We had an invitation to a party Saturday night, but we declined and saw a movie instead. Don't remember what movie, but I do remember it was depressing.

Sunday was no better. There was no fight, no argument. Just . . . distance. She was moody, and she was getting more withdrawn as the weekend progressed. I asked her what was wrong. She wouldn't or couldn't articulate a reason. Defensively—and selfishly—I became distant and uncaring myself. When I took her to the train station to see her off, the skies had fulfilled their gloomy promise. It rained. It was cold. And the coldness was inside us both, as well as on the outside. As we stood beside the train that was waiting to take her away, I kissed her. It was a very perfunctory kiss. And I was aching inside.

"Good-bye, Bev," I said, searching her eyes. I could read nothing there.

"Good-bye, Bert," she said. And then she stepped onto the train. She was nearly the last passenger to board, and the train began moving just seconds after I lost sight of her.

I stood and watched to see if I could catch another glimpse of her.

I felt hurt. I didn't want to lose her. A wall had come between us that I didn't understand. She doesn't care, I thought. Okay, I don't care either.

Then I saw her. She was framed in one of the parlor car windows. She didn't see me. As the train slowly moved away, I caught a glimpse of her—no more than a second. But what I saw in that brief glimpse pierced me like a shot. Her face fell into her hands and her shoulders trembled. She was crying!

I saw everything in that one glimpse. I knew she still cared. And I instantly dropped my own defenses and was more in love than ever. I could barely wait for her to get back to Smith so we could talk on the phone. All those decisions and feelings from a fraction-of-a-second look.

That is how the First Brain works. It understands at a preconscious, nonverbal level. It transforms a gesture, a glance, an inflection into instant feelings and emotion. It sees everything in one glance.

First Brain Friendly Makes Presidents

These days, there's a lot of emphasis on making computers, VCRs, and other technological devices "user friendly." In communicating, our emphasis must be on making ourselves First Brain friendly. Our goal is to become open, unaffected, spontaneous—in short, we want to disclose the Natural Self within us. A natural communicator is confident and at ease, not stiff, nervous, or aloof. When we are confident and at ease, we put our listener's First Brain at ease, allowing our listener to trust us and believe our message.

A person who is First Brain friendly is likable—and likability is the shortest path to believability and trust. Pollster George Gallup proved the importance of likability. He conducted a series of political polls that showed a phenomenon he called "The Personality Factor." The results can be seen most dramatically in his polling for presidential elections.

One of the most vivid examples of "The Personality Factor" is the Gallup poll conducted during the 1984 presidential election. In September, two months before the election, Gallup measured candidates Ronald Reagan and Walter Mondale for three factors—issues, party affiliation, and likability. To scientifically quantify the likability factor, he used the Staples Scalometer, a five-point variable where people state their emotional response to a candidate.

Let's look at the first two factors, issues and party affiliation. On issues, Gallup found that Reagan and Mondale were dead even in the polls. Two months before the election, if people were voting strictly on the issues, the election would have been a toss-up—42 percent to 42 percent. But on party affiliation, you have a very different story: Mondale had a clear edge because of Democrat-registered voters: Mondale 42 percent to Reagan's 28 percent.

But on the scale of likability—still another story. Using the Staples Scalometer, Gallup found that on a feeling level, the level of trust and likability, Reagan had a clear advantage over Mondale. The poll showed that 42 percent of those questioned found Reagan likable versus 26 percent for Mondale—a 16-point spread.

If all three measurements were equal in importance, the '84 election would have been a photo finish, with Mondale edging out Reagan by a mere two percent. But that's not the way it went down. Because these three measurements are *not* equal in importance. Sure, we pride ourselves on our rational assessment of the issues facing our nation, and some of us even pride ourselves in our loyalty to the party of our

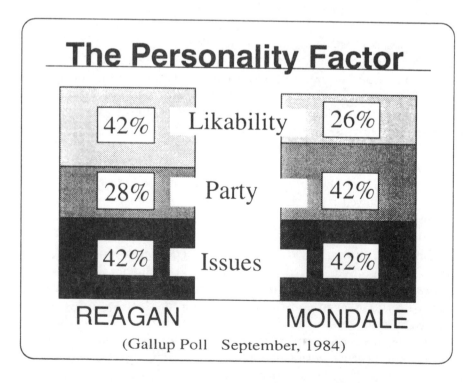

The Personality Factor

42%	Likability	26%
28%	Party	42%
42%	Issues	42%
REAGAN		MONDALE

(Gallup Poll   September, 1984)

choice. But when the chips are down, it's the likability factor that wins.

The final election tally mirrors almost exactly the likability factor of the poll two months earlier—59 percent for Reagan versus Mondale's 41 percent.

And it's not just a fluke of the "Reagan personality." George Gallup has conducted the Personality Factor poll prior to every presidential election since Nixon-Kennedy in 1960—the beginning of the television age of politics. In all that time, there has been only one of the three factors—issues, party affiliation, and likability—that has been a consistent prognosticator of the final election results: the likability factor.

Can we draw an inference regarding likability from these results? What do *you* think?

The personality factor dominates in politics. It also dominates in business. And it dominates in our day-to-day lives. Likability is the key to trust and believability. That truth was brought home to me in a dramatic way.

A Business Personality

There came a time in 1986 when I realized my company would not get very far without someone better than I to run it. Day-to-day management is not my strong suit, and the demands of leading seminars, making speeches, and managing the company were getting too hefty. So I began a search for that person who could lead and manage, someone who loved this business, someone who would be a good complement to my personality.

Several months later I was having lunch with my friend Tom Fife and I happened to mention my quest for an executive partner. I had no candidates. My search had led to a dead end. Tom said he knew a guy who would be great. His name was Dan Toth.

Dan had managed a multimillion dollar division of Computer Sciences Corporation, and was looking for exactly the kind of opportunity I offered. He loved the speaking business. I was enthused from our first few phone calls, but when Dan walked into my San Francisco office for our first face-to-face meeting, I was let down. He didn't "look" like the guy I had imagined.

Dan kids himself about being the kind of guy who only goes to the barber shop to reminisce. "I don't mind being bald," he says. "It just means I come out on top." He was also a bit overweight. I don't have anything against bald people or people who are a little out of shape. After all, I was looking for a guy to run my company, not star in a movie. But these things make an impression, and I was expecting something different. Suffice it to say that my First Brain was not exactly bowled over by Dan Toth during our first few minutes.

Fortunately for both of us, Dan and I had two more hours to talk after that first handshake. Soon thereafter, we cemented the deal. In July of '86, Dan became president of Decker Communications, Inc. He's an indispensable part of the business, an able associate and partner—and he's my friend. Not only does he make money for the company, but he's actually fun to work with!

Does Dan have weaknesses in this area or that? Doesn't everybody? But he has so many strengths, including one outstanding strength: that special touch he has with people. Whatever minor weaknesses Dan may have (and there aren't many) are vastly overshadowed by his strong likability.

Dan's not a "public speaker" in the classic mold. He says it's ironic that, as president of Decker Communications, he doesn't even reflect our program—but of course he does. He's natural. When he speaks, he's funny, engaging, involving—not by adopting the techniques of a "speaker" but by simply letting his natural warmth and humor shine through. People *love* to hear him speak. *I* love to hear him speak. The man is a hit—even with our company of experienced communication trainers—whenever he conducts company meetings.

Why? Simple. Dan Toth is a *likable* guy.

A Crisis at the House of Barbie

John Amerman is also a likable guy, and he needed that quality in his time of crisis. He is chairman of Mattel, Inc., the toy company that has parlayed the Barbie Doll into a billion-dollar organization. But just before Amerman took over it looked like Barbie might be headed for the bankruptcy court rather than the dollhouse.

John Amerman had just completed a great year as head of international sales at Mattel when the board of directors was casting about for a new chairman. The company was on hard times in 1987, except for the 150 percent increase in sales in Amerman's division. So he was asked to do the same for the world as he'd done in Europe—to make Barbie a star again.

John Amerman

The first thing he did was to cut expenses to the bone. Sounds smart, and typical, but was not something easily done at the house of Mattel. For Mattel was a "family," and cutting expenses in this business meant cutting people. John Amerman hated this part of the job. But he was the right man to do it. Because he was likable. He had a face you could trust—and he *was* trusted. He looked kind, and *was* kind—even though behind that warm exterior was a razor-sharp mind that could, and would, do what was necessary to survive. And to lead.

In the first six months of John Amerman's reign he had to lay off 250 people. Morale could have plummeted, but it didn't. Amerman communicated to everybody what had to be done, and why. He met people face to face. He walked and he talked. He held continuous meetings with those who remained on his team, and exhorted them to work harder. He was gentle yet firm. He had to do many things to turn Mattel around, but above all he communicated, and he succeeded.

In four years Mattel has rebounded from a $113 million loss to record earnings of $91 million in 1990. To announce earnings to his work force in 1989 Amerman himself went onstage and performed a funky rap routine, and it brought the house down! "All of the employ-ees came up and hugged me. It was like I hit the home run in the ninth inning of the seventh game of the World Series."

Fortune calls John Amerman one of the "champions of communica-tion," and describes his communication style as one of informality. He speaks without a written script and develops a "structured format" in his mind. And most often "this cheerful, white-haired CEO is seen wandering around the place, eating in the cafeteria, and meeting regularly with employees." He is likable and he is informal. He connects with the First Brain—and he *reaches* his audience.

Reading Speeches, Losing Audiences

Once during a layover at Chicago's O'Hare, I was making phone calls in the Red Carpet Club, waiting for my flight, when I noticed a couple of businessmen sitting at a nearby table. They were working on a sales presentation while waiting for their flight. They had their jackets off, their sleeves rolled up, and they were poring through a *mountain* of 35mm slides. Next to Mount Ektachrome was another mountain—this one made of paper. It was the script for their presenta-tion—and it had to be every bit of twenty or thirty pages long—*single-spaced*.

I thought to myself, woe betide the listeners doomed to endure this content-laden slide marathon. Imagine the boredom, the mass tune-out, the glazed stares! Pity those poor, tortured First Brains in the audience, all silently crying out for sustenance and relief! They will drown in data while thirsting for knowledge.

Don't do that to your listeners. And don't do it to yourself.

I've seen it so many times. One of the most glaring examples occurred when I was keynote speaker at the National Fire Sprinkler Association. The meeting was held at a major downtown hotel for over a hundred owners and managers of fire sprinkler manufacturing and distributing companies.

There were several speakers ahead of me, most speaking on fairly technical subjects—manufacturing processes, the financial climate, and government regulations. The first speaker had lots of detailed information, lots of handouts, and an annoyingly whiny voice. With all those handouts in their grasp, everybody was too busy reading to listen to the speaker. Which was just as well.

"We could be in for a long day," I thought to myself. And unfortunately for me I was the *third* and final speaker scheduled for the morning.

The next speaker had slides. *Lots* of slides, almost as many as those guys in the Red Carpet Club at O'Hare. Some people in the audience watched that slide show as if hypnotized. Some tried to read newspapers or magazines by the light from the screen. Some of the slides went by upside down. Didn't matter. Meanwhile, the speaker read his speech in a phlegmatic drone. At the end of his speech, there was no applause, only a weary sigh of relief.

The energy in that room was so low, I almost hesitated to do my normal opening, which almost always works. I deliberately start a presentation *the wrong way*. I mean, the *worst* possible way. I lay a stack of pages (supposedly the text of my speech) on the lectern and start reading. Eyes glued to the page. Flat monotone voice. No gestures. In other words, just like my two predecessors on that podium.

I decided to go with it anyway. After I was introduced, I stepped up to the lectern and proceeded to do everything I could to sabotage my own likability and drive the energy of the audience into the ground. It worked beautifully. In seconds, the boredom in that room was so thick you could cut it with a chainsaw.

I glanced up a couple of times as I droned on—not to make eye contact with my listeners, but just to make sure that they were still tuned out. It was perfect. I saw people yawning, gazing blankly, reading newspapers, checking watches.

Then, about a minute into my speech, I raised my voice, picked up my "notes," tossed them behind me, and stepped out from behind the lectern. A ripple of surprise and murmur of suspense went through the audience. I could see it in their faces: "What is this guy up to?" No question, I now had their undivided attention.

"How many of you completely tuned out while I was talking from that lectern?" Lots of sighs of relief, but no hands. "Oh, come on! Be honest! I just got through boring you to tears! Admit it! How many of you tuned me out completely in the *first five seconds* of my so-called 'speech'?" Grins now, expressions of relief, and a *massive* show of hands.

From that point on we were off and running. The energy level of the audience soared. Those poor suffering souls were so relieved—no, ecstatic!—that somebody finally cared enough to *communicate* with them. They were starving for someone who would give them real human contact, not just shovel some facts and figures at them. They were hungry for someone they could listen to.

Someone they could *like*.

A Memory Test

Whenever I open a speech that way with that dry, lifeless reading, I use real content, not nonsense. I start by talking about how we, as communicators at all levels, need to make emotional contact with our listeners and keep them involved *while at that very time I'm doing my best to turn my listeners off!* In fact, to underscore my message, I always give some simple facts and figures that support my content.

Then, after I move out from behind the lectern, make the transition, begin to *contact* the people, with the energy level leaping, I ask, "Does anyone remember those four points I made? . . . Two of the points? . . . One? Oh, come on! Somebody here must remember at least one out of four!"

I can usually find one or two volunteers who can remember one of my points, maybe two. Everyone else draws a complete blank. *They got absolutely nothing of the facts I just read to them only a couple of minutes before!* But when I bring the energy up, retention zooms! Clearly the primary variable is not how great your content is or how many facts and figures you have to buttress your argument. If you want to be memorable and persuasive, the primary variable *is your behavior*.

The wrong behavior turns people off. They won't hear you. They won't remember you. They won't even like you. They certainly won't be persuaded to action by anything you have to say. The First Brain has shut the doors and barred the gates—and you're left out in the cold. Here's an example from one of our own meetings.

Facts Versus Humor

Actually, it was the battle of the giants.

Tom Troja is big. He stands 6 feet 7 inches and he heads up our New York office in a big way. He is intense, direct, and well-liked. He also loves the New York Giants, and those of us in San Francisco never heard the end of it after their 1991 Super Bowl victory. But to let you know what a great guy he is anyway, Tom has given me permission to share this story with you.

In 1990 Tom had a great sales year. At the fall quarterly review he came in on a roll. He was doing an outstanding job in New York, and he knew it. He arrived on a red-eye flight, direct from Kennedy International to San Francisco, but came in full of pizazz anyway. He made his presentation, and it was a great one—up until the last few minutes.

As he unveiled the sales quotas he had projected for October, November, and December, the eyes of everyone in the room were drawn to the December quota, which was down dramatically. Several people in the room jumped on that December projection and started to quiz Tom about it. "Where did that number come from?" "Why so pessimistic?" "What do you base that on?"

Tom became defensive and tried to justify the number. A heated but bantering dialogue set in, and at that point Tom's enthusiasm dissipated—and his irritation began to show. A lot. He clearly felt he was being picked on because of one number on a chart.

And he probably had a right to feel that way. Tom was a top producer for our company, and he was having a great year. But still, when he let a flurry of questions throw him, upsetting his equilibrium and his good humor, this competent, effective, likable guy seemed— just for that moment—not quite so likable. And it killed the end result of his presentation.

And in contrast we have Fred Verhey. Fred is shorter than Tom Troja, but not by much. At 6 feet 6 inches Fred is impressive and effective—our vice president of Training and Operations.

In real contrast to Tom Troja, Fred was not having a great year in the Speaker Services division. He had poor revenues, well under plan for the whole quarter, and the year was not much better. And we all knew it. And he knew it. So what did he do?

In comes Fred Verhey for his presentation and he starts off with a variation of the game of "Jeopardy." With a big smile he puts up three figures and says, "So what's the question?" Dan Toth rattles off the first answer, and we quickly get into the swing of the game. And have fun with it. The questions (numbers) are all "bad"—the facts aren't made any better—but the total mood is different. People are *with* Fred, not just because he is smiling, or trying to varnish the facts and give them a different slant. No, we are with him because we *like* him. He is earnest and enthusiastic about getting those numbers up, and doesn't let himself get beaten down. He ends his presentation on a high note. The general feeling in the whole room is one of positiveness. Even though we know the facts are not good. *Direct contrast. Great feeling but lousy numbers for Fred Verhey. Lousy feeling but great numbers for Tom Troja. What carries the day?*

Likability! Like it or not.

Let's Take a Vote

In the spring of 1991, I was invited by Radius Scientific to address a large gathering of neurologists at the Silverado Country Club in the heart of the Napa Valley. I was speaking on a subject familiar to you by now: "Communicating Is a Contact Sport." The group was interested in relating the link between communication and the human brain to their work. Much of the morning had been devoted to talks about a new drug treatment for strokes, and most of the content revolved around technical minutiae—the effects of certain pharmacological agents on the hematology of the brain, and the like.

Again I found myself about to go before a low-energy audience. Should I use the turnaround routine again? Would it work again? The academic nature of the audience introduced a new variable into the equation. This group might be harder to turn than the previous low-energy audience.

But this group also presented an opportunity I had never had before: IRIS.

IRIS is an audience interactive device. Each listener in the audience is given a remote keypad so they can immediately vote on questions or issues. Radius Scientific had brought in the IRIS system in order to get instantaneous reaction to questions. I couldn't resist this opportunity to get instantaneous feedback on the issue of emotional connection and likability.

So I began with my customary boring, flat opening. I read my speech for a minute, then—still reading in my bone-dry monotone—I said, "I would like you all to use your IRIS device and answer *very honestly* the following question: At this moment, how open are you to the ideas of this presentation and this presenter? (1) Like very much; (2) Like; (3) Neutral; (4) Dislike; (5) Dislike very much."

The immediate vote came in predictably adverse (see chart).

Then I shifted to my normal presentation mode, and the mood swing was dramatic. For the rest of the hour I told them—and showed them—what it means to make emotional contact, to speak the nonverbal language of the First Brain. I think a lot of those very cerebral, intellectually oriented men and women had a hard time accepting what I was telling them. It's hard, when your lifelong focus has been on the cognitive, on content, on facts and figures and data, to suddenly adopt a new paradigm regarding the way the brain processes communication.

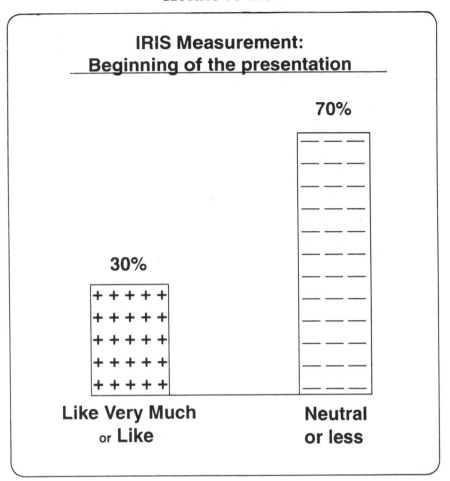

We had a lot of fun together. They laughed. They responded. You could see it in their eyes and in their smiles: I had won them over. Toward the end of the hour, I again asked for a vote. The result was immediate again, but different (see chart on next page).

This was nearly a threefold increase in likability. Here is a precise measurement of communication effectiveness—the kind of scientific measurement that even our reasoning New Brains can understand. And consider this. What kind of communication occurs in a group that is *70 percent neutral or disliking the speaker?* Precious little. But a lot occurs in the group that is *80 percent liking the speaker.* That's dramatic evidence for the case of likability.

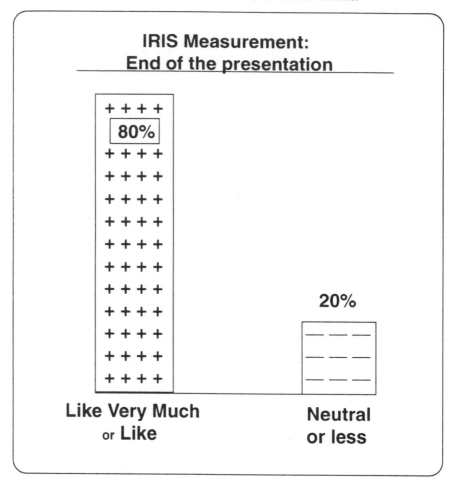

Trust under Pressure

The primary time to be open, to gain trust, and to exude the confidence that engenders believability is under pressure. It is here that our believability is often betrayed by the behavior of tension—right when it counts most.

One of the most vivid examples of this was by a cabinet official in response to a retaliatory air strike in Libya several years ago. Then Secretary of Defense Caspar Weinberger gave a press conference, speaking for three minutes. There were tens of millions watching in the

United States, and many millions more in the world beyond. Believability was crucial, and it was sorely lacking. Oh, it wasn't the content. The facts sounded plausible. But not believable. Not trustworthy. Not the truth. *Because his behavior gave him away.* Weinberger had 59 "ums" and "ahs" halting his speech flow in those brief three minutes. (They were so distracting I went back and counted them later from the recording.) And his darting eyes betrayed him, for he was anxiously glancing everywhere—and thus looking nowhere. He never looked at his audience, or the camera, or *anywhere*. His glances were all fleeting, nervously scanning his environment. He looked jumpy, lacked confidence, and did not earn our trust.

His behavior had nothing to do with content. But it had everything to do with whether we believed his content. He looked nervous. At the preconscious level we were reading a lot of cues. Why was he so tense? People are jittery when they feel they are under attack, when they are dissembling, or when they can't be open or honest. If one is telling the truth there is nothing to be nervous about. And confidence will show. And listeners will see it. The continuous mind chatter of a listener will tell him or her about the behavior of the communicator. And what will be believed and trusted. Or not.

Getting to Trust

Mind chatter occurs at this preconscious level. It is important self-talk, for it is the First Brain talking. It is either opening up the floodgates for content to reach our New Brain, or shutting down. The nonverbal behavior and nervously darting eyes impact the First Brain directly, immediately, and adversely. The mind chatter says "Not truth. No trust."

So we need to establish trust immediately if we are to be believed. In your first meeting with a huge potential client in a selling situation—you need to establish trust. When you are in a seemingly compromising situation that is perceived erroneously—you need to establish trust. When you are the leader of a new group—you need to establish trust. You must get to trust, or you get nowhere. Think of the reception of my audiences if I had continued to read my presentation. (I certainly wouldn't be in the communications business, you can trust that to be the truth.)

The communicator says his first words, and establishes trust or not. But even before that, the First Brain makes an evaluation as soon as it *sees* the speaker. The visual connection is actually the beginning of establishing trust and believability.

In the next part of the book, you'll learn how and why two primarily visual principles—what I call The Eye Factor and The Energy Factor—are so critical in establishing the trust you need to communicate effectively.

Part III

TWO KEY PRINCIPLES

THE SIX-DAY WONDER: AN INTRODUCTION TO YOUR PERSONAL TRANSFORMATION

When Rich Casey came aboard as Syntex Corporation's new national sales manager, he was an unknown quantity in an uncertain situation. Energetic, aggressive, and extremely savvy at the tender age of thirty-three, Casey was viewed with a mixture of expectation, apprehension, and skepticism by the people at Syntex. Top management saw him as an up-and-comer, while old hands in the business saw him as the brash and brassy new kid on the block—just a flash in the pan.

A once-thriving pharmaceutical giant, Palo Alto–based Syntex Corporation was going through hard times, and needed a new infusion of energy and ideas. Its new wonder drug Naprosyn was hanging under a cloud, harmed by some earlier flawed studies. With the expected high growth rate retarded, Syntex could no longer rest on its past reputation. Rich Casey's job: return this now lagging, sluggish pharmaceutical company to a robust and rambunctious force in the marketplace.

For the past ten years, tall, lean, dark-haired Rich Casey had stood out in a field of 400 Syntex salespeople. Suddenly, a worried management had thrust him into the top sales job in the company, with orders to put Syntex back on the fast track. Could he do it? Some in the company thought so. Many others doubted. But most just didn't know who Rich Casey was or what kind of stuff he was made of. An atmosphere of "wait and see" hung over the organization. What everyone was waiting for was the National Sales Meeting at the luxurious Doubletree Inn in Monterey, California, where the new national sales manager would be introduced.

Casey, who had been tapped for the position just three months before this crucial meeting, knew that his talk would be—for good or ill—the turning point of the meeting. It might well be the turning point of his career. It might even be the turning point of the future of Syntex.

I met Rich Casey just six days before the conference was to begin. I knew his wife, Shelley, from a Decker Communications seminar she had taken six months earlier. A charming and gifted executive for Saga Foods (now a division of Marriott), Shelley had enjoyed and benefited from her training in our program. She was sure Rich would benefit as well, since he had never seen himself on videotape before, and was very apprehensive about his upcoming speech. Shelley urged Rich to take the program, but he was unable to find the time until it was almost too late.

With just six days to go before one of the biggest deadlines of his life, Rich was in my San Francisco office, showing me the speech he had written. And it was a pretty good speech—on paper. I had Rich deliver his speech before a video camera, then had him watch the tape playback. The tape had only been rolling for a few minutes when he said, "My gosh! I had no idea I looked so stiff and boring when I give a speech! I can't go to the National Sales Meeting with that kind of presentation!"

I didn't have to say a word to convince him. Rich intuitively understood that his audience was going to be appraising his confidence, his competence, his ability to lead. They weren't going to be impressed by a man who lifelessly reads a speech while standing behind a lectern, no matter how well-written the speech is on paper.

"Bert, what do I do?" Rich asked. "I'm facing an impossible challenge! I've only got a few days to reshape myself into a dazzling speaker and energize the entire sales force of my company! This is the most important presentation of my life—and I don't have time to memorize it! Help!"

"I wouldn't help you memorize it, even if you *did* have time," I replied. "It would only sound as stiff and stilted as if you'd read it. But there is a better way."

For the next day and a half, we worked on that "better way." Were we successful? Did Rich prevail over his "impossible challenge"? Was he able to convince the skeptics, energize his sales force, and turn the company around?

Well, let me just take you back to that autumn day in the Grand Ballroom of the Monterey Conference Center on the craggy coast of California. In contrast to the crisp, salty ocean-scented air outside, the room was hot and stuffy. Though the lights were low, people were perspiring—but no one was sweating that moment more than Rich Casey. The chairman of Syntex, Dr. Bert Bowers, finished his opening remarks, then turned to introduce the new national sales manager of the corporation. As his name was spoken, Rich stood and crossed the darkened stage, stepping into the small pool of light that haloed the lectern. The houselights came up, revealing an audience of several hundred men and women—the entire Syntex sales management team and most of its corporate officers. The applause was respectful, but brief. *Okay*, thought Rich Casey, *this is it*!

"This is a crucial moment for you, for our company . . . and for me personally," he began. His wireless microphone picked up the keen intonation of his words, propelling them through the dense, stagnant air. "I've thought long and hard about the sales direction this company should take in the coming years, and about what I need to say to you this morning."

At that moment, Rich took up the manuscript of his speech, stepped out from behind the protective barrier of the lectern, and walked boldly to the center of the stage. "I wrote out a speech full of goals and objectives," he said, lifting the manuscript up, "but I got to thinking that maybe the most important thing for this company right now is *not* so much the goals and objectives for the next few months. What is important for us right now is the spirit that drives us. It's the spirit of each and every one of us. It's the spirit and vitality that is Syntex."

With a dramatic flourish, he ripped the speech from top to bottom. "So let's forget the speech," he said as the pieces of the manuscript fluttered to the floor. "This morning I want to talk to you from the heart."

Then Rich Casey proceeded to give one of the most dramatic, powerful and memorable talks Syntex had ever heard. Most of the ideas in that talk were the same ideas he had assembled in his written speech. But Rich delivered them with feeling, with spontaneity, with impact. In those few crucial moments, Rich Casey reached the First Brains of 200 key people in his company.

Standing on the edge of the stage, moving easily from one side of the room to the other, he ceased to be a performer on a stage. He became a person. People later remarked how he looked directly at each person in the room, how his eyes communicated with each individual. He stood tall and smiled easily (although, with his underlying nervousness, he certainly didn't feel like smiling). He gestured comfortably and confidently as he moved easily across the platform. His voice rose and fell dynamically, sometimes to underscore a point, sometimes to rivet attention, sometimes to convey emotion.

In those moments, Rich Casey did not merely give a speech. He became the leader of the Syntex sales force. He inspired his people to meet the challenge ahead with new energy and resolve. And, as people often do in the presence of genuine leadership and command, the audience gave Rich Casey a standing ovation.

Somewhere during the twenty-five or so minutes of Rich Casey's talk, the Syntex corporation turned a corner. Naprosyn later grew from under $100 million to over half a billion in sales, and the sales force itself grew from 400 to over a thousand. The career of Rich Casey would never be the same again. (He has since become the president of another biotech company.)

The story of Rich Casey is the story of a six-day wonder, an amazing personal transformation. Rich succeeded because he learned—just in the nick of time!—how to reach the First Brain of his audience. He did it by emphasizing just two key principles.

And you can do the same.

Skeptical? By the end of the next two chapters, I expect to make a believer out of you.

"Give us the tools, and we will finish the job."

WINSTON CHURCHILL

The Nine Ways to Transform Your Personal Impact

In The Decker Program™ we have identified nine skill areas that enable you to reach the First Brain of your listener. Each of these skills relates to Two Key Principles—The Eye Factor and The Energy Factor.

The Nine Ways to Transform Your Personal Impact are:

Chapter 6: The Eye Factor	**Chapter 7:** The Energy Factor
1. Eye Communication 2. Posture and Movement 3. Dress and Appearance 4. Gestures and the Smile	5. Voice and Vocal Variety 6. Words and Nonwords (The Pause) 7. Listener Involvement 8. Humor

Although all of these first eight skills contain at least some aspect of the visual dimension and some aspect of the energy dimension, one or the other dominates each skill set. However, the final skill combines both the Eye and Energy Factors equally, and will be explored in Chapter 15. It is:

> **9. The Natural Self**

These skills are simple to acquire and sharpen. That's why Rich Casey was able to transform himself as a communicator in only six days. If you focus on the visual impact of The Eye Factor and the personal dynamism of The Energy Factor, you'll be transformed too!

6

The Eye Factor

"What you do speaks so loud I can't hear what you say."

RALPH WALDO EMERSON

THE DOMINANT SENSE

The visual sense is very, very powerful. The nerve pathways of the eye to the brain are twenty-five times larger than the nerve pathways from the ear to the brain. The eye is the only sensory organ that contains brain cells. Memory improvement experts invariably emphasize techniques that link the information you want to remember to a *visual* image. Over the past few years, a huge body of research has been amassed, demonstrating that of all the sensory input the brain registers, it is the visual input that makes the greatest impact. Clearly, it is the *visual* sense which dominates *all* of the senses.

A Picture of Health

My partner in founding Decker Communications was my late wife, Deborah. She was a lively, vital woman who fought a valiant three-year struggle with cancer. Although she lost the battle, her fight was an inspiration to all who knew her, particularly our three children.

81

Allison, Sam, and Ben were impressionable teenagers. Obviously their mother was not herself at the end. The images of the last year were unflattering—that was not the eternal image I wanted the kids to have. So I took one of her typical, laughing pictures, had it blown up, and put it up in the family room right after the memorial service. And for months afterwards that three-by-four-foot picture of Deborah smiled down on us, a reminder of the person that was. And now, many years later, that is the singular image that is embedded in each one of our minds.

The Visual Reigns in Today's World

Why is the visual sense so dominant? It is estimated that the nerve endings of our eyes are struck by literally 700,000 stimuli every instant. We cannot escape the massive impact of this bombardment on our brain. Psychologists have said that viewing something three times has the power of one actual experience. This fact alone has enormous consequence, in our movie and TV habits, and in how we use our powers of visualization (see Chapter 9). Consider the impact of three viewings of *The Texas Chainsaw Massacre* or *Deep Throat*. The psychological, emotional, and destructive impact in your mind of seeing those acted-out scenarios three times would be similar to seeing the actual event just once. The power of vision can be used for good or ill. But there is no question that it is a strong, strong power.

The advent of television has exaggerated this natural phenomenon of visual dominance. Most of today's adults were raised on television, and are much more visually sophisticated than their parents. The subtleties of a glance or a coy smile are significant—and they communicate. Such nuances weren't as critical in the previous age.

Look at the laughably primitive acting methods and facial expressions of the silent movies of the 1910s and 1920s. Observe how they became more subtle and less exaggerated in the 1930s and 1940s, and how even our favorite actors, the best of that period—Cagney, Lombard, Bogart, Bacall, Tracy, Gable, Garland, Grant, and the rest—appear posed, affected, and exaggerated compared with their counterparts in the 1980s and 1990s. It is because the audience has become more visually attuned; a slightly upturned eyebrow conveys more than a leering grimace did fifty years ago.

Clearly, the visual channel communicates with power and impact. To communicate effectively in today's business and social world, you *must* be aware of the language of the First Brain—and you must *use* it. The language of the First Brain is a *visual* language. The Eye Factor dominates.

The Inconsistent Message

A spoken message is made up of only three components: the verbal, the vocal, and the visual. A few years ago, Professor Albert Mehrabian of UCLA conducted a landmark study on the relationships between the "Three V's" of spoken communication. He measured the effect that each of these three components has on the believability of our message. The verbal element is the message itself—the words you say. Most of us tend to concentrate *only* on the verbal element, mistakenly assuming this to be *the* message, when in fact it is only *part* of the message.

The second part of the message is the vocal element—the intonation, projection, and resonance of your voice as it carries the words.

And the third part is the visual element—what people see—the motion and expression of your body and face as you speak. Professor Mehrabian's research found that the degree of consistency (or inconsistency) between these three elements is the factor that determines the believability of your message. The more these three factors harmonize with each other, the more believable you are as a speaker.

Let's do an experiment—write your estimate of the percentage of impact each element has on the believability of your message:

What Counts: *Believability*

Verbal	————
Vocal	————
Visual	————
Total	100%

What happens when these three components contradict each other? We transmit an inconsistent message. We literally send out mixed signals. Which signals will our listener find the most convincing? Which signals will our listener believe? Which will he or she ignore?

In his research, Albert Mehrabian found that when we send out an inconsistent message, our verbal content is virtually smothered by the vocal and visual components. Just look at his results:

What Counts: *Believability*

Verbal	7%
Vocal	38%
Visual	55%
Total	100%

How did Mehrabian's actual results compare with your estimate? Surprised? Yet it's absolutely true! When the vocal and visual components of our message are inconsistent with the verbal content of our message, we will simply not be believed.

But when we learn how to coordinate all three of these components to form one totally consistent message, we are not only believable, *we have impact*. The excitement and enthusiasm of your voice work with the energy and animation of your face and body to reflect the conviction of your message. When your words, your voice, and your delivery are all working in harmony, your message dynamically and persuasively saturates your listener's First Brain.

But when you appear nervous, awkward, or under pressure, your verbal content is blocked by your inconsistent vocal and visual message. For example, when someone says, "I'm happy to be here," but looks at the floor, talking in a halting, tremulous voice, clasping his hands together in front of his body in an edgy, inhibited "fig-leaf" posture— he is sending out an inconsistent message. Those words will not be trusted, because it is the visual channel that dominates what is believed.

AND WHY USE VISUAL AIDS WHEN YOU SPEAK?

- Various studies show retention increases from 14 percent to 38 percent when listeners see as well as hear.
- Speaker's goals are met 34 percent more often when visuals are used than when they are not.
- Group consensus occurs 21 percent more often in meetings with visuals than without.
- Time required to present a concept can be reduced up to 40 percent with the use of visuals.
- When visuals were used in teaching a course on vocabulary, learning improved 200 percent.

What does the visual channel tell the listener about us when we send out an inconsistent message? Perhaps it says we are insincere or lacking in confidence. Or perhaps it says we have something to hide. Or perhaps it just conveys to the listener a feeling of anxiety or out-and-out boredom.

WYSIWYG is a computer term that stands for "What You See Is What You Get." It applies to personal impact as well. The message you *see* is the message you *get*. Clearly, the primary path to First Brain believability is through the visual channel. How, then, do we use the visual elements to enhance rather than inhibit our message?

1. Eye Communication

"An eye can threaten like a loaded and leveled gun; or can insult like hissing and kicking; or in its altered mood by beams of kindness, make the heart dance with joy."

RALPH WALDO EMERSON

Eye communication is your number one skill. It ranks first because it has the greatest impact in both one-on-one communications and large group communications. It literally connects mind-to-mind, since your eyes are the only part of your central nervous system that are in direct contact with another human being. When your eyes meet the eyes of another person, you make a First Brain-to-First Brain connection. When you fail to make that connection, it matters very little what you say.

Some Examples

- Judy Sandler, an outside salesperson for a major corporation, has a problem with "eye-dart." Even in casual conversations, her eyes flit about like those of a high-strung thoroughbred filly. When she talks with clients or her peers on the sales force, her "eye-dart" goes into

"Eye-dart"

high gear—and she fails to connect with her listeners' First Brain. People find her continually shifting gaze to be distracting and annoying. As a result, a lot of sales that could have been hers are going to the competition.

- Marion James is a personnel director for a major corporation. When she interviews people she rarely looks them in the eye, and often gazes out the window while talking. This unconscious habit makes her appear uninterested and distant.

- Doug Thomas is the minister of a small church. When he leads worship, he keeps his eyes closed two to three seconds between glances at his audience. Perhaps he is unconsciously imitating the "godly" stance of another preacher he admires, but in doing so he creates an impression of aloofness. This habit carries over into his personal conversations. His parishioners tend to view him as cold and detached—the exact opposite of the way Doug sees himself. Could it be that some of the tensions he feels around some of the people in his church are not caused so much by any doctrinal differences, but by his undiagnosed "slo-blink"?

Do you see yourself in the examples of Judy, Marion, or Doug? If so there's hope, for their eye communication problems are curable—and so are yours. But don't assume making "eye contact" is enough. I don't use the term "eye contact" often because it implies a short glance. Good eye communication is more than just a glance. You are actually looking at an individual—making a First Brain–to–First Brain connection—when you genuinely communicate with your eyes.

"Slo-blink"

The Basic Rules

Use Involvement Rather than Intimacy or Intimidation. Intimacy and intimidation mean looking at another person steadily for a long period—say, ten seconds to a minute or more. In business and normal social conversations, both intimacy or intimidation make our listeners feel uncomfortable. But over 90 percent of our business and social communications call for involvement. How do you achieve that "just right" level of eye connection that conveys a feeling of involvement?

For Effective Eye Communication, Count to Five. A feeling of involvement requires about five seconds of steady eye contact. That is about the time we take to complete a thought or a sentence. When we talk to another person and are excited, enthusiastic, and confident, we usually look at them for five to ten seconds before looking away. That's natural and comfortable for most listeners in one-on-one communications, so it's logical that we should try to meet that expectation in all our speaking situations, whether we are addressing one listener or a roomful. Push for longer eye communication—beyond your comfort zone—for it's too easy to revert back to "short" eye-contact habits unless you work at it.

Beware of Eye Dart. When we are under pressure or feel a lack of confidence, our instinct is to avoid the eyes of our listener. The problem is the listener can read our anxiety in our darting eyes. We give the appearance of a scared rabbit. We exude an "aroma" of fear and nervousness—and this undermines our credibility and makes our listener feel uncomfortable.

Beware of Slo-Blink. On the other hand, it is equally disconcerting to talk to a person with the "slo-blink" habit. This is where a person closes his or her eyes for up to two or three seconds while speaking. It conveys the message, "I really don't want to be here." It doesn't take long before the listeners decide they feel the same way.

Some Basic Exercises

Get Video Feedback to make yourself aware of your eye movements—both length of contact and idiosyncrasies like eye dart or slo-blink. Do this when you are making a presentation, practicing in your company's training room, in a video feedback course, or even at home. (See Chapter 12.)

Practice One-on-One at every opportunity. Ask a friend to keep track of your eye patterns and length of movements during a normal conversation. Have your friend silently count while you make contact, and record it so that he or she can tell you later. Then get an average count on how long you tend to look at a person. Work on pushing that average to five seconds or more.

Practice with a Paper Audience when you have a presentation coming up. Draw happy faces on Post-It™ notes—or, if you prefer, unhappy faces (tough audience). Stick those notes on chairs, or on the wall in the room where you practice your talk. Put a face at each "fringe," right next to the corner.

Now, give your presentation to your paper audience. Talk to the chairs or wall—the whole wall, corner to corner. You can practice your movement, too (see below). Be sure to give at least five seconds of "look" to each face—and be sure to include the faces at the fringes.

Watch TV to increase your awareness and "eye savvy" by seeing *real people* in pressure situations. And I don't mean watching actors wrapped in a role in soaps or sitcoms. Observe people being themselves—talking under pressure—and notice their eye communication patterns. Watch shows like "60 Minutes" or "20/20"—where people are put on the defensive and the heat is on. The First Brain reveals

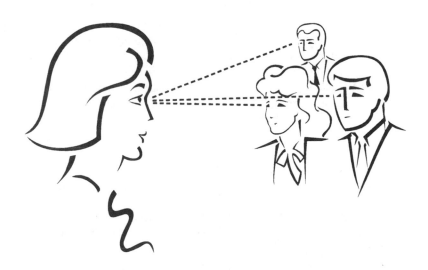

"A Confident Five Seconds"

"EYE CONTACT SAVED HIS LIFE"

He began by telling about being a soldier in Vietnam. One evening he and his buddies were pinned down in a bunker. His fellow soldiers were killed and he was hit three times—once each in his right shoulder, his right thigh, and his left side.

Lying on the ground, he thought that any moment he'd die. He visualized his heart pumping all the blood out of his left side . . . and then just quitting . . . and he'd be dead.

About that time the Vietcong soldiers came up and started going through the dead American soldiers' bodies—taking their valuables—watches, rings, money, even knocking gold fillings out of their teeth.

One of the soldiers came up to him, reached down for his watch, and discovered he was still alive when the young man jerked his hand away. Immediately the enemy soldier pointed his gun between the young man's eyes. The young man just knew he was about to die.

He told how he looked up into the soldier's eyes, with as much feeling and emotion as he could muster, shook his head from side to side, and said, "No . . . no . . . please don't kill me!"

After a moment the enemy soldier could no longer handle it emotionally, broke eye contact, and pulled his gun away. Just then another Vietcong soldier yelled something. The young man assumed he asked if he was still alive, because the soldier yelled something back, which he assumed was "Yes." Then the other soldier yelled again. My friend assumed he yelled, "Kill him!" because once again the soldier pointed his gun at him and was about to pull the trigger.

Again, the young man looked deeply into his enemy's eyes, nodded his head from side to side, and said, "No . . . no . . . please don't kill me . . . please don't!"

After an incredibly painful pause, even though he couldn't understand the language, the Vietcong soldier once again backed down, broke eye contact, pulled his gun away, pointed it into the ground a few feet away, and pulled the trigger. He then yelled something to the other soldier, and walked away.

From *Integrity Selling* by Ron Willingham

itself in eye communication. Notice telltale signs of fear, anger, harassment, humor, arrogance, or sadness in the eyes. Or you might see confidence and believability. Catch the morning shows, the news shows, the variety and talk shows. Sensitize yourself to how eye communication enhances—or betrays—a person's credibility and likability.

The Benefits of Good Eye Communication

- You feel less nervous (like having a series of one-on-one conversations with people).
- You appear confident (whether you are or not).
- You focus your thoughts.
- You can motivate your movement.
- You "read" your audience by seeing individuals.

Remember: Contact eyes, not faces. Look at people for four, five, or six seconds. And exercise particularly on eliminating rapid and/or distracting eye movements.

2. Posture and Movement

"Stand tall. The difference between towering and cowering is totally a matter of inner posture. It's got nothing to do with height, it costs nothing and it's more fun."

MALCOLM FORBES

"Dress for success," the saying goes. But the most powerful visual first impression you make comes not from your clothes but from your posture.

Think of a public figure you see frequently on TV. Can you think of any "slumpers"? Not many—and the reason is clear. Confidence is best expressed through good, upright posture. How you hold yourself physically is an indicator of how you hold yourself mentally—and a decisive factor in how others regard you.

Some Examples

- Phyllis Manning runs her own consulting firm. She thought she had a big tummy as a little girl, so she consciously sucked in her stomach at all times. This caused her shoulders to go back, so that as an adult she has very erect body posture. Because of the confident way she walks, she commands attention when she enters a room.
- Denise Elliot was a typical seventeen-year-old. She was in the audi-

ence when I appeared on the "SFO Evening Magazine" television show to demonstrate the impact of our video seminars. Denise volunteered to give an impromptu on-camera talk, then participate in the Decker Program. The following week, she would return to the show and talk on-camera again—a live "before and after" experiment.

In the "before" segment she talked rapidly—a lot of "ums" and "ahs," a few giggles, the normal kind of nervousness you would expect from a first solo performance before a large TV audience. Moreover, she slumped a little, with all her weight on her left hip, arms akimbo—a stance that gave her an anxious, insecure look. As I accepted the challenge of transforming this awkward teenager into a confident communicator, even I had my doubts. Under this kind of pressure could Denise dramatically improve her habits and her posture before next week's show?

She completed the two-day training on the very afternoon of the live broadcast. Her repeated comments about how nervous she was about the show did nothing to help my peace of mind! As we waited backstage, I was nervous for Denise—but just as much for myself and my company! We had a lot of credibility riding on the performance of this seventeen-year-old girl.

I went out first to explain to the audience what we had done. Then came the dramatic moment as Denise was announced. She proudly strode from behind the curtain. She stood tall and coolly composed. Before she opened her mouth, her posture exuded a sense of assurance that was almost tangible. I'll never forget that moment and the remarkable visual impact of her bearing of confidence. She was terrific—and she made me look good, too!

• Al Ellis is president of a major transportation company. He enrolled in our Senior Executive Program along with several of his vice presidents. Not having met him before, I tried to spot the company president out of the group who entered our training center that morning. I was sure it couldn't *possibly* be the fellow with the sagging shoulders and slumping posture—but I was wrong. *That* was Al!

People make a lot of assumptions about us in the first few seconds after they meet us—assumptions about our attitude, our confidence, our competence, even our rank and position. Many people have posture habits that undermine trust and convey a lack of self-assurance. Even if you inwardly *feel* confident, your poor posture will invariably communicate a lack of poise and confidence to your listener, because that's the impact on their First Brain as it forms first impressions.

Many times upper body posture comes from outdated habits. For example, many tall men walk around hunched over because they grew fast as teenagers and didn't want to stand out. Height was not their problem—self-consciousness was. Others simply never considered posture to be important and allowed the slouching and slumping "teenage" period to extend into adulthood. There are some things you can do.

The Basic Rules

Stand Tall. Poor upper body posture often reflects low self-esteem. Stand with your shoulders back and your stomach in. Be conscious of looking out from eyes that are an inch or so taller than they were before you "stood tall." It may help to imagine a string from above tied to the center of your scalp and pulling you upward. Whether you are walking into a room or speaking before an audience, for maximum visual impact stand straight (but not starchy) and move naturally. Remain fluid rather than locked into a rigid position.

Watch Your Lower Body. The second part of posture that often

"Back On One Hip"

gets neglected is the lower part. When speaking to others, you may limit your effectiveness and squander your communication energy through inappropriate body language. One of the most common posture problems is "going back on one hip." This position communicates, "I don't want to be here," and literally distances you from your listener. This goes for casual conversations as well as presentations. Other common variations are rocking from side to side or going forward and back from heel to toe.

"Some men are born to wear a tuxedo, and David Coronet is one of them. Standing ramrod straight at the single microphone of the ballroom's low stage, he looked like the chairman of the board of the entire world. He waited calmly, hands clasped in front of him, until the room quieted down."

From *The Choice* by Og Mandino

Get in the "Ready Position." The Ready Position means basically "weight forward." Communication rides on energy, and your posture either communicates energy and interest to your listener's First Brain—or it communicates apathy and disinterest. When you are speaking confidently from a self-assured stance, your energy is directed forward, physically and *psychologically*, toward your listener. The Ready Position looks like this: Lean slightly forward, knees somewhat flexed, so you can bounce lightly on the balls of your feet. You should feel like an athlete ready to move easily and quickly in any direction. When your weight is forward, it is impossible to go back on one hip or rock back and forth on your heels. With the Ready Position as a posture habit, you'll always be ready to communicate, whether formally or informally.

Move. Tradition says speakers should always be rooted to one spot when they speak. Well, tradition is *wrong*! To make emotional contact with our listeners, we need to convey excitement, enthusiasm, and confidence when we speak. That means we've gotta *move*! Motion is visual! Motion is energetic! How can we expect to move people to action when we are standing still?

In large groups, think of the lectern as the eight-ball. *Don't get trapped behind it!* Get rid of any physical barriers between yourself and your audience. On a platform and in meetings get out from behind

"Trapped By Tradition"

the lectern so you can gesture with your hands and arms. If you're in a seated situation, consider standing—or even getting out of your chair and walking around—when it's your turn to speak. If that's not appropriate, *lean forward* to give yourself more impact. Just make sure you move as you speak. Movement adds energy and variety to your message and imbues you with an aura of confidence.

When talking to a group, move naturally—a few steps at a time rather than just a single tentative one-step. With eye communication motivating you, take a few natural steps toward one person, pause as you complete your thought, then move on to another set of eyes. Beware of repetitive and mechanical movement though—it can be worse than standing still.

Some Basic Exercises

The Miss America Exercise or **Walk Away from the Wall.** Have you ever seen a Miss America pageant, and been astounded at the fabulous posture of almost every contestant? Ever wonder how they got that way?

Former Miss America Donna Axum once told me about an exercise almost every contestant uses for good posture. It's simple, and *you* can gain from it.

Find a bare wall in your home or office. Set your heels against the wall. Then set your shoulders against the wall. Then your buttocks. Now comes the hard part: Press as much of the small of your back as you can against the wall. You should be ramrod straight against the wall.

Now walk away from the wall, and give a slight shake. How do you feel as you step away from the wall? Straight as a telephone pole, even after the shake? Probably. But you *look good*. You have *great* posture. And not too stiff either.

Videotape yourself before and after the Miss America Exercise. You'll be convinced. You *can* improve your posture. Practice this exercise daily, and use it before giving a presentation.

Use the Ready Position in all situations. When you are in the Ready Position, your energy is directed forward, toward your listener. Whether you are standing around at a coffee break or in a conversation, practice the Ready Position, leaning slightly forward, knees slightly flexed, so that you *could* bounce lightly on the balls of your feet. But don't actually bounce—people might think you are *over*-energetic.) Make the Ready Position a habit. Then, when the pressure is on in a speech to thousands you won't have to think about "leaning forward"—it'll be an ingrained habit. Practice the Ready Position—always.

Begin the Two Step. In our training programs we find many people often resist coming out from behind the lectern. Some only take a tentative step—or even just a half step—and then take root in a little patch of the carpet. That doesn't do it. So we push them further—we urge them to do the Two Step.

The Two Step is simply a technique to help us remember to *take at least two full steps*—then keep moving. Remember, we communicate with *all* of ourselves, and movement is a reflection of energy, excitement, and enthusiasm. If you do the Two Step you can't get away with a halfhearted overture toward movement. *You have to move.* The Two Step forces you to move *toward* somebody at the side or in the middle of an audience. It forces you to direct your kinetic energy forward. Get in the habit of using your energy. Do the Two Step.

Practice with a Paper Audience. (See Eye Communication exercise above.) With Post-It™ notes on chairs, give your presentation to your paper audience. Let your eye communication motivate your movement, so you talk to one person on one side of the room, and

"The Ready Position"

then move to the other side. Really move around the space. Stretch yourself.

See Your Posture and Movement on Video. The most definitive form of feedback is video feedback. It's fine, when you practice your posture and movement, to get feedback from other people. But people are subjective, video is objective. People can only give you their opinion, but a video camcorder sees all, tells all.

As you push yourself to stand straighter, focus your energy forward, and move out to people in a more open way, you will actually see that it doesn't look as exaggerated as it feels. Video feedback will help you become comfortable with your new posture and movement habits. In fact, you'll realize you look *great* with these new behavioral habits at your command. Never miss the opportunity to videotape yourself and learn from the objective feedback experience.

The Benefits of Good Posture and Movement

- You feel taller and more powerful.
- You look more confident.
- Your movement makes eye communication easier (they work to-gether).
- Your habit of being "forward" in the Ready Position helps you be "psychologically" forward.
- Your movement gives variety to the eye of the audience.

Remember: Stand tall; use the Ready Position; focus on "energy forward." Most of all, get out from behind the lectern and *move*!

3. Dress and Appearance

"You never get a second chance to make a good first impression."

JOHN MOLLOY

After posture, the most immediate visual impression we make on our listener's First Brain is that of our dress and appearance. I have a theory that I call the two-by-four rule, which has been validated in the experience of training many thousands of people: The impressions made in the *first two seconds* are so vivid that it takes another four minutes to add fifty percent more impression—negative or positive— to that communication. And those first two seconds are almost entirely *visual*, made up of how we look. This means that if we make a poor first impression, even before we open our mouth, it takes a *really* long time to overcome any damage done.

The Odd Couple

Not long ago, my teenaged son Ben and I spent one hot, fun, noisy summer day at the Taste of Chicago in Grant Park. All up and down Lake Shore Drive, along Lake Michigan, foods from every country and culture imaginable were displayed, sold, and enthusiastically con-sumed against a background of loud music and boisterous good cheer.

"The Odd Couple"

But there was one couple that I'll never forget because they stood out even in *that* crowd. To say they were "funky" or "new wave" does not begin to do them justice. They were *beyond* the beyond. The fellow had a neon-orange Mohawk hairdo, two inches wide and fully two feet high, swooping halfway down his back. His head was shaved at the sides and a large gold earring dangled from one ear. His black leather jacket was festooned with colorful braids and silver studs.

His girlfriend made it a matched set. Half of her face was garishly grease-painted in a clash of Day-Glo colors. The other half of her face had no makeup whatsoever. Half of her briefly cut top was see-through. Needless to say, they attracted some attention.

Ben and I turned and followed them around for about fifteen minutes—not just to watch them but to watch other people watching them. It was fascinating. As people approached this couple, they were careful not to stare. But as soon as people passed this couple's line of sight, they *all* invariably turned and gazed in wonder.

I don't know why people thought they had to wait for this odd couple to pass by, since they obviously wanted the attention. I suppose it's part of the socializing process we all go through: we're taught that it's not polite to stare, even when staring is not only an understandable reaction but practically mandatory.

Dress and appearance are a crucial aspect of communicating who we are—our values, our self-image, our self-respect. That gaudily plumed duo on Lake Shore Drive clearly chose their attire *not* for the sake of protection from the elements, but for the purpose of *communicating something about themselves*. They were sending a message.

In our own communicating settings, we need to be aware of the message *we* send with our own dress and appearance. Even more, we need to be aware of how our dress and appearance serve to make (or break) an emotional connection with our listener. Our goal is to enable the listener to feel a comfortable sense of identification with us. We should dress and groom in such a way that our appearance is not only appropriate to who *we* are, our own values and identity, but also to the values and culture of our listeners.

Since about ninety percent of your body is covered with clothing, the way you dress is crucially important. Yet the ten percent of your body which is *not* covered by clothes is the most crucial ten percent of all: your face and hair. When you are speaking, your listener's eyes are focused on the area around your face. The impression others receive from you is largely influenced by the way you groom yourself from the neck up—hairstyle, makeup, and jewelry if you are a woman; hairstyle, facial hair or lack of it if you are a man.

Some Examples

- For almost fifteen years I had a beard. People seemed to like me in a beard, and they responded positively. When it began to turn gray, I thought of tinting it but felt that besides being a little vain, it was a waste of time. So I shaved off the beard. After a week or so I learned that the majority of the people I talked to liked the beardless me better! Again and again people said, "Bert! You look ten years younger!" Some male faces are no doubt improved by a beard. But me? What a difference a shave makes!

- Back in my film producing days I usually sported the casual, tieless "uniform" of a filmmaker. Today I am embarrassed to think of the reaction some must have had of me. I vividly remember the time I spoke before fifty top managers of *Sunset Magazine*, selling a film concept to this notably conservative company. I wore a plaid sports jacket, a solid black knit tie, and a dazzling red shirt. Silhouetted on the bright scarlet background of the shirt were the outlines of women dancing under swaying palms. (For some reason I did get the job and made the film, but I still wonder how I got over what must have been a pretty negative First Brain impression!)
- Paul Green heads his own company, Behavioral Technologies, out of Memphis. He travels the country speaking and training on hiring and firing—he has a head for personnel. He also has a bald head, clean as the pate of a Telly Savalas or Michael Jordan—and just as appealing. "My hair was thinning," he said, "and I consciously decided to go all the way. It was truly one of the best decisions I ever made. I look better, and people remember me—positively."

The Basic Rules

Be Appropriate. There is not so much a right or wrong way to dress as there is an appropriate way. This means you should, first, be appropriate to your environment and, second, be appropriate to *yourself*. You want to dress and groom to make others comfortable with you—and to make *you* feel comfortable with yourself. In practice, this means you should have a style that allows you to feel relaxed and at ease, but which can accommodate flexibly to the norms of the group, the social setting, the time of day, and the weather.

Some tips for appropriateness:

- Conservative is better for business.
- Dress and groom up, not down. It is safer, and more comfortable, to be overdressed than underdressed.
- For women, if in doubt about a pantsuit, don't. A suit, dress, or skirt and blouse is fine in almost all business settings. A pantsuit often makes a statement you might not want to make.
- Pick the two or three basic colors that look good on you, and then get all your clothes in those colors. Mix and match those basics, and let accessories provide the accents (scarves, ties, etc.).
- In a business setting that makes its *own* statement by going against

the basic "dress codes" of business (i.e., the film business, the original Apple Computer, some ad agencies, etc.), throw out these tips as inappropriate—and act appropriately.

Dress and Groom at the Conscious Level. Most of us dress according to habit. For optimum Eye Factor, take a conscious look at how you dress and groom. Do you pick out certain colors because you always have? Do you wear certain ties or bows because that's what you did in college? Is it effective today? Do you wear one style of earrings, without experimenting? Have you ever changed your haircut? Is it effective today? Make sure all your choices are at the conscious level.

And remember, the effect of your first appearance is far greater than you think. Your appearance *instantly* communicates how you feel about yourself—and how you feel about your audience. Your appearance may also show what you sometimes do just to get attention.

Button Your Jacket. Not a hard and fast rule, but for you men, it generally looks better. For women, some caution is advised since many suits are tailored to be unbuttoned. But all men's suits and jackets are tailored to be buttoned when you want to look "smart." And when you are presenting yourself, it's smart to look smart.

Some Basic Exercises

Get People Feedback. The area of Dress and Appearance is one area where people feedback may be more important than video feedback. Style is subjective. It pays to find out what *others* think of you. You do that by asking. Find out how you come across to others in terms of your visual aspect: For men—clothing, hair, beard, and mustache (if any), accents and jewelry (watches and rings—earrings not recommended); for women—clothing and accents, haircut and hairstyle, makeup, and jewelry. If you come in close contact with your listeners, consider the appropriateness of your fragrance as well. Seek *honest* appraisals from a variety of people. Make it clear that you value their opinion and that you really want to know.

Then sift the answers as objectively as possible. Some will tell you what they think you want to hear. Others will give you off-the-wall comments. But a few will give you valuable, honest criticism. That's what you're looking for.

Be Observant. Read current magazines on style. Read John Molloy's classic *Dress for Success*. Learn from it, but don't take it as gospel.

"To Button, Or Not To Button"

Molloy is very opinionated, as are many other fashion writers, and what such people say is "right" may or may not be be right for *you*. But Molloy *has* done extensive research on the subject.

Keep a keen watch on your coworkers and friends. Notice who is on the fast track. Learn from other people—but don't become someone else's carbon copy. Just be *you*—but be the best and smartest you possible! Experiment with various styles. Get feedback. Observe. Sift. What you feel comfortable in has a lot to do with what you will feel confident in.

Test Out Your First Two Seconds. Remember that people form their first and often lasting impressions of you in the *first two seconds* after meeting you. Those impressions are primarily from your dress and appearance. Find out what people *really* think by asking them.

The Benefits of Good Dress and Appearance

- You feel confident in how you look.
- You take less time dressing and grooming when you know what you are doing, and why.
- You make a positive impression that *adds* to your effectiveness (and you don't have to *overcome* a negative first impression).
- You can more easily make positive changes in your dress and appearance than any other skill, and thus gain immediate benefit.

Remember: Be appropriate, be conscious, and be smart.

"Looking Good"

4. Gestures and Smile

---

*"We don't 'know' our presidents. We imagine them.
We watch them intermittently and from afar, inferring from only a
relatively few gestures and reactions what kind of people they are
and whether they should be in charge. Much depends on our intuition
and their ability at a handful of opportune moments to
project qualities we admire and respect."*

MEG GREENFIELD

Your listener's First Brain is wary and watchful. It is looking for the nonverbal cues that prove you can be believed and trusted. The First Brain knows that if we *believe* what we are saying, we will be *animated* while we are saying it.

When you communicate, are you enthused? Excited? Do you speak with conviction and passion? Your listener's First Brain wants to know not just what you are saying, but how you really *feel* about what you are saying. It is responding to The Eye Factor—those visual cues that communicate your emotional state.

There are few things that do more for effective communication than open gestures and a warm open smile. An open-armed greeting is welcoming. It says, "Come in." Your smile dominates your listener's impression of you as you communicate. A smile shows not only on your mouth but in and around your eyes. It demonstrates openness and likability. The First Brain just naturally has an antipathy toward a closed body and an unsmiling face—and may even perceive it as a threat.

Gestures and smiles are the dominant visual component of spoken communication. Our gestures and smiles reveal our inner state and propel our message with energy and emotional force.

Some Examples

- The winner of the Super Bowl endorsement battle is New York Giants' coach Bill Parcells—by a smile—so reports *USA Today*. "What a great face," says Vangie Hayes, talent director for the J. Walter Thompson ad agency. "It's such a witty, expressive face."

Parcells, who has been in Ultra SlimFast ads, has an appeal that goes beyond football followers. "Even if Bill Parcells wasn't a Super Bowl coach," she says, "he should be in an ad."

He will be in more than one ad—and big in broadcasting as well. When Parcells resigned from coaching after his Super Bowl win NBC hired him. Though his heart may be in football, looks like his expressive face will earn him many millions more in endorsements and sportscasting.

• Ted Mallard had a problem with gestures. He went through the Decker Program where he was videotaped giving his opening two-minute introduction. He started with a classic nervous gesture called the "fig leaf"—then he switched to something much worse! Every few seconds he would raise his cupped hands for a moment, then

"Fig Leaf Flasher"

drop them back into the "fig leaf" position. When he saw the effect later on video playback, he called himself the "fig-leaf flasher." He was so shocked at the distraction that he made it his first priority to drop this habit. He never "flashed" again.

- Charles Levitt rose through the ranks to become senior vice president of a major advertising agency. His employees thought he was always in a bad mood because his face looked grim and serious. He wondered why his children sometimes asked, "What's wrong, Dad?," when inwardly he felt fine. It wasn't until he did some experimenting in front of a video camera that he saw what everyone else saw; even when smiling on the inside, nothing showed through on the outside. He tried a smile. It looked good. Then he tried exaggerating that smile. To his surprise, it didn't look exaggerated at all! Instead, he looked happy and enthusiastic. Charles Levitt was always a dynamic, energetic man—but now he puts that energy on his face for the world to see!

- Poor former President Jimmy Carter. Often derided for his toothy smile, he was a low-energy communicator when it came to gesturing. Carter's media advisor, Jerry Rafshoon, inadvisably suggested that Carter try to gesture more for a TV speech. Ironically, the topic of the speech was the "Energy Crisis." President Carter's TelePrompTer was marked at certain key words to cue him to *gesture*. The effect was so awkward that the media raised a chorus of derision for Carter's "wooden" and "puppetlike" performance. The moral is that everyone—even Presidents!—should work within their natural energy framework.

Your goal is to become a natural communicator. So take it easy! Keep your hands and arms relaxed at your sides when you are at rest. When your message calls for animation, enthusiasm, and underscoring, gesture naturally. Learn to smile under pressure. Cultivate the same natural smile when you're on the Hot Seat as when you are at ease among friends.

Always be conscious of the Personality Factor when you communicate. Remember the Gallup poll of the factors that have influenced all the presidential elections in the television age (Chapter 5). The Personality Factor—each candidate's likability—was the *deciding* factor in each race. It's also the crucial factor in *your* business communication, social communication, and family communication. Your gestures and smile tend to show you as either open or closed to your listeners. It's a truth as old as the biblical book of Proverbs (18:24): "He who would have friends, let him show himself friendly."

The Basic Rules

Find Your Nervous Gesture, and Stop Making It. We all have "nervous gestures." We all have a place our hands seem to stray to whenever we are speaking and don't have anything to grasp. If you don't know what your "nervous gesture" is, give a short talk before a video camera. Once you've identified that gesture, do *anything but* that gesture. Don't try to plan a gesture at certain words or phrases— remember the example of our "wooden puppet" President. Just concentrate on not doing your nervous gesture. After practice, your hands should fall naturally to your sides when you are not emphasizing an idea or a point. When you need the physical emphasis that comes from natural enthusiasm, the gestures will come naturally. But it can't occur

"*Fig Leaf*"   "*Napoleon*"

if your hands are continually locked in the "fig leaf," the "arm lock," or any of the other common nervous gestures.

You Can't Overexaggerate. There is a wide disparity between how *we* perceive our gestures and expressions and how *others* perceive them. For example, a person with a naturally unsmiling face may *think* she is expressing her inner happiness in a big smile while others around her think, "What's she so glum about?" The fact is, very few people truly exaggerate their gestures or facial expressions even when they try to—yet most people don't believe it until they experience it and see themselves on video.

We have an exercise in our workshop called The Disparity Exercise. It enables people to experiment with exaggerations that feel uncomfortable, but don't look uncomfortable. Believe me, it's virtually *impossible*

"Sisters of Mercy"

"Jangler"

for you to overexaggerate. Get up in front of a camcorder and prove it to yourself. Push yourself. Big positive smile! Big energetic gestures! Don't worry about overdoing it. Exaggerate! You'll be surprised how normal and natural they really look. (More on this in Chapter 13.)

Smile, and Find Out Which "Third" You Are In. We all think we smile much of the time. In reality, the people around us may view us quite differently—and it's *their* opinion that counts. Experience from the thousands of people in our training programs has shown that approximately one-third of us have naturally open and smiling faces. The middle third tend to have neutral faces that can readily go from a smile to a serious and intense look. The "lower third" have faces that are naturally serious and intense (if not downright grim!)—even when they *think* they are smiling!

Find out which third you are in. (You can ask people, but the best way to objectively find out is to observe yourself on videotape.) If you are in the top third—the group that smiles easily and often—you have a built-in advantage in your communications with others. People will naturally perceive you as open and friendly, and will be more open to your ideas. Another advantage is that you can also convey bad news more readily than others. (Remember Mattel chairman John Amerman in Chapter 5.)

If you are in the neutral third, easily moving from a smiling face to a serious one, you have flexibility—but you should still be conscious from moment to moment of the energy level and enthusiasm your face is registering.

If you are in the bottom third—the "grim group"—you have your assignment: *exaggerate*! Practice your smile in front of a mirror or a video camera. Ask your spouse or a friend to tickle your ribs whenever your face sags into its grim position. Make yourself conscious, moment by moment, of what your facial muscles are doing. And remember, you're not alone. I know how you feel, because I've got a grim exterior myself. Unless I'm consciously working at it, my face projects a low-energy, stern appearance—even when I'm grinning from ear-to-ear inside! I have to work at letting my inner energy show through my face—and you may have to as well. In the eyes of the beholder, perception is reality.

Lift Your Apples. There's nothing mysterious about a smile, except the magical effect it has on others. A smile is the result of the physical operation of facial muscles—and these muscles can be exercised. The best way to practice smiling is not by moving your lips to form a smile. Think rather of raising your cheekbones. Consider

"Lift Your Apples"

the upper part of your cheeks as apples and just "lift your apples" to smile.

Your Smile Affects You. Not only does your smile affect others, it has an effect on you physically. It is a fact that you will *feel* your smile throughout the rest of your body. It makes a difference in both your mind *and* body. Try it—you'll like it.

Caution: Phony Smiles Don't Work. I stress the importance of smiling because a smile establishes the perception of how you feel. It sets the emotional tone of the conversation. People look at your face and the smile dominates everything they see. But be careful not to paste on a phony smile. Phony smiles look phony. Instead, season your facial muscles to smile naturally—and never forget this truth: A true smile comes from within.

Some Basic Exercises

Practice Exaggeration. Exaggerate your smile. Exaggerate your facial expressions. Exaggerate your gestures. There's no better way to desensitize and defuse our inhibitions than to find out what feels exaggerated does not really look exaggerated. You should especially try to exaggerate your facial expressions and gestures during informal times when you can experiment without risk. Practice when there is nothing riding on the outcome; then when the pressure is on you will automatically be *bigger* without thinking about it.

Exaggerate in a Mirror. Look at yourself in a mirror and just talk normally. Do a winger (an impromptu presentation)—talk about your favorite hobby or your favorite book. As you talk, observe how your hands and arms move. Do they stray to an inhibited position, such as the Fig Leaf, or do they stay lifelessly at your sides—or do they communicate the energy and passion you feel about your subject?

Try it again. Give the same talk you just gave to the mirror—but this time *exaggerate*. Try to overdo it. You may feel awkward, but you'll be surprised how much more energetic and effective you will *look*.

Exaggerate on Videotape. Video feedback is the most powerful tool we have for learning effective communicating. It gives us a sense of observing ourselves that a reflection in a mirror can't come close to. The best use of video feedback is in situations where there is at least a small audience for you to communicate with. Having an audience present causes you to be less aware of the camera. Instead of playing to the camera, you are more focused on communicating with real people. The camera can then capture the way you *really* communicate with people. On playback, you will be able to observe the disparity between how exaggerated you might have felt and how energetic and effective you actually looked.

Even when you're practicing alone, however, a video camera can be a powerful learning tool. Practice before the camera as you rehearse your presentation, pretending to talk to an audience. In low-risk speaking situations, feel free to experiment. Pick one behavior, such as gestures, and work on exaggeration in front of a real audience. Afterwards, study the playback. Does your exaggerated behavior *look* exaggerated? You'll be amazed at how effective and natural those "exaggerated" behaviors seem when put into real life practice.

Get Big. As you exercise your gestures, look for phrases and concepts in your talk that *demand* bigger gestures. Find ideas that are larger, greater, better, more wonderful—ideas that push you into expressing them with energetic, visually dynamic gestures. Find ideas that are so big that the only way to convey them is by reaching for the ceiling, stretching your arms out wide, putting a lot of kinetic power into your motions, and physically moving from wall to wall. And a mental bonus will occur—as you think in terms of big gestures, your mind will automatically gravitate toward larger, more dynamic ideas. The content of your message will become more dynamic, and that content will be powered by bigger, more dynamic gestures. It's a nice upward spiral.

"Get Big"

Imitate an "Expressor." Pick a "temporary" expressive role model. Select as your model a highly exciting person you know well enough to imitate. It doesn't have to be someone you like. It just has to be an *expressor* that you can have fun imitating in an uninhibited way. Try to get inside the skin of that person and play the part with gusto! Robin Williams. Robert Schuller. John Madden. Joan Rivers. Jesse Jackson. John Belushi. Tom Peters. Roadrunner. Try to *become* that energetic, expressive person, and you'll unleash and discover the hidden energy in your own personality.

The Benefits of Good Gestures and Smile

- You are *free* to express your thoughts fully.
- You smile—and the world smiles with you.
- Your natural energy can be released.
- Your open gestures *show* your openness, and thus a willingness to listen as well as talk.
- You are capable of emphasizing important points or concepts with ease when you are in the habit of freely gesturing.

Remember: Put movement and energy into your gestures. Use *big* gestures—but make sure to gesture within your natural energy level. Affected, unnatural gestures make you look artificial and wooden. Yet even basically shy and low-key people can express energy by practicing the exercises listed above. And above all, *smile*!

"Yes"

To summarize, the first four of the Nine Ways to Transform Your Personal Impact are:

1. Eye Communication
2. Posture and Movement
3. Dress and Appearance
4. Gestures and the Smile

Appreciate the *fact* that it is the *visual* sense which dominates *all* the senses. The Eye Factor rules! The language of the First Brain is a *visual* language. If we learn to "speak" this visual language every time we communicate, we will make emotional contact, we will gain our listeners' trust—and we will be effective and persuasive.

COMPUTERIZED EMOTION

Computer enthusiasts communicate with each other via computer "billboards" where messages can be posted and read by anyone with a computer and modem. Interestingly, computer users seem to have an intuitive understanding of the importance of the Eye Factor in effective communicating. They know that words on a computer monitor are not enough. To really make contact with your "listener" (even via computer), a message has to be visual.

An ingenious development in computer communication was the invention of Emoticons. The word comes from emotion and icons (icons are little pictures or symbols used to convey a function on a computer). Emoticons are pictures of faces made out of keyboard characters. These pictures are used to convey emotion. They are an attempt to put the Eye Factor back into faceless, voiceless, keyboard-only conversation, and to convey the mood in which a line of computer text is typed. *Emoticons lie on their sides, so you have to tilt your head to the left in order to read them.* Some examples:

Emoticon	Meaning
:-)	Feeling happy. (Grin.)
:-(	Feeling sad.
:-<	Feeling very sad. Or maybe grumpy.
#-(	Feeling hung over from last night's party.
:-¢	Feeling undecided.
:-p	Sticking tongue out at you!
:-&	Feeling tongue-tied.
:-D	Yak yak yak. (I talk too much.)

(cont. on page 116)

Emoticon	Meaning
:-#	My lips are sealed.
:-l	Blank expression.
l-)	Hee hee!
l-D	Ha ha!
:-o	Oh! I'm shocked!
:-6	Bleccch!
:-I	Hmmmmmmm.
:-9	Yumm! Licking my lips!
:-c	Bummer!
:->	Hey! All right! Feeling lecherous.
;-)	A wink is as good as a nod.
:-0	I am pontificating.
:-}	I'm wearing lipstick.
:-Q	I'm a smoker.
8-)	I'm wearing glasses.
B-)	I'm wearing horn-rimmed glasses. (I'm stuck in the 1960s.)
:-{	I wear a mustache.
{:-)	I part my hair in the middle.
*:o)	Just clowning around.
8-#	I'm dead.

7

The Energy Factor

THE "SECRET" OF BOBBY KENNEDY

Robert F. Kennedy was not a great communicator in the classic sense. He certainly did not possess the natural oratorical skills of his brother John. Yet there was *something* about Bobby that worked. When he spoke, he made contact with his audience. He had *energy*—and he used it.

I got to watch Bobby Kennedy in action—behind the scenes as well as onstage in front of the cameras—as a twenty-eight-year-old film director. I was young and not too experienced. I just happened to be in the right place at the right time to observe a piece of history. And though I hardly knew it then, the seeds of the First Brain concept were already being planted in my mind as I watched this legendary man at work.

It was an unusually hot spring night for Washington when I got the phone call at home that plunged me into the dizzying whirl of Kennedy's 1968 Presidential campaign. The call was from my boss, Charles Guggenheim, the renowned Academy Award–winning documentary filmmaker. He wanted to see me at the office. "Immediately," he said, and that was not like Charles. When I arrived, he spoke quickly. "Bobby Kennedy just threw his hat in the ring. He's picked California for the first leg of the campaign. I want you to put together a couple of film crews and follow him everywhere he goes."

Guggenheim Productions had been contracted to produce Kennedy's TV commercials. Our job was to get everything on film so it could all be edited down to a series of thirty- and sixty-second spots and short films. I hastily assembled the film crews, and the next thing I knew we were on the press plane, part of a three-jet entourage winging through eight California cities in three days.

Kennedy was a fascinating man to watch. I have to confess that I wasn't a big RFK fan at first. But as I watched him—in closed-door meetings, before the press, grabbing a few moments rest, delivering his "stump speech," shaking who knows how many outstretched hands—I became intrigued with the energy that flowed from him. It was not so much his message that impressed me, but the extraordinary personal impact with which he delivered it. He clearly made a powerful impression on every person he touched.

Certainly, there were times when his style struck my First Brain as abrasive and abrupt, which gave resonance to the "ruthless" charge that was circulating about him. But the communicative power of his presence seemed to excite everyone—both his staff and the crowds who flocked to hear him. Amazingly, even those who disagreed with his politics seemed as deeply affected by Kennedy's persona as those who supported him.

In city after city, our cameras captured every word, gesture, and nuance. Soon it dawned on me that I was seeing something that was definitely not what is ordinarily described as "charisma." That hypnotic, spellbinding quality that surrounds most so-called charismatic speakers just didn't fit Bobby Kennedy. His delivery was much more down-to-earth, much more subtle and real. His was almost an entirely new brand of communication.

Kennedy's speaking style broke every rule. His pronounced Boston accent and halting delivery would have been a fatal handicap for most speakers, yet he somehow turned his eccentricities into assets. Many years later, in a *Newsweek* article, Meg Greenfield would make a similar observation of Bobby's brother John, reflecting that "he managed to retain and impose his stylistic eccentricities on the public consciousness—he wore what he wore and spoke the funny 'Cube-er' way he spoke. So he established authenticity and then, in the first debate, he established that his personality was that of a leader, a plausible president."

Throughout that grueling jet-tour through California in the spring of '68, I saw Kennedy repeatedly face all the incredible pressures and frustrations of the campaign trail: last-minute schedule changes, inadequate accommodations, malfunctioning sound systems, staff conflicts, and hostile questioners. Yet he never lost the ability to put himself across in that amazing way that was his style alone.

Near the end of that tour, I saw the Kennedy energy tested to the limit.

It was another hot spring night as Kennedy approached the podium in front of the California State Capitol in Sacramento. To me, it seemed the man had been squeezed dry by the pressure and the pace. As he walked, his legs literally shook from exhaustion. I was a couple of feet away, watching him take his place before the vast milling crowd. I wondered how he could pull himself together for one more delivery of what had essentially been the same speech in city after city. I was exhausted myself, short on temper, wanting nothing more than to just go somewhere and sleep—and I was just a guy in the entourage. But Kennedy had been under continuous pressure and nerve-racking scrutiny the whole time—and the dream of a whole lifetime was on the line. I couldn't imagine how he could summon the gumption for each new speech, meeting, and TV interview.

As our cameras rolled, I thought, *look at him! There's no way he can make it! He can barely stay on his feet!*

But as soon as he was introduced, something happened to him. He seemed to spring forward, evoking the image of a runner sprinting from the blocks or a fighter coming out of his corner. All evidence of his exhaustion was erased from his face. His legs still trembled, but few people were aware of it. Within moments, he propelled himself into one of the most effective speeches of the tour. A speech filled with passion. With power. With *energy*.

Our crews captured some of the most memorable footage of the entire tour during those moments.

Three months after that tour, Kennedy was well on his way to winning the Democratic nomination for President of the United States when he was fatally wounded by an assassin's bullet at the Los Angeles Ambassador Hotel. From what I saw of Kennedy as a leader and a communicator, I'm convinced that, were it not for that bullet, the history of our nation would have been written very differently.

Reflecting on those memories of Bobby Kennedy, I can clearly understand why this man consistently got to the heart of his listeners. His sheer use of personal energy enabled him to connect with the First Brains of his listeners. He was a master at using humor, unforgettable language, and personal involvement to connect with his audience. There was energy in his voice, but even more so in his face and in his body language. The vocal and visual power of the man conveyed to the millions who saw him in person and on TV that *here is a man who believes what he says*. A line of narration from Guggenheim Productions' Academy Award–winning film, *Robert Kennedy Remembered*, captures it well: "He entered the Senate in characteristic style—leaning forward." People respond to that kind of conviction. That's why people responded to Bobby Kennedy.

His best asset as a speaker was his *energy*. And there is simply nothing mysterious or magical about energy. It's a dynamic quality that anyone can use to reach and persuade his or her listeners. Spoken without energy, the most eloquent and profound words in the world will be instantly forgotten. But even an average person with ordinary credentials can get people to respond to him and even follow him— *if he has energy when he speaks*!

THE BEST TEACHER

Not convinced? Then let's try a little experiment. Think back to your high school and college days. Now, think quickly: Who was the *best* teacher you ever had?

I've asked this question of literally thousands of people, and almost without exception people instantly "flash" on a certain type of teacher. And it is not necessarily that teacher with the more impressive degrees, or more published works to their credit, or even the teacher who was better prepared and more knowledgeable.

The teacher who stands out as the *best* in our minds is almost always the teacher who had *energy*, who was interesting to listen to, who had dynamic and creative ways of getting the message across. It's that teacher who was the most excited, enthused, and eager for you to get the information and principles from the class. It's that teacher with a big extra ingredient called The Energy Factor.

When I was at Yale I had to take a History of Art course to satisfy a requirement—and I liked neither history nor art. The morning of the first class, I approached Woolsey Hall with a cloud of ennui over my head, dreading the next fifty minutes of unrelieved tedium. The auditorium was dimly lit—perfect for catching up on the sleep I had missed the night before. In fact, I was just beginning to doze when Professor Vincent Scully walked into the spotlight. *Yes, a spotlight.* For Vincent Scully had no intention of letting anyone sleep in *his* class!

His voice rang out as he announced the importance of this course. Without pause he flashed the first slide on the screen, strode across the stage, and used his pointer to bang against the screen, making his points. He roamed the stage like a restless tiger as he drove home to each student in that room the subtle intricacies and nuances of each painting, sculpture, or architectural design. It didn't matter what medium, or what artistic period, or what artist he was talking about. This man knew how to light the fire of fascination in the eyes of his students.

Now Vincent Scully is a Yale legend. Even up to his recent retirement at seventy, his courses continued to be standing-room only. I learned to appreciate both history and art—and do to this day. Because of one man. Because of his energy, enthusiasm, and excitement. Because he *communicated*.

The Two-year-old Speaks

Who are the best communicators in the world? Teachers? Actors? Politicians? Network news anchors? Stand-up comics?

No! Two-year-olds!

That's right, two-year-olds—those little Gerber-fed, Pampers-clad toddlers who have just been introduced to the power of speech are the *best* communicators in the world! Why? Because they have not been socialized yet. They have no inhibitions. They have just added the artillery of *words* to their arsenal of unrestrained energy. They don't care what anyone thinks of them, so they will shout, gesticulate, tug at you, make faces, cry, rant, and rave in order to get their message across! It's not that they are necessarily the most articulate—far from it. But they very often are the most persuasive.

Good persuasive communication is driven by energy. In the previous chapter, we saw that our personal energy is most forcefully conveyed through such visual components of communication as gestures and facial expressions. Those of us who are born with high levels of communicative energy—a naturally expressive face and voice or the gift of humor, movement, or untrammeled gesturing—have a natural advantage in reaching the listener's First Brain. But whether we are high- or low-energy communicators by nature, we can *all* become more aware of our energy levels—and we can all learn to increase our energy output.

Unlocking Your Energy

As communicators, we can learn (or relearn) a lot from two-year-olds. We can begin to shed some of the uptight, inhibited, self-limiting habits we have acquired over the years. The "secret" that Robert Kennedy had, that your favorite teacher had, that every two-year-old has, is essential and profound yet so simple to grasp: To unlock the communication process and get our point across, we must unlock our inner energy.

There's nothing mystical or magical to unlocking inner energy. It's not a matter of chanting a mantra or getting zapped by spiritual enlightenment. It's a simple matter of sharpening our skills and changing our behavior. And I do mean simple.

In the Decker Method™ training program, we divide Personal Impact into its component parts, then we focus on each part, one by one. We practice one skill, then the next, then the next. Before we know it Personal Impact is in the process of positive change, and on its way to becoming literally transformed!

At the beginning of this section, we listed The Nine Ways to Transform Your Personal Impact. In Chapter 6: "The Eye Factor," we explored four of these nine skills:

1. Eye Communication
2. Posture and Movement
3. Dress and Appearance
4. Gestures and the Smile

Those four skills are designed to transform our *visual* impact. The next four skills are designed to help us pack more *energy* into our message. They are:

5. Voice and Vocal Variety
6. Words and Nonwords (The Pause)
7. Listener Involvement
8. Humor

Now let's take a closer look at these four energy skills. You'll see how real people in real-life situations use them to be more effective communicators—and you'll see how easy it is for you to put the Energy Factor into your communication.

5. Voice and Vocal Variety

---

*"The Devil hath not, in all his quiver's choice,
An arrow for the heart like a sweet voice."*

BYRON

Your voice is the vehicle of your message. Learn to drive that vehicle like a Lamborghini. Push it, open it up, and, as my sixteen-year-old tells me, "Floor it!" Transmit the energy you have inside you through the vehicle of your voice!

Indeed, the voice is such an expressive instrument, and the First Brain of our listeners is so finely attuned to the signals carried in the voice, that a single word you speak can reveal volumes of information about you. Skeptical? Call a friend or family member on the phone and listen as they say, "Hello." Chances are you can tell that person's precise mood by the tone in which that one word is spoken.

What kind of voice do you have? Have you ever listened to your own voice on a tape? Did you like what you heard—or did you think, "That doesn't sound like me?"

Most people are surprised when they hear themselves on tape, and are absolutely convinced that the tape recorder has distorted their "true" voice. The fact is, the voice on the tape is much closer to what others actually hear than the voice we ourselves hear as we speak. So to hear ourselves as others hear us, we have to record ourselves—on the phone, in a meeting, or just in casual conversation—and listen carefully to the playback. It's the only way we can truly become aware of how much or how little energy we transmit when we speak.

Some Examples

- These days, few people recall how George Bush sounded when he was a candidate in the Republican primaries, running against another fellow named Reagan. Back then, one of the biggest complaints people had about George Bush was not his views but his voice, often described as high-pitched, reedy, and whiny. Critics cruelly dubbed him "The Wimp."

  Eight years later, Bush was again running for president. But this time he had been coached by Roger Ailes, the political media advisor to several Republican presidents and senators, including Reagan himself. One of the dramatic changes Ailes helped Bush make was to bring his voice down into a deeper, more authoritative range. In interviews, on the stump, and in the clinches of the Bush-Dukakis debates, Bush's voice had just the right tone of strength and sincerity. The rest is—quite literally—history.

- Sensational accounts of steamy illicit sex guaranteed that videotape from Pamela Smart's murder trial would be carried on all the TV networks. At the end of the trial, she was convicted of conspiring to kill her husband. Because of her muted, monotone voice and aloof composure, observers of the trial called her "The Ice Princess."

  After the trial, radio call-in shows buzzed with opinions about the convicted murderess. This remark by one caller was typical: "You could tell she was guilty by the way she talked. Flat, no emotion. If she was innocent of the accusations against her, you would have heard some emotion in her voice." The jury, of course, had a lot more evidence to go on than a First Brain impression of the defendant's voice—but it's clear that her stony demeanor and toneless voice did little to help her case.

- A well-known corporate CEO was invited to give the dedication speech for a new building in a major city. A thousand people gathered for the event. After being introduced, he stepped up to the lectern and began reading his speech out of a manuscript his speechwriter had prepared. His voice was a deadly monotone. But deadlier still was the fact that page ten of the manuscript had been copied twice. Without even noticing, he read it twice. No one else noticed either, because no one else was listening. Actually, many had already left by the time he got to page ten.

- Jennifer Morales, a graduate student at Stanford University, was asked to give a talk to a community group on the life of John Steinbeck. She asked her English Lit professor to come to her talk, then evaluate her performance. The prof obliged, making himself comfortable in the center seat in the very front row.

  Throughout her talk, Jennifer stood glued to her lectern, speaking in a voice that would have left a perfectly flat trace on an oscilloscope. Within the first five minutes, the professor was quietly snoring way. Afterward, Jennifer indignantly confronted her professor. "You know I wanted your opinion of my speech," she said. "How could you go to sleep like that?" He simply replied, "My dear, sleep *is* an opinion."

It is often a shock to hear our voice on tape. It sounds different to our ear because the voice on the tape (and the voice others hear) is conducted by airwaves. The voice we hear when we speak is conducted through the bones in our head. If you want to know what others hear when they listen to you speak, you *must* listen to yourself on audiotape. That

"The 'Reel' Voice"

is where you will discover the strengths and weaknesses in your vocal quality and variety. And once you really *hear* your voice you'll be able to *change* your voice.

The Basic Rules

Make Your Voice Naturally Authoritative. If you discover you have a high, nasal sounding voice, you can work on bringing it down into a lower register. One of the more valuable exercises that follow is the "King Kong" exercise, which will deepen your voice and give it flexibility. All it takes is practice—just a few minutes each day.

Is a rich, resonant voice really all that important? Have you ever heard such expressions as "listen to the voice of experience," or, "that's the voice of authority?" Have you ever seen a movie or a TV show in which the voice of God was heard? Did that voice sound more like Orson Welles or Pee Wee Herman? (There's a reason Charlton Heston always plays Moses-like figures.) Clearly, people associate a rich, well-projected voice with authority and competence.

The Voice on a Roller Coaster. Does your voice have a pleasing dynamic range? Does it rise and fall with the meaning of your words? Does it express emotion? Does it emphasize and underscore your message? Or do you speak in a monotone? Most of us do. To cure a monotone voice, visualize your voice as a roller coaster: lift it over the summit, then let it plummet. This mental exercise forces you to be aware of the dynamic range of your voice and puts you in the habit of extending that range by adding variety to your voice.

Be Aware of Your Telephone Voice. Professor Albert Mehrabian's research (Chapter 6) shows that your voice—the intonation, resonance, or auditory delivery of your message—counts for as much as (are you ready for this?) *84 percent* of your emotional impact and believability when people can't see you—such as when you're talking on the phone!

Does your telephone voice differ from your speaking voice? If so, why? Are you more expressive and energetic on the phone? How can you become more expressive and energetic in face-to-face situations? The exercises that follow will get you there.

Put Your Real Feelings into Your Voice. Does the tone of your voice send out a different message than your words? Do you ever say, "It's good to talk to you," or, "I'm really excited to be here," in a flat, emotionless voice? Do you know how to put a "smile" into your

"The Roller Coaster"

voice? That one is simple—just smile, and then talk. Try it when you practice with a tape recorder. Notice the difference? Be conscious of the emotional signals your voice sends. If you feel happy, excited, and enthusiastic, *let your voice show it.*

Some Basic Exercises

The voice has four basic components: *relaxation, breathing, projection,* and *resonance.* All of these components work together to make your voice uniquely your own. Each of these components can be altered and strengthened to allow your inner energy to come through when you speak. Here are some exercises to help you develop a more dynamic, authoritative voice:

Tone and Relax. This set of tone and relax exercises is especially valuable just prior to giving a presentation. Find a place where you won't be disturbed—backstage, in the restroom, behind a potted plant. Then physically prepare yourself to communicate. Here's how:

Your Head and Neck. Relax your jaw and let your mouth hang slightly open. Gently allow your head to settle so that your chin rests on your chest. Raise your head. Then let your head drop gently to your right shoulder. Raise it. Drop it gently to your left shoulder. Raise it.

Now roll your head two times to the right. Then roll your head two times to the left.

Monitor your breathing as you do these exercises. Breathe deeply from the diaphragm, but easily. The goal is to relax. Don't hold your breath. Keep your jaw loose, your mouth slightly open.

Your Shoulders. Hands relaxed at your sides. Now . . . make two fists! Clench them. And with your fists still clenched, lift your shoulders all the way to your ears! . . . Okay, then, just get them as close to your ears as you can. Keep trying. Then stop.

Drop your shoulders. Unclench your fists suddenly—shoot those fingers *out!* Sigh (let yourself hear it) as you exhale.

Your Face. For reasons that will become obvious we call this exercise The Prune.

First, make a tiny face. Try to push all your facial features in toward your nose. Pucker your lips. Squinch your eyes. Scrunch your face muscles. Be a prune! Then . . . *go w-i-d-e! Surprise* your face! Open it as *wide* as you can!

Now make another prune face! Then try to move your entire face—puckered lips, squinchy eyes and all—all the way to the right. Now move it all the way to the left.

Then make that wide-open, surprised face again. Repeat the process several times.

Your Lips. We call this The Motorboat—again for obvious reasons. Take a deep breath. Stick your lips out. Now force air through your puckered lips so that they vibrate and make a rolling *B-r-r-r-r* sound. Those vibrations help to relax your lips and prepare them for speaking.

Breathe from the Diaphragm. Good vocal expression demands good breathing. This exercise will enable you to put real power into your voice.

Place your hands on your lower rib cage and inhale deeply through your nose, mouth closed. Your shoulders should remain still. Feel that expansion in your rib cage? That's caused by the expansion of your diaphragm muscle.

Now exhale *slooooooowly* through your slightly open mouth. Feel the contraction of your rib cage? That's caused by the diaphragm muscle contracting, rising, expelling the air from your lungs.

Do it again. And again. Keep practicing and experiencing that sensation of deep diaphragm breathing until it becomes effortless.

Now repeat the exercise with one hand over the front of your abdomen. When you breathe in, your abdomen should expand, shoving your hand away. The abdominal area of your body should fill up more fully than your chest. If not, then you are not inhaling deeply enough for the diaphragm to do its job.

Keep practicing. Make deep, diaphragm breathing a natural part of your daily "communication calisthenics." When you practice this exercise, you should feel a sensation of being relaxed, yet full of energy.

Do the "King Kong." This is great to relax your vocal chords before a speech—and to lower your voice. Let your mouth drop open. Inhale deeply through your nose—a deep breath from the diaphragm.

Now, exhale. And as you exhale, say or sing the words, "King Kong, Ding Dong, Bing Bong," in an up-and-down, singsong fashion. Start at a medium pitch and lower the tone, word by word, toward the deepest range of your voice. Let the words drop in tone like stones falling down a hilly mountainside into the valley below. Make that last "Bong" into a three-syllable word, and drop it in steps to the bottom of your range.

Gently, now! Don't strain your throat muscles reaching for that basso profundo! Again, the goal is to relax your voice so that it can find a deeper register.

As you exhale, relax your jaw. Let your mouth and throat open wide and easily, just like yawning. But gently, gently.

"The King Kong"

Repeat this several times. If you do this regularly (daily) you can permanently lower your voice. It's much like daily weight lifting—as long as you keep it up you will get the desired result: increased strength in the muscles that control your vocal cords. But stop, and the muscle turns to flab.

Learn to Project Your Voice. Say a test sentence in your normal conversational voice. Then inhale through your nose—a deep breath from the diaphragm.

Now exhale, saying that same test sentence as you breathe out, and mentally *push* your voice out beyond the last row of an imaginary audience. Don't push the sound from your throat. Propel it from your stomach and diaphragm. Make your diaphragm support your voice.

Practice Varying Your Pitch. Say various test sentences in a lilting, singsong fashion, up-and-down. Use poems or songs for your test sentences. Practice pumping feeling and conviction into your words as you say them. Let your voice be like a roller coaster.

Practice Varying Your Pace. Try varying the speed of your delivery. Practice using a long pause. Record yourself with a tape recorder, phone answering machine, or camcorder as you speak. For material, read a passage from a book or a newspaper article. Read it with expression and conviction.

Use Voice Mail. Many of us now have access to voice mail systems in our companies. It is growing fast in the home market too, so most will be able to use it now, or soon, in a new way—to practice communication skills. Use it as a feedback tool. Send yourself a copy of a real message you are sending to a colleague or friend, and listen to the sound of your voice. Do it daily at first.

The Benefits of Good Voice and Vocal Variety

- You are more effective on the telephone.
- You can convey emotions when you have a flexible voice.
- You are attractive to the ear.
- You have the capability to emphasize certain points and ideas with vocal energy and variation.
- You are First Brain Friendly.

Remember: The world of business is a world of lower (resonant) voices. Join up, and project authority, vocal variety, and energy. Practice makes permanent!

6. Words and Nonwords

Another good way to put the Energy Factor in our communication is through our use of *words*. And a good way to drain the Energy Factor *out* of communication is through a bad habit I call *nonwords*. Let's take them one at a time. First, let's discover how to energize and ignite our message with the use of . . .

Words

---

*"Perhaps of all the creations of man,
language is the most astonishing."*

LYTTON STRACHEY

Mark Twain once said, "The difference between the right word and *almost* the right word is the difference between lightning and a lightning-bug." To put the energy of *lightning* in our message, we have to select the right words for the right situations. A rich, varied vocabulary and the ability to use it appropriately can spell the difference between "good enough" and "*great!*"

Some Examples

- Mario Cuomo's keynote speech before the 1984 Democratic Convention was seen by a TV audience of nearly eighty million people. In those few electronic moments, Cuomo was instantly transformed from a newcomer to a national contender on the political scene. As conservative radio personality (and confirmed Cuomo critic) Rush Limbaugh fumed in a 1991 broadcast, "There is only one thing Mario Cuomo has done: The keynote speech at the '84 Democratic Convention in San Francisco! Nobody's lived off a speech—except maybe Nixon and the Checkers speech—like Cuomo has lived off of this one! . . . You know, if he runs for President in '92 it will have been eight years since that speech. And do you know what his TV commercials will be? That speech!"

  And what was it about that speech that made it so powerful and effective? Cuomo's articulate and inspiring use of *language*, his love for the power of *words* to motivate and move people. Although Cuomo has a speechwriter on his staff, the speech he gave that night was one he drafted himself. "[Cuomo is] the only person I ever met in politics who has a real feel for words," said Cuomo's speechwriter Peter Quinn, "and not just for putting arguments together, *but for the sound and power of words!*" [emphasis added]

- The dramatic use of words sent Cuomo's career into the stratosphere. In the wrong hands, language is lethal. And no form of language is more deadly than jargon. It can kill a conversation—instantly—as in this case:

  Overheard at a cocktail party: "I've been a systems programmer on DECs, OS/2s, and VM/CPs for six years, and I swear QMS has the friendliest command-line–oriented user interface in the field. It comes with the whole toolkit bundled in—editor, sort, text search, the whole whiz-bang! And the kernel interface supports every processing paradigm in the book—stop, suspend, wait, even hibernate. Of course, it has one humongo drawback. I mean, who wants to fork over a cool ten K for the same basic compiler you can get for five bills on your MS-DOS machine?"

"A word fitly spoken," says Proverbs 25:11, "is like apples of gold in pictures of silver." With just a little bit of effort every day, you too can make apples of gold every time you speak.

The Basic Rules

Build Your Vocabulary. The English language is a powerful tool, loaded with extra attachments and gadgets called "synonyms." Because

"Jargon"

of the wealth of synonyms in our language, we can take a single thought and express it in virtually hundreds of ways. With a well-stocked vocabulary at our disposal, we can speak with precision, with subtle shades of meaning, with evocative imagery, and most of all with *energy*.

Does this mean we need to know a lot of "big words"? I beg to contravene. But we should have at our disposal the power to say "meticulous" instead of "careful," "conundrum" instead of "riddle," "pivotal" instead of "crucial," "endow" instead of "give," "disciple" instead of "follower," "rebuff" instead of "refuse," and "ad infinitum" (or even "ad nauseum") instead of "and so on and so forth."

It's easy to stretch your vocabulary. Just try to use one new word a day. If you come across a new word while you're reading a book or a magazine, jot it down, look it up in a dictionary, start using it in conversation, make it your own. Don't use words to show off, but continually be on the lookout for new words that can help you communicate in the clearest, most colorful, most interesting way for every situation.

Paint Word Pictures. Language can do a lot more for our message than merely give us multiple ways of expressing an idea. Language can pack the Energy Factor into our communication by enabling us to paint intense, colorful word pictures. We can lend the energy of both *motion* and *emotion* to our speech by the use of metaphors and vivid expressions.

With a little imaginative language, the night sky becomes a "sparkling cosmic ocean." An F-16 fighter-bomber becomes a "screaming bird of prey." A freeway at night becomes "a river of glowing red coals." The stock market didn't just rise, it "broke the price barrier." The politician didn't just evade the question, he "bobbed, weaved, and jinked."

These are not "big words" used to impress other people with how smart we are. They are, for the most part, fairly simple words, but put together in ways that create memorable, exciting images that make vivid impressions on the First Brain of our listener. Our goal is not to impress, but *to make an impression.* A rich and varied language can be one of the best tools at our command for getting our point across with energy and impact.

Beware of Jargon. If you are in a profession that uses a lot of jargon—careful! Jargon can be a convenient form of shorthand communication when educators talk to other educators, doctors talk to doctors, lawyers talk to lawyers, computer programmers talk to computer programmers, and so on. But when you are moving in circles outside your professional field, you have to speak English again!

Like the fellow talking about "OS/2s," "kernel interfaces," and "processing paradigms" at the cocktail party, jargon-addicts don't communicate. They just turn people off. Jargon-addicts convey the impression that they feel superior to their listeners. Those who have to endure the babble of acronyms and technical language soon slam their First Brains shut. Whatever the jargon-babbler says bounces uselessly off the closed doors of his listeners' minds.

Nonwords (The Pause)

"The notes I handle no better than many pianists. But the pauses between the notes . . . ah, that is where the art resides!"

Artur Schnabel

Everyone knows that language is made out of words. But did you know that language is also made out of nonwords?

To communicate effectively, you must be aware of nonwords that

"Nonwords"

obstruct your message. The most common nonwords are "uhh," "ahh," and "umm." Others include such sounds and phrases as, "so," "well," "you know," "and," "okay," "like," "sort of," and similar nonsense noises we use to fill the empty spaces in our communication. As in, "Well . . . uhhh . . . my name is Joe Smith . . . uhhh, annnnnnnd . . . I'm here to sort of talk about Effective Communicating: . . . umm . . . the Key to, uh, Success. And . . . uhhh . . . I want to thank you all for being here . . . soooo . . . um, let's get started, okay?"

Nonwords bleed the Energy Factor right out of your message. They make you appear hesitant, uncertain, incompetent. The listener's First Brain is put on guard against your message. Your listener wonders— usually at a preconscious but very real level—"If this speaker isn't confident about his or her message, why should I believe it?"

Some Examples

- Joyce is an account exec with a large advertising agency in southern California. Her job is to persuade corporate clients to spend money with her firm so that their companies can sell their products and services more effectively. Joyce is good at what she does. She has a pleasant, authoritative voice and a confident presence. But she has an unfortunate habit of ending many of her sentences with, "Okay?"

She continually seems to be asking for agreement—a habit that undermines her air of confidence and the effectiveness of her communication.
* Secretary of Defense Caspar Weinberger's press conference (mentioned in Chapter 5) was an embarrassing, high level, nonword disaster. Speaking on national television before millions about the Libya air strike, he had fifty-nine "ums" and "ahs" getting in the way of his message. And that was in a brief three minutes.

Let's face it: Most of us are *addicted* to using nonwords that choke our energy level and retard the effectiveness of our communication. In short, we are "uhhh-dicted." But there is a way out with the help of some simple behavior modification techniques.

The Basic Rules

Find Your Level of Nonwords. Years before I knew very much about communicating, I recorded a speech I gave and was *shocked* to hear thirty-five nonwords in the first two minutes! I can't overemphasize the power of feedback to uncover your communicating weaknesses so you can deal with them. Listen to yourself on tape. Count the nonwords you use. You will probably wince a lot as you listen—but you'll also become more aware. That awareness will help you control the nonword habit.

Replace Your Nonwords with Something More Powerful. You're probably thinking, "But what if I can't live without my nonwords? What happens if there's a big silent *gap* in my sentence while I'm thinking of the next phrase? Don't I need to fill those gaps with some sort of sound?" No. You fill those gaps with something *infinitely* more powerful than meaningless sounds. You fill those gaps with something that gives energy and drama to your message: The Pause.

Use the "Power of The Pause." Did you know that The Pause can be one of your most dynamic communicating tools? You can pause for as long as three or four seconds, right in the middle of a sentence—and it will not only seem perfectly natural to your listener, it will give extra punch to your message.

The problem with pausing is that most of us have never tried it. We are afraid of silence in our communication. We're not used to pausing, so we rush to fill the silence with inane and meaningless sound—sound which dampens our Energy Factor and blunts the point of our message.

"The Pause"

Let me suggest an experiment. The next time you have a conversation with a close friend, pay attention to your nonwords and replace them with a pause. Instead of saying "uhhh" or "ummm," just wait three or four seconds while you gather your thoughts for the next phrase or sentence. Sure, it'll *seem* like twenty seconds in your own mind, but your friend won't even notice. In fact, a beat or two of silence now and then actually heightens the intensity and the energy of your message, while helping to hold the interest of your listener.

Some Basic Exercises

Exercises in *pausing* probably have the second biggest and most immediate payoff in your communications effectiveness. (Eye Communication is number one.) You will not *only* get rid of nonwords, but in gaining the power of the pause you gain thinking time and can add drama to your impact.

Record Yourself. Use video- or audiotaping regularly to practice leaving pauses, and to sensitize yourself to your nonword patterns. It won't take long for you to sharpen your ear to those irritants. In fact, you'll soon begin catching yourself *before* the nonword comes out of your mouth! You'll replace it with a pause. Being conscious of nonwords is the first step to eliminating them.

Use Voice Mail. Use your voice mail system as a feedback tool. Send yourself a copy of a real message you are sending to a colleague or friend, and listen to your pauses, or nonwords. Do it daily at first.

Practice with a Buddy. Have a friend listen while you give an impromptu talk. Ask him or her to instantly say your name every time you use a nonword. For some of us, the nonword habit is so ingrained that we will not even notice it when it is pointed out to us. We may even feel picked on unfairly: "I did *not* say 'Uhh.'" It helps to work with a friend who is trying to get rid of his or her own nonword habit so you can trade off.

Practice The Pause. When you feel tempted to lapse into a nonword, just *pause*. Let The Pause hover lightly in the air—three, four, five, six seconds, or even more—while you gather your thoughts for the next sentence. Push your pauses to the limit. Then get feedback on your pauses: Did they seem forced or natural? Did they heighten the drama of your message and grab your listeners' attention? Remember the disparity that you will feel. It is valuable to get this experience of disparity many times over. You'll be surprised to discover how natural and confident you sound when you have learned the Power of The Pause.

The Benefit of Good Words and No Nonwords

- You are memorable in your language.
- You appear confident and intelligent.
- You can use The Pause for dramatic emphasis.
- You no longer belong to the great mass of nonword irritators.
- You become more First Brain Friendly.

Remember: Use colorful, jargon-less language, and replace nonwords with a good three-second pause.

7. Listener Involvement

> *"Your listeners won't care how much you know until they know how much you care."*
>
> ANONYMOUS

Human beings communicate. Books dispense information. There's a big difference. The question is: Are you a human being—or a book?

Every time you communicate with another human being via the spoken word, you are doing much more than merely imparting information. You are revealing ideas, opinions, and emotions. You are attempting to move that person to action, or to persuade that person to agree with you. In other words, you are trying to *involve* your listener. If all you want to do is impart information, you might as well be a book!

Right now, I'm coming to you in the form of a book. You can read me, but I can't read you. Are you bored? Fascinated? Irritated? Yawning? Excited? Are you smiling? Frowning? Giving half your attention to the TV? Are you sitting in a comfortable chair? Lying down? Do you sit at a desk and study this book intently—or is it bathroom reading? I don't know! I can't see you! I can't adjust my message to better involve you! At this moment in your life, I'm nothing but words on paper!

But if you were sitting in my office, in my living room, or in my audience—even if you were just one face in a sea of faces—I could *involve* you in a conversation. I could see if you are falling asleep or leaning forward in anticipation—and I could adjust my message and my behavior accordingly. I could change my strategy to keep your First Brain open to the flow of my message.

Some Examples

- John Rogers was asked to give a talk to a church group. His subject was "Conflict." As he stood up in front of the group, the babble of various conversations continued from different portions of the audience. "Shut up!" John shouted at the top of his lungs. "I'm tired of listening to you! From now on I talk and *you* listen!"

  At that moment, all eyes—some of them as big as saucers—were looking at John. You could have heard a snowflake drop. John went on: "The man who shouted those words in my face was about six feet tall and 200 pounds. At that moment, I knew I was in for a heap of conflict." The tension broke—but John's listeners stayed quietly, attentively involved for the rest of his talk.
- Fred Hillman is a computer engineer. He has a brilliant mind and a keen sense of humor. Talk to him in informal situations, and you will find him bright, engaging, and fun to listen to. But when he speaks formally, he turns into a dull, dry, computer nerd. He reads his speeches without making eye contact, without inflection, without

humor. Even a roomful of his colleagues—all computer enthusiasts themselves—find him a crashing bore.

There are eight key techniques you can use to involve your listener.

The Eight Basics

1. Use Drama. You can immediately involve your listener with a strong opening. Start with a striking statement, a dramatic story, or a question that forces the listener to focus on your message. Make your message visual and energetic with the use of action and motion. Use your voice to create drama: vocal tone or pitch variation, dramatic pauses, and strong emotional content (anger, sorrow, joy, laughter). Close your talk with a motivational call to specific action, or with a memorable quotation.

2. Maintain Eye Communication. Don't look over the heads of your audience; *meet them in the eye!* Survey your listeners for a few moments before you begin speaking. Maintain three to six seconds of eye contact with as many individuals as possible. Don't forget to include people in the "fringes" at either end of the audience or conference table. Read the eye contact they give back to you. Gauge whether

"Drama"

your listeners are bored, wary, hostile, interested, or enthusiastic— and *adjust* your approach accordingly.

3. Move. Don't nail your shoes to the carpet—*move*! Avoid using a lectern. If a lectern is provided, move out from behind it. Make your movements purposeful and authoritative. Never back away from your audience—it makes you look intimidated. In fact, at both the beginning and end of your talk, it lends force to your message to take a few steps *toward* your listeners.

4. Use Visuals. In addition to making your own presence as interesting as possible, give your listeners something to look at. Make your communication memorable with the use of bold, striking graphic aids, props, overheads, flip charts, or other sensory enhancements. Mix assorted kinds of media (for example, use both overheads and video clips) in order to keep the visual dimension varied and interesting.

"A Visual Array"

Rehearse the visual part of your presentation so that transitions will be fluid rather than fumbling. Involve your listeners with your visuals; for example, ask questions of your audience and briefly tabulate their answers on an overhead transparency.

5. Ask Questions. Rhetorical questions will keep your listeners thinking and focused. Asking for a volunteer is even more involving. You actually feel a surge of intensity go through an audience, and you can read the thoughts of many of your listeners right on their faces: "Should I answer that question?" Asking for a show of hands also generates involvement—and it gives you a quick gauge of your audience's mood and opinions.

6. Use Demonstrations. Plan and time every step or procedure. Have a volunteer from the audience assist in the demonstration. Above all, make sure your demonstration *works*.

THE "REVERSE" DEMONSTRATION

Charles Fort, the late author and investigator of paranormal phenomena, used to tell about a high school science professor who attempted to illustrate scientific principles with visual demonstrations. For example, this teacher tried to show that a bullet and a feather fall with equal speed in a vacuum—but the bullet landed first. On another occasion, he tried to show that white is a mixture of all colors, so he mixed several colors of paint together, expecting to produce white—and got a muddy gray-brown. Fort said that his faith in science never recovered from the "demonstrations" of this science teacher. The lesson is simple: When you demonstrate a concept for your listeners, make sure the demonstration doesn't backfire!

---

7. Use Samples and Gimmicks. Have fun with your listeners. If you are promoting a product, have samples available to give as rewards for volunteer participants. Be creative with using gimmicks—but be careful. Gimmicks can backfire, so proceed with caution. When they work well, they work very well. But when they bomb, they explode with a big bang.

8. Create Interest. Remember that your listeners have a short attention span. Pace your various involvement techniques to keep the level of interest high. Use eye contact to gauge your listeners' involvement. Most of all, keep *your own* interest level high, even if you are giving a "stump speech" for the thousandth time. Change the order, change techniques, vary the stories you use. If you demonstrate genuine enthusiasm for your message, your emotional involvement and energy will be infectious!

Some Basic Exercises

Be Creative. Use your imagination in dreaming up listener involving actions and techniques. After watching someone give a presentation, make a list of the things that person could have done to involve people. (Chances are there was not much.) Think of what could have been done to involve you. Always look at what you could do *differently*.

Try Something New. Push yourself to try something new in each

"One Man Band"

speech or meeting that you give. Take these eight involvement techniques and concentrate on one a day in all of your communicating situations.

The Benefits of Good Listener Involvement

- You keep your listeners' energy up.
- You keep your energy up.
- You can get more of your concepts and ideas across when you have the interest and involvement of your audience.
- You have more fun.
- Your audience has more fun.
- It reinforces other good communication habits, like eye communication, movement, etc.

Remember: You are a human being, not a book. Don't just dispense information. Involve your listener and *make emotional contact*.

8. Humor

"The one who causes them to laugh, gains more votes for the measure than the one who forces them to think."

MALCOLM DE CHAZALL

Humor creates a special bond between you and your listeners. It's virtually impossible to dislike someone who makes us laugh, who helps us enjoy ourselves. A sense of humor—whether sharp and explosive or dry and witty—makes you appear more genial, more warm, more likable. The strong, pleasurable emotions people associate with good fun and high spirits make your message enjoyable to listen to—and *memorable*.

Our First Brains use strong emotions—including the emotions that trigger smiles and laughter—to saturate our New Brains with vivid impressions that result in greater retention of the message.

Some Examples

- In 1984, running for a second term in the White House against Walter Mondale, seventy-six-year-old Ronald Reagan knew that age was a concern in the campaign. A fumbling performance against Mondale in the first debate had already created the impression that Reagan was getting a little foggy, if not senile. So when a reporter served up the age question to Reagan during the second debate, the President was ready for it. "I will not make age an issue of this campaign," he replied. "I am not going to exploit for political purposes my opponent's youth and inexperience." The press and the audience howled. Mondale himself could not contain a laugh—even though his fate was perhaps sealed at that moment. The age issue never came up again during the rest of the campaign—and that one exchange was the most remembered event of the debate.

• Bill Dromm's topic for the Instructional Systems Association convention in Key West, Florida, was "Quality in Finance"—a guaranteed yawner. On a two-day program filled with dynamic professional speakers, he was the professorial, academic type who would be sweating bullets. As Bill was introduced, many in the audience steeled themselves for a dull, dry, statistic-laden lecture. But not those who knew Bill.

Within the first sixty seconds, Bill had already garnered half a dozen laughs. Within half an hour, he had delivered his talk— painlessly and engagingly. In fact, Bill was easily one of the best speakers of the entire convention.

"Sweating Bullets"

"Let me try to get through this stuff 'cuz I'm dying a slow death up here" was typical of his commentary during a rough Q & A session. His humor was dry, but his presentation was anything but! He was entertaining. He got his information across. He got a rousing round of applause. He was a *star*.

Humor can be a powerful tool for packing positive energy into your communication. Keep in mind the principle to *make the formal informal*. It doesn't come naturally to most of us, but is definitely worth working on.

The Basic Rules

Don't Tell Jokes. Leave comedy to the comedians. How many people do you know who are really good joke-tellers? I would estimate that perhaps one person in a hundred is a good joke-teller—and unfortunately, about ten times that many *think* they are good joke-tellers. If your joke falls flat, you'll go down with it. Everyone in the room feels uncomfortable and embarrassed when a speaker's joke does the old lead zeppelin. First Brains snap shut. Persuasion screeches to a halt. Unless you are in that rare ninety-ninth percentile who can actually tell a joke successfully—with timing, delivery, and flair—*don't*.

The great improvisor Jonathan Winters said, "I don't do jokes well. I think you can be funny just by commenting on the present scene or on things that have happened in the day. I try to create verbal pictures."

Fun Is Better Than Funny. Your goal is not comedy but *connection*—creating an atmosphere of fun, friendliness, and openness. You want to put your listeners at ease, not do a stand-up at the Improv. Unless you're Jonathan Winters.

"Laughter is the shortest distance between two people."

VICTOR BORGE

Find the Form of Humor That Works for You. If jokes don't work for you, what does? Perhaps you can use stories and anecdotes. Or perhaps a slightly skewed outlook on life. Of course, a warm, genuine smile *always* works.

What's your sense of humor like? A dry, subtle wit? The ability to poke gentle fun at yourself, to not take yourself too seriously? A flair for earthy, gut-level humor? A unique outlook on everyday life? Do you find unexpected amusement in the things that happen around your home or the office? What kinds of things do you do and say in private conversations that make people laugh—and how can you work them into your presentations? Do you have a gift for seeing the humor and the opportunity in a crisis?

Use the Humor in Language. The right emphasis of a single word can provoke a laugh and cement the connection between you and your listener. Example: the speaker who defined "ageism" as "prejudice against the aged by the *temporarily* young."

THE GREAT COMPENSATOR

"Carrie Fisher was born to Eddie Fisher and Debbie Reynolds, and grew up in the spotlight of America's most publicized divorce. 'My mother was pretty and I knew I didn't look like her—I remember thinking I looked like a toe—so I figured I'd better develop some compensating feature.' A peculiar sense of humor did the trick, a quality she stuck with in adulthood. 'When I read in the *Star Wars* script that Leia was "staggeringly beautiful," ' Fisher recalls, 'I thought, that can't be me. So I crossed it out to read, "staggering beautifully." ' "

From *Vis a Vis* magazine, June 1991

Some Basic Exercises

Think Funny. Humor is the hardest communication skill to exercise, and the best exercise to do is actually working at a mind-set. Think funny, and you will begin not only to *see* the humor around you, but to *use* humor in your communications. What makes you laugh? Is it wry wit, personal asides, puns? Find out, and use it in your own communications. Look for the humor in the serious—it is almost always there. There is even laughter at funerals, and it is appropriate.

People like to laugh. They like to be with people who are light-hearted. So do you. Look at those who make you laugh or feel light-hearted, and emulate them. Think funny.

"Think Funny"

Think Friendly. This is also a mind-set, and you can exercise your attitude on this one. The next person you see, think of being friendly, rather than judging or advocating or questioning or however you might set your attitude. With this mind-set, humor and humanization are much more likely to occur, and it will become a habit. Here's what habit forming good humor can do: I recently went to a new dentist, and I had to go back *three times* for adjustments. I never would have put up with that inconvenience if Dr. Ron and his charming reception-ist-wife were not so darn friendly. She smiled, had a warm telephone manner, and was interested in everyone. He was informal and easy-going—they both were so *nice*. And they weren't just putting it on— that's the way they really were. Thinking friendly can become a habit, and it's good for business.

Write Down Your Humor. Keep a journal or diary of observations and funny quotations, anecdotes, and stories—especially those stories that happen to you. When keeping a story diary, don't write the entire story down—just a few trigger words to bring it back to mind when you're preparing your talk. Review it regularly, and it will add to your mind-set of thinking funny.

The Benefits of Good Humor

- You will be more likable.
- You will have more fun.
- Your listeners will have more fun.
- People will be more eager to be with you, and to hear you speak.
- You will be *much* more First Brain Friendly.
- You will find more energy and vitality in your life.

Remember: Life should be *fun*—so have fun with life. Think funny, and then speak up and share that fun with others!

Unleashing the Energy Within

People like and trust the person who puts all of his or her conviction into motion, expression, vocal variety, and memorable language. People respond warmly to the speaker who displays humanity and humor. The Energy Factor is right there inside you, waiting to be unleashed.

It was unleashed for General H. Norman Schwarzkopf in his famous press briefing at the conclusion of the Gulf War in February 1991. On ABC's "Nightline," Ted Koppel called the Schwarzkopf briefing "quite an extraordinary performance."

He communicated effectively, persuasively—and *energetically*. Stormin' Norman's performance was commanding and punctuated by moments of visible emotion. His voice choked as he expressed sorrow over the loss of American lives. His face shaded with anger as he described the senseless waste of Iraq's soldiers and "the absolutely unspeakable atrocities" against Kuwaiti civilians. But the most memorable and effective moments of Schwarzkopf's presentation were his sudden and disarming flashes of humor.

The most frequently replayed excerpt showed the general being asked by a reporter for his assessment of Saddam Hussein as a military strategist. "Hah!" Schwarzkopf laughed. Then, leaning toward the audience of reporters, his voice dripping with derision, he said, "He is neither a strategist, nor is he schooled in the operational art, nor is he a tactician, nor is he a general, nor is he a soldier." A short pause, then, "Other than that, he's a great military man."

Perfect comedic timing. The line not only got a laugh, but extensive network airplay as a choice and memorable sound-bite. More importantly, that light moment revealed a lot about the human heart within the uniform. Schwarzkopf's emotion, his energy, and his sense of humor helped define his humanity and likability before an amazed press and a grateful nation.

You too can use the four components of The Energy Factor:

5. Voice and Vocal Variety
6. Words and Nonwords (The Pause)
7. Listener Involvement
8. Humor

All the communicative energy you need is right there inside you. Learn to release and direct The Energy Factor—then watch it ignite your communication, inspire your listeners, and *change* the direction of your life.

Part IV

MASTERING YOUR
FIRST BRAIN

Up to this point we have been talking about what you can do to affect and reach the First Brain of your listener. Not your audience. Your *listener*. Remember, every person within the sound of your voice is a *singular* person, whether you are communicating one-on-one, or to a packed house. The first seven chapters of this book have been focused on reaching the First Brain of your listener.

Now, in Part IV, it's time to look inward, to the First Brain that powers *your own* personality. Through the next four chapters, we will examine what you can do to better *control* and *utilize* the driving force of your own First Brain. We will discover how your *First* Brain—the unreasoning, feeling part of your mind—can be brought under the conscious control of your thinking, reasoning, decision-making *New* Brain.

Until now, we have seen the First Brain as passive, an important but helpless gate in the listener's mind that opens and closes according to the signals and cues the speaker sends forth. But at this point we will explore the enormous active power of your own First Brain—power to transform your life for the better, or, if poorly understood and directed, power to strangle your future.

The four chapters of Part IV are:

Chapter 8: First Brain Fear. This is *the* crucial issue for many of us: *The fear of public speaking.* In this chapter we will discover why we feel the way we do about speaking, what the fight or flight response is, and why it wields such enormous power.

Chapter 9: First Brain under Control. How to *conquer* our First Brain fear of speaking is the important subject of this chapter. And how to harness the energy of our own First Brain to make us more effective and persuasive.

Chapter 10: Gatekeeper on Guard. So far, we have talked almost exclusively about reaching other people at a preconscious level, about being effective and persuasive communicators, about getting others to respond, to buy, to follow our leadership. Aren't we really talking about *manipulation*? Isn't this book *really* about how to exploit and unfairly influence others? Find out why the answer to these questions is a resounding *"No!"* And discover how you can guard against others who would try to manipulate you.

Chapter 11: Opening the Gate. This book is about opening the two-way gates of communication—both our listener's *and our own*. To communicate effectively and persuasively, we must not only talk, but we must *listen*. There's enormous power in the ability to truly listen to our own listeners. In this chapter we learn how to tap the power of the First Brain and open our mental floodgates to this potent force.

8

First Brain Fear

"Do the thing you fear and death of fear is certain."

EMERSON

FEAR ON THE RUN

Speaking is what I do, and I do it all the time. I speak to large audiences. I speak in small workshop and seminar settings. I speak on TV. Public speaking holds no terror for me anymore—but it used to. Much more than I like to admit. In fact, it wasn't too long ago that I first discovered how to overcome the fear of public speaking.

It was in 1981—a little over a year after I founded Decker Communications. I had accepted an invitation to be the main presenter at a regional meeting of ASTD—the American Society for Training and Development. After I accepted, the first thing I thought was, *"Why did I get into this business anyway?"*

In those days, when my knees were in better shape, I used to exercise many days by running up and down the hills of San Francisco. Right on my running path was the Holiday Inn on Van Ness Avenue—the site of the upcoming ASTD meeting. I have vivid memories of those morning runs, sucking in that crisp Pacific air as I chugged to the crest of a hill, my Nikes snick-snickering on the pavement—and then I would see . . . *it*.

By *it* I mean the Holiday Inn. I shouldn't make it sound so horrible, because it's a nice enough building, really. But to me it was as ominous and forbidding as the old house on the hill above the Bates Motel in *Psycho*. Here it was, a full *six months* before I was to give that speech, and the mere sight of the Holiday Inn made my blood congeal and my stomach turn somersaults. And this didn't happen just one or two times. It happened *every time* I passed that building.

Sure, it was an important speech. After all, this was the first major exposure of my fledgling company before many potential buyers of my services. A lot was riding on it.

But I had to wonder why I was even in the communications business if I had such an intense fear of public speaking. It was like the president of Bank of America keeping his money in a mattress, or the president of McDonald's being a vegetarian, or the president of General Motors owning a Yugo, or the president of Philip Morris not smoking. I realized that if I couldn't conquer my fear of public speaking, I was a fraud and didn't deserve to be in the business.

I tried to talk myself out of my fear. I tried to psyche myself up. But as the day of the speech grew closer, my fear only increased.

Then the day came. Shark music thundered in my head, as the theme from *Jaws* grew louder and louder: "Dum-dum. Dum-dum. Dum-dum. Dum-dum!" As I stepped up to speak, I was one big jangling terrified nerve. I faced the audience. I opened my mouth. And I spoke.

My presentation was videotaped, and I got to see that videotape the next day—and I was utterly amazed. I knew of the disparity phenomenon—heck, I even taught it—but it was profound to experience it so personally. You couldn't tell how nervous I was! It didn't show in the slightest! What an astounding difference between the way I felt and the way I looked. (More on that in Chapter 13).

Not only that, I wasn't bad. I was even persuasive—so persuasive that I convinced a skeptic. Fred Verhey was in the audience. I didn't know him then. He was a trainer for a restaurant chain at the time, and was impressed enough to come and do the Decker Program. Within six months we hired Fred, and today he is a vice president in our company. He's a great speaker, too. That terror-drenched speech was my first connection with Fred.

Public speaking used to spook, scare, rattle, and unnerve me—but no longer. I learned how to disarm the fear of public speaking. I knew I had to if I was going to stay in this business. The ASTD speech in 1981 was the spark that sent me on a search for answers and solutions to this fear.

I have learned those answers and found those solutions. Today I practice what I preach. I've gone through the confidence-building process that I hope you embark on—and in the coming pages I'm going to tell you exactly how to get there yourself.

Sure, I still have an emotional reaction before a speaking "performance." But it's an excitement and exhilaration, not raw fear. It's the kind of reaction a sprinter feels as he steps into the starting blocks—the healthy edge of tension that powers a Class A performance.

The fear of speaking is a First Brain fear. It's irrational—and knowing it's irrational doesn't help one bit. But knowing *where* this irrational fear comes from, *how* it affects you, and how you can *control* it helps immensely.

By the end of these next two chapters, you'll know everything you need to know to send fear on the run.

The Fear of Speaking

The following chart of people's greatest fears is best known from *The Book of Lists* but it was originally researched some years ago in a

Greatest Fears

1. Speaking	41%
2. Heights	32
3. Insects & bugs	22
4. Financial	22
5. Deep water	22
6. Sickness	19
7. Death	19

survey by the Sunday *Times* of London. And I can affirm that the facts are true from my own experience with Decker Communications. We have trained over 50,000 people and I can assure you that, almost without exception, everyone who comes through our programs can testify to the truth of this research.

But why? Why should the fear of speaking loom larger than any other threat in our lives? Why would we literally rather *die* than get up before an audience and communicate? It's totally irrational—and you and I both know it. And we also know that the fear of communicating limits our effectiveness and hinders our careers and our relationships.

Irrational though it may be, the fear is *real*. It has real causes—and fortunately, it has real solutions.

The fear of public speaking has its genesis in the way our First Brain works.

The Source of Fear

The fear of public speaking is actually many fears bundled together. Broken into its component parts, the fear of public speaking—often called "performance anxiety"—becomes easier to understand and to overcome. The first thing to understand about this anxiety is that it is actually the fear of making ourselves vulnerable before others (exposure). Added to this is the fear of failure (ridicule). These component fears, which become exaggerated to wildly unrealistic proportions in our minds, have the power to stimulate genuine mortal dread within us at the prospect of speaking in public.

The reason this fear can be so overpowering and paralyzing is that it is First Brain fear—unreasoning, preconscious animal fear, related to our instincts for survival. Remember that the First Brain does not reason or analyze. It reacts emotionally. It registers needs and it responds to threats of danger and it controls certain physiological responses as part of the body's autonomic and sympathetic nervous system. When our New Brain analyzes a situation (such as speaking before an audience) as a threat, it sends many stimuli—siren alarms of danger—to our First Brain. The First Brain responds with naked animal fear and physiological responses that are not under our conscious control.

Our palms sweat. Our hearts palpitate. Our throats constrict. Blood pressure increases. Adrenaline surges.

That's the reaction I experienced while running past the Holiday Inn on Van Ness Avenue. It was a First Brain reaction. That's why I couldn't control the way I felt, even six months before the day of the speech. I didn't know then what I know now.

You can't reason with your First Brain. You can't control its responses. But there is a way to bring First Brain fear under control. It all takes place in your New Brain, the thinking and reasoning part of your brain. You control First Brain fear by modifying the attitude in your New Brain that triggers the fear.

Fight or Flight

The basis of First Brain fear is a psychological and behavioral principle called the Fight or Flight response. It's a survival mechanism that developed in very primitive forms of life, and which has grown more powerful and elaborate in more complex forms of life, such as you and me.

A primitive survival mechanism is the way freshwater snails jerk into their shells when touched by a predator, or the way baby chicks instinctively crouch and freeze in response to an alarm call by the mother hen. In reptiles and lower mammals, this survival mechanism includes the ability to fight and attack a predator alongside the ability to run and hide.

Your First Brain and mine are like computers with very basic programming written in their circuits. The program is called Fight or Flight. When faced with a perceived threat (whether that threat is objectively real or not), the primitive computer of the First Brain analyzes the situation in terms of a very simple decision: "Should I flee and hide—or should I stand and fight?"

All the First Brain cares about is survival. The Fight or Flight response is one of the survival programs etched in the hard-wired circuitry of your First Brain.

There was a time, millennia ago, when the Fight or Flight response served our prehistoric ancestors quite well. If you've ever seen pictures of prehistoric predators, you know there were times that our predecessors needed to make some lightning-fast, life-or-death decisions. There wasn't time for analysis. Whether the choice was to fight or flee, they literally had to move it or lose it.

So if Mr. or Mrs. Australopithecus happened to be on the way to the watering hole when a saber-toothed tiger leaped out from the underbrush, he or she wouldn't have to think. Everything would take place at a preconscious, First Brain level—a virtual reflex reaction. Blood would rush to the muscles of Mr. or Mrs. A's body, preparing it to run. Glycogen would be changed to glucose for energy. Adrenaline would move the mind to think more quickly. A flush of perspiration would occur instantly and automatically to cool the body, now ready and heated for action.

Of course this primitive individual is not completely at the mercy of his or her reflex responses. If the tiger in question has teeth as long as your forearm and weighs 400 pounds, there is only one choice: get the hell out of here! But if Mr. or Mrs. A is a big-boned individual armed with a stout club and Mr. Tiger is a cat of modest size and ferocity, our prehistoric ancestor may be confident enough to whup the tar out of that kitty.

Now, my suspicion is that you don't encounter too many saber-toothed tigers on the way to the office watercooler. But the physiological reactions that Mr. or Mrs. A experienced in the presence of the saber-toothed tiger are probably very familiar to you. Perhaps you experienced those sensations one time when you were confronted by a mugger. Or when a speeding car came at you while you were in the crosswalk. Or when you stood in front of an audience, about to give a speech.

Strange, isn't it, that a natural survival response that served our ancestors so well—and that *still* serves us well in dangerous situations—can also hurt us, limit our effectiveness, and mess up our performance at those times when we desperately want to do our best. But it's true.

So what can we do? We can teach our thinking, reasoning New Brains to stop shouting "Danger!" at our First Brains. We can teach our New Brains the difference between real and imagined threats.

A Friendly Experiment

It was one of those perfect summer evenings—a dinner party at our home with three other couples. The sun had just set as we finished dinner and went for the view in the living room. From the picture window of our hillside house, we could see the headlights prowling the valley below. Over the mountains, stars were just peeking through the deepening twilight.

"Just perfect," said Emily, one of our guests. She was looking out the window at the gathering dusk, cradling a tulip glass of cabernet.

I didn't know Emily well. I knew she was a very successful sales executive for a large company in the Bay Area. I could tell from talking to her that she was a confident person. She exuded poise and competence, and she was a good conversationalist.

"Bert," she said, "I know you have a communications company of some kind, but I don't understand what kind of communications you're involved with. Do you work with telecommunications? Computer networks? Phone systems?"

"I work with people."

"Well, you could say we *all* work with people, but—"

"No, I mean I really work with *people*," I said. "I help people communicate more effectively, giving speeches or sales presentations, or communicating one-on-one. I teach people how to get their message across more persuasively, and how to overcome the fear of public speaking."

"Fear of public speaking?" she said. I detected a glint of condescension in her smile and in her tone. Maybe it was always there—but I now just recognized it. "Are there really that many people who are afraid of something as simple as giving a talk in front of an audience?"

"It's the number one fear," I replied. "People are more afraid of speaking in public than they are of death." And I proceeded to tell her about the results of the Sunday *Times* of London survey.

"You're joking!"

"I'm not."

"That's too bad. I've never felt that way," she said. And then went on to talk effusively and enthusiastically about a new project she had just launched for her company. While she talked for the next few minutes, the wheels in my mind were turning.

"Emily," I said during a pause in the conversation, "would you try an experiment?"

She glanced at me from the corners of her eyes, intrigued but wary. "What do you have in mind?"

"Trust me," I said. "I think you'll find this very interesting. Maybe even educational."

"Okay," she said, even more wary than before. "What do I do?"

"Very simple. All you have to do is tell us the story you just told us. About the new project with your company. Tell it exactly as you did before, but with one little difference. This time, stand up while you speak."

"Sure," she said, relieved that the "experiment" turned out to be a piece of cake. She stood up and took a few steps back from the table, then began to speak. "As I was telling you—the, uh, project I—"

We all saw it. Although it wasn't exactly a hunted look that came into her eyes, it was no longer that cocksuredness either. Her hands assumed the classic "fig-leaf" position in front of her—a sure sign of nervousness.

She didn't finish her first sentence before saying, "This *is* different! Standing up here with all of you looking at me like this, I don't feel I'm just chatting with friends anymore. I feel . . . *judged*."

Our Mind Does It to Us

What happened to Emily? What caused her to freeze up?

Just moments before, she had been talking effectively, excitedly, confidently as she described something in her life that she felt enthusiastic about. What changed? The room was the same. The listeners were the same. The message was the same. In fact, *nothing at all changed* except the fact that Emily was now "presenting" instead of just communicating with friends.

Her mind did it to her. Even though she was still among friends, she felt she was standing in the hot glare of the spotlight. She imagined her "audience" was gauging her "performance" with a critical eye. Even though nothing had changed, *everything* had changed in Emily's mind because *she felt she was being judged as she spoke.*

The conclusion that she was being judged came from her New Brain. Her New Brain sent a message to her First Brain: "Danger!" Now she not only felt she was performing, but she also felt threatened. The Fight or Flight response took over her physiological responses. Adrenaline, nervousness, and fear suddenly replaced her former excitement, enthusiasm, confidence.

And communication ceased.

Childhood Disasters

Poor little Janny. She learned about hurt at a very early age. Her parents loved her and never abused her. But still she experienced some very deep hurts, and her First Brain still bears the scars.

Janny's older sister Beth had a cruel streak. She resented Janny from the day she was born, because baby Janny got all the attention and Beth got shoved aside. So, whenever her parents weren't looking, Beth took her resentment out on Janny in small ways. Inflicting pain. Inflicting humiliation. Name-calling. Telling Janny she was stupid or ugly or unloved or unwanted.

Once, when Janny was two years old and Beth was six, big sister punched little sister in the face to make her stop laughing. It split her lip—four stitches.

But one of the most emotionally devastating events in Janny's young life had nothing to do with the cruelty of her older sister. It happened at the church picnic when Janny was eight years old. The children were playing softball in the park next to the church.

Janny stood behind the chain-link backstop, awaiting her turn at bat. At the plate was eleven-year-old Jeff—the pastor's son and object of Janny's infatuation. He had just taken a mighty swing and knocked the ball deep into left field.

Janny started to shout, "Great shot!" but in the split-instant before the words came out of her mouth, she tried to change it to, "Great hit!" But what came out of her mouth, what everyone at the church picnic heard, what her horrified parents could not ignore, were the shrill words, "Great shit!" And at the top of her little lungs. That was not at all what she had meant to say. Suddenly all eyes were staring at her. Even Jeff looked over his shoulder in amazement as he ran to first base. He laughed. Janny burst into tears.

She never forgot the shame and embarrassment of inadvertently shouting an obscenity before a crowd of people. Never.

In her college speech course (which she took only because it was required), she painfully stammered her way to a C minus—nothing more than a sympathy grade. In her church and her job, she carefully avoided situations that might require her to speak.

The First Brain fear that was hammered into her at an early age by a resentful sister and a traumatic childhood experience is with her to this day. Janny—or Janice, as she is now known—is thirty-eight years old and scared to death of public speaking.

There's nothing unusual about Janice's story. Her childhood was, on balance, no more unhappy or painful than that of most people. But her future is crippled by the First Brain fear that she learned at a very early age.

NORMAN VINCENT PEALE ON SELF-ESTEEM

"I once spoke in New Orleans at a convention of elementary school principals. There were 9,000 there and I got to visiting with a lot of them. One of the things we talked about was self-esteem. When a child is born he is born as a positive personality, but they said that by the time they get to the fourth or fifth grade, eighty to eighty-five percent of them have a low self-esteem. They are negative and that low self-esteem tends to continue during their high school and their college careers, and on into their adult life. And I had never heard that before, so I interrogated all the teachers that I have spoken to in various states and nationally and they corroborated this. Low self-esteem is a major problem in today's world."

From a conversation with Dr. Norman Vincent Peale.

Does Janny's story remind you of your own story? Could it be that your own First Brain fear is rooted in things that happened to you in your own childhood? Could it be that the taunts and petty cruelties and abuses you suffered twenty or thirty or forty years ago are still hurting you, still holding you back, still keeping you from achieving the grown-up goals of your life?

When our cerebral cortex—our New Brain—is just being imprinted and developed in early childhood, the First Brain is the driving force. We are extremely vulnerable to the pain of judgment and criticism. The cruel taunts of siblings and other children and the appraisal of stern parents are quickly and indelibly etched into the wet cement of a child's mind.

Patterns of insecurity, fear, self-doubt, and self-criticism are set, for most of us, at a very early age. These patterns emerge in our adulthood as a lack of confidence in situations where we are called upon to perform, to expose ourselves to the appraisal of our peers. Hence the term "performance anxiety."

Think for a moment: What is it you are really afraid of when you contemplate speaking in public?

Is it judgment? Are you afraid of what other people will think of you? Are you afraid of embarrassment? Of failure? Of taking further crippling blows to your self-esteem?

All of these things sound pretty horrible. But now that we are adults, do we *really* have so much to fear from the judgment of other people?

The Ninety-five-Percent Solution

The deeper and more profound truth about our fear of being judged is that this fear is so terribly exaggerated and misplaced. The tragedy is that we needlessly limit ourselves by our fear, because we aren't faulted by others anywhere near as much or as often as we think we are.

Both psychologists Abraham Maslow and Karen Horney did extensive work on the development of self-esteem and self-worth in an individual. Maslow's "hierarchy of needs" theory leading to self-actualization is now classic, but I think Horney's work has perhaps an even stronger application. She found that when an individual actually attempts something—intellectually or physically, be it a memory verse, an athletic event, going for a promotion, or even a speech—the great majority of the time the individual will succeed. Yet when a person does not make the attempt, they have an impression of failure. The dramatic finding is that for most people their self-impression is one of failure more than success, *because most of the time they do not make the attempt*.

I have tracked this with myself and others and found that about ninety-five percent of the time we attempt to speak—to communicate—we succeed. The first time I realized that, I thought, "Wow! Ninety-five percent?" (Major league ballplayers are doing great if they are batting above .300.) But I've tested the thesis, I've done the experiment. My test has been anecdotal rather than scientific, to be sure, but I have verifed Dr. Horney's theories. Looking objectively at my meetings, communications and speeches over a set time period, I had to say I really *was* batting around .950, just as Dr. Horney indicated. That's pretty dramatic.

And the same is true of *you*. About ninety-five percent of the time, you're going to succeed at communicating. So why not play the odds? Every time you attempt a speech and feel the tug of self-doubt, tell yourself that this is going to be one of your "ninety-five percent" performances. If, when it's all over, it turns out to be one of those rare "five percent" duds, so be it. Accept it, learn from it, and move on.

Consider this: *Why should you jeopardize every performance for the sake of that five percent?* Yet that, unfortunately, is what most of us do.

You don't have to do that to yourself any longer. Here you have already acquired some insights that can help your New Brain quell the irrational fears of your First Brain. You know that your physical survival is not at stake when you stand up and communicate with others. You know that you have little if anything to fear from the judgment of others. You are batting .950, and that puts you in a class *beyond* the major leagues. In short, you *are* better than you think you are!

And the best is yet to come.

9

First Brain under Control

THE CASE OF THE POUNDING HEART

My late wife, Deborah, was my partner in founding and operating Decker Communications, Inc. Deborah was a very articulate and engaging lady. When questioned, her responses not only exuded confidence but were also stamped with her own special sense of humor. Her wit and insight were always right on the mark, and audiences and interviewers were invariably charmed by her personality.

Just a few months after Deborah and I formed our training company, we were asked to appear on a TV panel show. The subject was "Fear of Speaking."

During the show, she fielded the first question with great poise and apparent ease. It was clear that her answer was very persuasive. As she spoke, I noticed her right hand cross her body and lightly touch the area just over her heart, then fall back onto her lap.

Later at home we were watching the videotape of the show. At the point where she began answering that tough question, I heard her murmur in astonishment, "You can't even tell how nervous I was!"

"Nervous?" I said. "You know, you said you were nervous, but I still don't believe you. It doesn't show at all."

"Wait," she replied. "Rewind the tape a little . . . "

I did, and we looked at the TV screen. Her right hand moved up, touched the area over her heart, then fell back into her lap.

"At that moment my heart was hammering so hard I thought it

was going to burst out of my chest!" she said. "I put my hand over my heart to cover up the fluttering. I really thought it showed."

As Deborah sat beside me and described her jangled inner feelings, I studied that *other* Deborah on the video screen. She appeared as confident and charming as ever. Her answer was bright and penetrating, her manner completely controlled and self-assured. Where was all this mortal fear she said was going on inside? It certainly didn't show in any heart flutter. And it didn't show on her face, in her eyes, or in her voice.

Clearly the Fight or Flight response was ringing off the walls inside Deborah's First Brain—though she was the only one who knew. Ironically, while she was talking on TV about the fear of speaking, that fear was raging inside her like a five-alarm fire. Yet on the outside she was the picture of poise and confidence.

Since those early days at the founding of Decker Communications, I have made an intensive study of the fear of speaking, its causes and its cure. And the cure for this near-universal fear lies in learning to bring our First Brain under control.

The Life Force

The greatest 400-meter hurdler in history is Edwin Moses. He won the Olympic gold medal in 1976 with a record-setting time of 47.63 seconds—a time he trimmed to a new record of 47.02 seconds in 1983. From 1976 to 1987, he astounded the world with a string of 119 consecutive victories.

What was going on in the mind of this phenomenal athlete each time he crouched at the starting blocks? Was he worried about survival? About what people would think of his performance? No. Was he worried about winning? I doubt it, because in nearly every race he ran, Moses won by wide margins. After thirty, fifty, or a hundred consecutive wins, I would think he had confidence.

But was he nervous? I'm certain of it. Not because he was afraid of losing, but because he wasn't sure *how well* he was going to do! Would this be the day he broke his own record again? Maybe—with just a little extra competitive edge.

Edwin Moses was a champion because he used the adrenaline-charged Fight or Flight reflex of the First Brain. He channeled the physiological force of the First Brain to power his performance over the hurdles.

You can speak like Edwin Moses jumps. Or at least make a grand stride in that direction. You can channel the awesome power of the First Brain that athletes use to give you that competitive edge every time you speak.

Your First Brain is an unbridled powerhouse of raw emotions, urges, and needs. It's the energy force that drives you—that powers your wants and desires, your sense of excitement and satisfaction, your feelings of joy and fear.

Picture the tremendous power of a 5,000 psi firehose. It's hooked up to the hydrant, water is roaring through it, but there's no one directing its force. It whipsaws like a wounded cobra, spewing a blast of water that knocks people off their feet and drenches everything within a hundred-foot radius. That's what the uncontrolled First Brain is like.

"Controlling the First Brain"

Now picture a firefighter confronting a five-story inferno. Alone he is a pretty puny challenger against such a raging force. But put that 5,000 psi firehose in his grip and watch what happens! Now you have a powerfully effective force for good. That firefighter is like your New Brain—well-trained, flexible, smart, with a fantastically potent tool at his command.

That's what the First Brain is like under the conscious control of the New Brain. The Fight or Flight response doesn't have to destroy us. We can command it. It is in our power. This is one of the things that separates human beings from other animals: our New Brain, and its capacity to rule the First Brain. All other animals—dogs, dolphins, lions, and even the primates such as chimps, gorillas, and orang-utans—are essentially motivated by primitive First Brain impulses. They have no conscious control over those impulses. You and I do. The smart thing is to learn how to effectively exercise that control.

Dynamic Tension

To some degree, we all exercise a measure of First Brain control— but we all could do much better than we do.

Let's face it: Public speaking means speaking under pressure. There is pressure and inner tension involved whenever we speak in public because we are exposing ourselves to public appraisal. And speaking under pressure is the most important kind of communication we do. There's a lot on the line: reputation, personal satisfaction, fulfillment of others' expectations, and even career advancement.

It's the *pressure* aspect of public speaking that suggests a parallel between speaking and athletic performance. Because we have so much on the line, we want to have all the natural excitement, enthusiasm, and confidence at our disposal *working for us*. That's what athletes do: direct the pressure and tension they feel into the energy needed to power their best performance.

That's why you never want to get rid of your performance anxiety. In its proper balance, performance anxiety is essential to a *great* perfor-mance. Ethel Merman once said, "I know my lines, what's there to be nervous about?" I suspect Miss Merman was a bit disingenuous. A little nervousness—let's call it dynamic tension—translates into energy to help us do our best. Obviously, there's a line between dynamic tension and fear, and it's a line we don't want to cross. But a mild case of "backstage jitters" can be an asset to a good performance.

NO MAGIC PILL

"The first couple of words, it's like—I get an immediate case of dry mouth, and that makes it difficult to talk. You stumble over your words and then you even get more nervous, because you know you are messing up, and it's frustrating."

Michelle Felde was the star of a recent "20/20" program on the fear of speaking. ABC brought their camera crews into our video feedback training, and Michelle was one of our students. She worked for Ingres Corporation—a fast-growing software company—and was making a transition from computer support work to marketing management. She was taking the Decker Program to help prepare for her new role.

The "20/20" camera crews followed her through the program and a consulting session with Bob Figari, one of our senior trainers. Then they covered a real presentation she gave a month later to see how she did, and what became of her fear of speaking. So Michelle had to "perform" with not only the normal pressure of a video training program, but with the possibility of being seen by a national television audience on top of that. How did she do?

Brilliantly, which is why the producers used her for most of this "20/20" program. It was a thrill for us too, to see the confidence that comes from video feedback training demonstrated on national television.

But the most telling piece of the program was in the last shot. From a closeup Michelle said, "Actually if they could just develop maybe a pill that you took, that took care of the sweaty palms and the adrenaline and all that, I mean that would be great."

But there is no pill, so the ABC interviewer asked why she subjected herself to this pressure.

"If I had stepped back and said, 'No, I couldn't do it,' it would have been real self-defeating. And so this was the chance to say 'OK, you had this problem of fear, so let's go for it and what the heck, let's do it on national TV.'

"It's been good, yeah. It's been real good."

Remember, we succeed at ninety-five percent of the tasks we attempt. So we know that we will almost certainly do well when we get up to speak—but sometimes we don't know *how* well. That little bit of surplus nervous energy can be the extra edge that sends our performance to unexpected heights!

> *"The object is not to get rid of the butterflies but to get the butterflies to fly in formation."*

When the Angels Descend

Patricia Fripp is one of the top professional speakers in the United States and Great Britain. She is a petite, winsome engine of communicative energy with a charming English accent. She's a pro, and she always knows she'll be good. She just never knows exactly *how* good.

Patricia's brother is Robert Fripp, one of the most popular guitarists in England. Patricia says the quote she often uses about her speeches originally came from Robert talking about his concert performances: "I know I'll always be good, but I never know whether the angels will descend."

I know what they mean—and you should too. We have confidence to know we will be effective, we will be good—but there will be those times when we will be *great*. You can never predict when those times will come, when "the angels will descend." But those times *will* come—and when those angels descend, they'll be riding on lightning bolts of First Brain energy.

You and I can have the same winning confidence of Robert Fripp, of Patricia Fripp—and of an athlete like Edwin Moses. Every time the starting pistol fired, Moses came out of the blocks knowing he would be good—but never knowing if he was going to soar over those hurdles in 47.63 seconds, 47.02 seconds, or maybe (if a whole heavenly band of angels came down) 47 flat. He never knew and neither do we.

But the possibility is always there. *That's* the possibility that should ignite our First Brain, not the slim chance of failure. The thought that maybe, just maybe, tonight is the night we "push the envelope," the night our energy propels us beyond what we thought we could accomplish.

It can happen to you. It *will* happen to you—if you plug into the power of your First Brain, and learn to direct its power in the direction of your goal.

So how do you harness this power, overcome fear and achieve these peak communicating experiences? It's a two-step process, and you begin by finding out where you are in The Four Stages of Speaking.

The Four Stages of Speaking

In my experience with thousands of business and professional people, I've found that there are four basic levels to communicating effectiveness. Each has different characteristics of *emotion, behavior, attitude,* and *position.* We all are in one of these four stages of speaking. What is important is to find out which one you are in, and go beyond. We grow from Stage 1 to Stage 4 as we learn more about ourselves and our ability to control First Brain fear, and as we practice, and as we speak.

The stages are:

Stage 1: The Nonspeaker, characterized by:
- *Emotion*: Terror. This person is virtually scared to death of standing up and speaking before a group. Even the prospect of stating his name and introducing himself before a group fills him with anxiety. Often the nonspeaker is characterized by extreme shyness.
- *Behavior*: Rarely, rarely speaks. Avoids speaking at all costs.
- *Attitude*: Passive, with excuses. "Gee, I'd love to, but I've got the flu." "Oops, that's my bowling night." "Sorry, got to take our goldfish to the vet." Occasionally this person will get trapped into making a presentation at the office or giving a toast at a wedding, but usually he is very adept at making excuses to avoid presenting himself publicly.
- *Position*: Support. Usually low skill-level because he has little experience or ability as a communicator, so he works in a job that doesn't require communication skills.

    Perhaps his job requires some speaking. Perhaps his spouse or a friend encourages him. For whatever reason, the Nonspeaker begins to blossom and graduates to the next stage . . .

Stage 2: The Occasional Speaker, characterized by:
- *Emotion*: Fear. Not paralyzing fear, but sufficiently serious to limit her effectiveness. It is this fear that keeps her from volunteering. On those occasions when she is cajoled (or conned) into speaking, her nervousness usually shows.
- *Behavior*: Speaks occasionally. She can be coaxed into taking a speaking assignment, but she would never volunteer.
- *Attitude*: Active reluctance. Marked with growing awareness of the importance of it. She probably knows she must be able to present her ideas in order to get ahead—but she may not know how to go about it.

- *Position*: A frontline-doer. Growing ability. The Occasional Speaker is not locked into a pattern of hibernation and abject terror. She has tried public speaking—and she has survived. She learns that she can improve with work.

    With enough practice, the Occasional Speaker emerges as . . .

Stage 3: The Willing Speaker, characterized by:
- *Emotion*: Tension. A trace of the old Fight or Flight response, but it's no longer a hindrance—more of an annoyance. Positive emotions pervade. This speaker has learned to anticipate rather than dread the speaking experience. She finds that extra edge of tension uncomfortable but stimulating, just like an athlete before a race. She knows she will do well—but she's coiled and tensed for the performance, not complacent.
- *Behavior*: Speaks often. She's vocal and articulate. She readily utters her mind in business meetings.
- *Attitude*: Willing. Butterflies—but they fly in formation.
- *Position*: Management. Proven ability. She may not think of herself as a "public speaker" but she has the skills to pull it off. And the confidence.

    With enough motivation and experience she can become . . .

Stage 4: The Communicator, characterized by the fact that speaking is part of his or her job description, raison d'être, meat and potatoes . . .
- *Emotion*: Stimulation. Excitement about speaking. He is genuinely stimulated by speaking. He enjoys the feedback he gets from the audience—not to mention the applause.
- *Behavior*: Speaks always. First Brain mastery. He has embraced the art of turning the Fight or Flight reaction into positive energy. Adrenaline is his ally.
- *Attitude*: Alacrity. Gusto. Enthusiasm. He doesn't hesitate to present himself and his "wonderful" ideas. In fact, he jumps at the chance! He knows the rewards to be reaped.
- *Position*: Leadership. He is recognized as a person who attracts, persuades, and motivates people by the way he communicates. He inspires and commands.

Whatever stage you are in, push on to the next stage. The way to do it is to just *do it*—using the power of the visualization principle.

The Visualization Principle

The way to conquer First Brain fear and put your New Brain in control of your First Brain is a technique called *visualization*. Visualization is not a new idea. It actually has its roots in the Bible. "As a man thinks in his heart, so he is," says Proverbs 23:7. Most of the success methods being sold today are based on some variation of this very real principle.

How does visualization enable us to master the First Brain? By transforming the emotive power of threatening situations into safe ones.

Maxwell Maltz, author of *Psycho-Cybernetics*, was an early exponent of the visualization principle. Over a quarter century ago, he captured a truth that can literally transform the way we think, act, and communicate. He wrote,

> The mind cannot tell the difference between an actual experience and one vividly imagined.

Today we know that Maltz's statement can be refined even further: *The* First Brain *cannot tell the difference between an actual experience and one vividly imagined*. The New Brain can, but the First Brain cannot. *That* is the foundation of the visualization principle. *That* is why the visualization principle works.

The First Brain cannot distinguish reality from fantasy. That's why scary movies *really* scare us, even when our New Brain knows it's "only a movie." That's why bad dreams can awaken us with our hearts pounding and our sheets soaked with sweat. That's why just remembering an embarrassing childhood episode can make you blush, and just imagining jumping off the George Washington Bridge can make you short of breath and send a quiver of genuine terror up your spine. All of these experiences—a movie, a dream, a memory, an imaginary event—are forms of visualization (the movie is externally created, while the other experiences are generated in your New Brain).

Now you begin to see how powerful visualization is—and how it works to change the way the First Brain perceives and responds. We can create images in our mind that the First Brain will interpret as experiential reality. We can take a situation that the First Brain perceives as threatening and turn it into a cozy, warm, safe experience—using nothing but the power of the imagination!

Some real-life examples will show you how it works in practice:

18 Holes in His Brain

Major James Nesmeth had a dream of improving his golf game—and he developed a unique method of achieving his goal. Until he devised this method, he was just your average weekend golfer, shooting in the mid to low 90s. Then, for seven years, he completely quit the game. Never touched a club. Never set foot on a fairway.

Ironically, it was during this seven-year break from the game that Major Nesmeth came up with his amazingly effective technique for improving his game—a technique we can *all* learn from. In fact, the first time he set foot on a golf course after his hiatus from the game, he shot an astonishing 74! He had cut twenty strokes off his usual average without having swung a golf club in seven years! Unbelievable. Not only that, but also his physical condition had actually deteriorated during those seven years.

What was Major Nesmeth's secret? *Visualization.*

You see, Major Nesmeth had spent those seven years as a prisoner of war in North Vietnam. During those seven years, he was imprisoned in a cage that was approximately four and a half feet tall and five feet long.

During almost the entire time he was imprisoned, he saw no one, talked to no one, and experienced no physical activity. During the first few months he did virtually nothing but hope and pray for his release. Then he realized he had to find some way to occupy his mind or he would lose his sanity—and probably lose his life. That's when he learned to visualize.

In his mind, he selected his favorite golf course and started playing golf. Every day, he played a full eighteen holes at the imaginary country club of his dreams. He experienced everything to the last detail. He saw himself dressed in his golfing clothes. He smelled the fragrance of the trees and the freshly trimmed grass. He experienced different weather conditions—windy spring days, overcast winter days, sunny summer mornings. In his imagination, every detail of the tee box, the individual blades of grass, the trees, the singing birds, the scampering squirrels, the lay of the course became totally real.

He felt the grip of the club in his hands. He instructed himself as he practiced smoothing out his down-swing and follow-through on his shot. Then he watched the ball arc down the exact center of the fairway, bounce a couple times, and roll to the exact spot he had selected—all in his mind.

In the real world, he was in no hurry. He had no place to go. So in his mind he took every step on his way to the ball, just as if he were physically on the course. It took him just as long in objective time to play his game of mental golf as it would have taken in reality. Not a detail was omitted. Not once did he ever miss a shot, never a hook or a slice, never a missed putt.

Seven days a week. Four hours a day. Eighteen holes. Seven years. Twenty strokes off. Shot a 74.

Vividly Imagine

Maltz emphasized visualizing a successful self-image in your mind as a way to overcome low self-esteem. This will increase your confidence, and greater confidence naturally leads to increased energy and enthusiasm in communicating, and greater success in life. *Confidence is built on the experience of success.* The secret is to *vividly* imagine. And that experience can take place right in the corridors of our minds.

A vividly imagined visualization is not just a mental picture, not just a detailed mental picture, not just a mental picture with color and motion and sound. To be vivid, our mental image must be drenched with *emotion.* It is emotion that reaches the First Brain. It is emotion that saturates the memory storage centers of our brain, so that the images we visualize become ingrained in us.

The key is to visualize those situations where you have the greatest fear. As you visualize those situations, reframe them in your mind as *opportunities* to present yourself, to be successful, to change the direction of your life. You can use visualization in virtually any area of your life where you want to create change, improvement, and success.

Do you want to be a better parent? Begin by visualizing a trip to the mountains or the beach with your child. Or just playing catch in the backyard. Experience the *joy* of spending time with your child.

Have a problem with procrastination? Visualize getting that report handed in or that suitcase packed a day early. Experience the *satisfaction* of having an unpleasant task out of the way with time to spare.

Have a book in mind that you've always wanted to write but can't seem to get started? Then just take a page out of a book by my wife, Dru Scott:

Visions of a Best-Seller

Dru is a nationally recognized expert on customer satisfaction. She speaks, conducts workshops, and writes books on the subject. She also is an expert on the psychological success principles of time management, and wrote the best-seller *How to Put More Time in Your Life*.

During the year she spent actually writing the book, and long before she even had a publisher, she visualized herself in New York autographing copies near the curving staircase of a classy bookstore on Fifth Avenue. She imagined wearing a burgundy wool skirt and burgundy silk blouse with white pearls. In her mind, she experienced the excitement of having crowds hovering around her as she signed copy after copy of her best-selling book. She visualized the setting, the color, and the emotion of that book-signing party, and kept that image in front of her every day as she did the hard, lonely work of producing that book.

Her vision came true in every detail, including the pearls, the burgundy outfit—and the fact that the book was a phenomenal best-seller.

Visualization and Work

A golfer once said, "Visualize all you want, but if you don't know how to hit the ball, you can't beat a player who does." Visualization often gets a bad rap as if it is some sort of magic. It isn't, for it doesn't work without work—but it does work.

It gives us a psychological, emotional, and *conscious* goal and focus; it magnetically pulls us toward the achievement we desire.

For example, let's say I want to become a professional speaker. Anyone can lean back, put both feet up on the desk, and daydream about thunderous applause and rave reviews. But that's not visualization. Accolades and ovations don't go to the daydreamer but to the person with *drive*. And *discipline*. And *talent*. And *perseverance*. And even some *luck*.

So what's the difference between daydreaming and visualizing? Simple. Daydreaming is a substitute for work. But visualization *is* work. It's a *tool* you use to get the job done.

If I want to be a professional speaker, I can use the tool of visualization every time I get blocked or feel lazy or find myself procrastinating and not getting around to practicing or preparing a talk. I can visualize speaking to an audience of hundreds—and I can close with a visualized standing ovation. That gives me the focus and motivation to punch through the ennui, the laziness, the pressures and make my "dreams" of a successful speaking career come true.

Visualization is no guarantee of success—but it gives you a "visible" target to shoot for. It powers your hard work. It motivates. It worked for Dru and for Major Nesmeth—but both brought considerable discipline, talent, and energy to the mix as well. Visualization is not just daydreaming. It's the battery that charges our engine so that *we can do the work* of making our dreams come true.

Visualization and Communication

Your vision of being a confident, powerful communicator can also come true. If you fear that next big speech or sales presentation, change the image in your mind. With your *consciously reasoning New Brain*, vividly imagine the setting. If it's a room or hall you've never been to before, try to visit it in advance so you can picture yourself speaking in that environment. If you can't see it beforehand, get a detailed description of the place. Bring as many senses into play as you can. Look at the surroundings, smell the carpet and the stale coffee, listen to the hum of the air conditioner, touch the lectern, or the overhead projector.

Then comes the key part—vividly imagine how you will do and how you will feel. This is where the First Brain comes into play—the emotions. Put your feelings of success out there. You are going to be great! Imagine it. Rehearse it. And suddenly you *are* great! You feel it. You love the response. They are buying your concepts. They like you. You are triumphant.

You have only imagined it, but your First Brain gets it ingrained *emotionally*. The unreasoning part of your brain doesn't know the visualization is not real. It experiences your imagined triumph as a *real* event! That boosts your confidence—and increased confidence plus conscious preparation equals a *great* performance!

What if the reality turns out *not* to be everything you imagined? At the very least you can be sure it is a far sight better than it would have been with a mind filled with fear and negative thoughts. *And* you can be sure you have moved at least a step up the ladder of the Four Stages of Speaking.

Principles of Visualization

When you visualize:

1. **Make It Real.** Think of an upcoming communication event or recall a past successful event, and immerse yourself completely in that experience. Then add the five senses—touch, taste, sight, smell, and sound—and make the image real.
2. **Make It Positive.** Experience the sights and sounds of success. Bask in the applause. Practice imagining the experience perfectly. (Practice is only practice, but perfect practice makes perfect.)
3. **Make It Regular.** Do it daily. Find a regular time. A strategic time is at the start of the day—it sets the day up. Another is at bedtime, before you go to sleep—so your last thoughts can be positively working on your unconscious. If you are visualizing a successful talk before a large audience, envision that success before *every* speaking situation.
4. **Apply It to All Things.** One-shot visualization is like your first flying lesson—it may be fun, and get you up and back, but it won't take you very far. Make visualization your daily habit—applying to all things—then watch how your life changes. Successful people actually visualize before any major event. It is their habit to envision themselves achieving success and reaping the reward. Make it your habit too.

Just Do It

When all is said and done, the best way to get through the fear of speaking (or any other fear) is to face it head-on and *just do it*. But before you do it, visualize doing it perfectly, splendidly, to the acclaim of your listeners.

"Do the thing you fear and the death of fear is certain."

EMERSON

10

Gatekeeper on Guard

A FAIR QUESTION

Jason was a successful sales exec for a high-tech Silicon Valley company. He had all the identifying accoutrements of a West Coast liberal yuppie—Rolex watch, Brioni suit, gold earring, moussed hair. He was brash and opinionated as he was going through our program, and his convictions came through loud and clear when he did his first impromptu "winger." He was given the subject "television," and he used that topic as a launching pad for an attack on President Bush, whom he considered "manipulative" and "Hitlerian."

Yes, Jason was a young man with an attitude, but I saw him as basically articulate and engaging beneath the surface. I also sensed that something was troubling him about the seminar. It's not what he said, but what he did—he looked away when I looked at him, did not laugh, tapped his foot continuously, and had a grimace on his face that was different from the smile he had coming in—among other things. Later in the morning he put words to the body language.

"You've been talking about making emotional contact," he said, "about being persuasive, about how people buy on emotion and justify with fact. Aren't you *really* teaching us how to *manipulate* people by appealing to their emotions? To tell you the truth, it seems like you're teaching us how to *sway* people emotionally. I'm not calling you a Hitler, but that's the way he manipulated the people of Nazi Germany!"

Jason's statement made some of the others in the room uncomfortable. Heck, it made me pretty uncomfortable, but I smiled and said, "Your question sounded a lot like an opinion." Jason did manage a grin, and some of the others laughed. The tension was broken. "But it's a fair question, and it deserves an answer."

Perhaps this same question has nagged at you as you've been reading this book. You wonder, "When I make emotional contact with my listener and reach his or her First Brain, am I actually engaging in manipulation?"

And my answer to you is the same answer I gave my friend Jason: a resounding *No!*

Lincoln Knew

There's no question there are manipulative "communicators" in this world. Some examples:

- There is the case Jason cited, Adolf Hitler. The German dictator was infamous for the hypnotic, emotion-charged sway he held over audiences, and even over his close subordinates. He skillfully and cynically played on the emotional forces of a country that was humiliated, devastated, and bankrupt after World War I. Hitler's Germany was ripe to be manipulated by fear, hatred, and the desire to shift blame and contempt onto the backs of Jews and other minorities— and Hitler was ruthless in exploiting those emotions. He was probably *the* classic example of a manipulative "communicator."
- Then there are those slick, fast-talking, chance-of-a-lifetime, sign-right-here, offer-ends-today salespeople. Not legitimate salespeople like you and me, but con men, hustlers, and high-pressure artists. Unfortunately a great profession gets condemned by the behavior of a few, but you'll still find too many of the manipulative ones selling stocks by phone quick-talk, hawking used cars, time-share vacations, water purifiers, and no-money-down real estate schemes.
- Not many years ago in the talk-show field, at the opposite end of the likability scale from Oprah and Donahue, was a ranting, raving, chain-smoking despot of the airwaves named Morton Downey, Jr. He thought that the key to talk-show success was angry, chair-throwing, sensationalized, top-of-the-lungs "conversation." And it worked—for a while. Downey's ratings zoomed because his freak-show attracted a lot of curious onlookers—but then, so do train wrecks. Within a few months, the show's offputting blare of confrontation and hostility had scared off most viewers, and Downey disappeared from the airwaves, leaving scarcely a ripple in his wake.

Morton Downey, Jr.: a shrewd manipulator of emotions—but ultimately a flash in the pan.

- Then there are the Elmer Gantry–type media preachers whose "ministries" always seem to teeter on the edge of bankruptcy, who suffer
for the Lord in palaces of opulent splendor, and whose "gospel" is,
"Send me your money, brothers and sisters! I'll pass it along to the
Lord, and he'll drop-ship a truckload of blessings on you by return
mail!" One televangelist used to talk about going out to the desert
to pray—but he neglected to mention that the "desert" he meant
was a lavish vacation home in Palm Springs. Sure, there are honest
preachers on TV, but the manipulators know that few emotions are
more susceptible to undue influence than the feelings of religious
fervor.

But understand this: *Not one of these people has a thing to do with what
this book is about.* What all of these people have in common is that they
exploit powerful emotions in order to compel, coerce, and manipulate
their listeners. Moreover, they all, to some degree or another, use
deception and slick technique to get what they want out of their
listeners. Many of them *are* knowledgeable and skilled in communicating, but they pervert it. The tragedy is that too many of the well-
meaning, right-hearted, nonmanipulative people often *aren't* as knowledgeable. I hope that this book will change some of that.

The fact is, effective communicating is the *opposite* of manipulating,
brainwashing, or swaying the listener. Far from trying to "package"
ourselves with deceptive and artificial techniques of coercion, we are
actually focused on becoming natural, unforced, and believable. We
want the real inner *us* to come through, not some phony image. Our
goal is to make emotional *contact* with our listener's First Brain—*not*
exercise emotional *control.*

Lincoln knew:

---

*"You can fool some of the people all of the time, and all of the people
some of the time, but you can't fool all of the people all of the time."*

In fact, his words are truer now than when he first spoke them. In
this video-saturated age, it is a lot harder to fool and manipulate people
over the long haul. We are a more visually sophisticated society than
ever before.

Can the First Brain Be Fooled?

Could a man like Hitler ever gain hypnotic sway over a Western audience today as he did more than fifty years ago? Impossible! If you've ever seen old newsreels of Hitler giving a speech, you've probably noticed how exaggerated, even buffoonish, his gestures and expressions now seem. You wonder how this clownish little man with the Charlie Chaplin mustache could have ever inspired a nation to launch a war against the rest of humanity. You wonder how he managed to move emotions and inspire such an intense degree of hatred and zeal in his followers.

The fact is, Hitler did not make emotional contact with his audience. He did not make a First Brain–to–First Brain connection with his listeners. Rather, he was an actor encased in a role. He communicated with exaggerated posturing from a distance. There was no television to be able to see him up close. His listeners weren't given the real Adolf Hitler; they were given a fraudulent persona. With the intense, adversarial media coverage we have in the 1990s—and especially when our leaders are continually scrutinized by tight closeup camera shots that reveal the slightest nuances of expression, eye contact, inner nervousness, and evasion—a fraud like Hitler would soon be found out.

You can use New Brain gimmicks and tactics to fool people in the short run. High-pressure salespeople do it all the time. But gimmicks and tactics can't fool your listener's First Brain in the long run. Trust and believability are a First Brain–to–First Brain function, rooted in the reality of who you are. The First Brain of your listener is like a child's mind—innocent, open, irrational, but devastatingly effective in forming judgments about people. Our goal is not to deceive the First Brain of our listener, but to put our listener's First Brain at ease by allowing the genuine, likable person that we are inside to come through.

Can the First Brain be fooled? Yes, for a while. The old saying, "First impressions are deceiving," is a restatement of this fact. All of us can think of people we have found disagreeable on first meeting, but who are now our closest friends. And we can think of people we have taken an instant liking to who later turned out to be intolerable. The fact is, however, that so many of our opportunities to communicate with others—speeches, presentations, business and sales contacts—*are* first-impression situations. And, as the saying goes, you never get a second chance to make a good first impression. So it's important that the real, likable person inside us *immediately* comes through.

Habits, mannerisms, and physiological cues can build trust between you and your listener—or needlessly tear it down. The goal of effective communicating, and of this book, is to make you aware of those nonverbal signals you give off, to enable you to master them, so that you can release the warm, vibrant, inviting self that will enable you to get your message across persuasively and effectively. There's nothing manipulative in that.

The Eye Does Not Lie

Faces can lie. Especially smiling faces. A smile may adorn the face of a pious saint—or mask the intentions of a congressman hip-deep in S&L bribery, a con artist peddling the Brooklyn Bridge, or a serial killer like Ted Bundy.

But while faces and smiles can lie for a while, physiological cues will ultimately give you away. To cite a specific example, there is one facial cue that is virtually impossible to fake. It's a subtle cue that hardly anyone consciously notices, yet it is a faithful indicator of the *truth* within another person's emotions. This cue is linked directly to our First Brain, and you find it in the eyes. It is the cue of *pupil signals*.

The colored part of our eyes is called the iris, and the black dot or opening at the center of the iris is the pupil. We all learned in grade school that our pupils dilate (enlarge) in dim light and contract in bright light. But few people are aware that the size of our pupils is also affected by changes in our *emotions*. Even when the amount of light falling on our eyes remains constant, our pupils *dilate* when:

- We feel joy or pleasure.
- We see something that excites us with pleasurable anticipation.

Our pupils *contract* when:

- We feel displeasure or discomfort.
- We see something we find unpleasant or disagreeable.

These changes occur without our knowledge or conscious control.

But what is perhaps even more surprising and significant is the fact that these pupil cues are not only unconsciously given off, they are also *unconsciously received* by others. As Desmond Morris writes in *Man-watching*, "Two companions will feel an added emotional excitement if their pupils are dilating, or an added emotional dampening if their pupils are contracting, but they are most unlikely to link these feelings with the Pupil Signals they are transmitting. It is a 'secret' exchange of signs operating below the level of contrived manners and posed expressions." We give off and receive pupil cues all the time without even being aware of it.

Research suggests that it is pupil signals that two lovers uncon-sciously seek when they look deeply into each other's eyes. Without realizing it, they are searching for that widening pool of blackness that reveals the truth of their beloved's emotions. Pupil dilation also enhances romance by giving our vision a hazy soft-focus that blurs any blemishes in the features of our beloved. This "halo effect" amplifies the "magic" of love and helps bond two lovers together emotionally. Many Hollywood filmmakers intuitively recreate the misty, soft-focus effect of pupil dilation by shooting love scenes through Vaseline-smeared lenses.

But pupil signals are not just for lovers only. They are transmitted in all human relationships, including business and professional rela-tionships. When Rob, a salesman, calls on his client Ted, they invari-ably look each other in the eye, shake hands, and spend a few minutes in warm and friendly conversation about mutual acquaintances, sports, or each other's families before getting down to business. Theirs is a business relationship, yet they are genuinely pleased to see each other. They can see it in each other's eyes, even though they are not con-sciously aware of pupil signals. There is no manipulation, but there *is* genuine emotional connection between Rob and Ted. The warmth of their relationship is reflected in Rob's hefty commissions, and in the fact that Ted knows he can expect an extra measure of service and commitment from Rob.

Kelli is in middle management in the consumer credit division of a major bank. She is well-groomed, but not stunningly attractive. She is competent at her job, though hardly a whiz or a wunderkind. Yet she has been marked by her superiors for growing responsibility and advancement. Why? Because her customers, her colleagues, and her superiors *like* her. They *trust* her. They don't know what it is, but there's *something* about the way Kelli meets your eye that makes you feel valued and cared for. It's not something Kelli affects or puts on, but something genuine that comes through when she meets you with her eyes. And it has to do with making emotional contact.

What do our eyes tell us about the way we communicate? They're telling us, "Don't try to fake it. Don't put on a mask. Don't try to manipulate the situation or the people around you. *Be yourself.* Let the *real you* come through."

You can't manufacture warmth and emotional contact. If the warmth is there, people will sense it in your eyes, even if they aren't consciously watching your pupils. And if your "warmth" is nothing more than a grinning mask you put on, they'll sense that too.

The Manipulators Are Out There

Pupil dilation is just one of many behavioral cues that we transmit. And there are even larger and more influential ones that we have talked about like length of gaze, gestures, standing, leaning back, etc. They cannot easily be faked, and some can't be faked at all.

Now that you are becoming more aware of the subtle nonverbal cues you give off when you communicate, you have probably noticed that you've become more aware of the habits, mannerisms, and nonverbal cues of others. This is good. In fact, one of the byproducts of becoming a more conscious and effective communicator is that you will be better prepared to sort out the manipulators from the communicators.

And believe me, the manipulators are out there. They want to sell you something—a product, a candidate, a political agenda, a new religion—and they will use every deceptive, manipulative trick in the book to sway your thinking. So put your Gatekeeper on guard. Use the power of your First Brain to guard against their deceptions before they get the chance to part you from your money or (even more important) from your beliefs.

How do you do that? How do you know if you are being persuaded by the truth—or merely manipulated? How do you know if you can trust another person?

The Hunching Skill

One way is to consult your hunches about that person.
How good are you at listening to your hunches? Most of us ignore

our hunches. Some of us reject hunches outright, believing them to be irrational or linked to ESP and the occult. But there's nothing eerie or otherworldly about hunches. Hunching is simply a form of thinking that takes place at a preconscious, First Brain level. It can be a valuable ally in life. In his excellent book *The Luck Factor*, Max Gunther defines a hunch as

> a conclusion that is based on perfectly real data—on objective facts that have been accurately observed, efficiently stored, logically processed in your mind. The facts on which the hunch is based, however are *facts you don't consciously know*. They are stored and processed on some level of awareness just below or behind the conscious level. This is why a hunch comes with that peculiar feeling of almost-but-not-quite-knowing. It is something that you think you know, but you don't know how you know it.

Let's say you're considering buying a piece of commercial property from a man named Cowles. You meet him and discuss the arrangement. In a pragmatic, logical, New Brain fashion, you look the deal over from all angles. Terms, financing, everything looks good. Survey and title search come back spotless. Still, there's something about Cowles himself that bothers you. Pleasant enough looking guy. Strong handshake. Seems confident enough. Seems honest, too. If only you could put your finger on what's nagging at you. But what the heck, you're doing business with him, not marrying the guy.

Six months after escrow closes, you get a notice in the mail that turns your blood to lime Jell-O. It's from the EPA. Turns out that piece of commercial property you picked up from Mr. Cowles has a hundred drums of toxic waste buried in it. Guess who has to pay a cool million to clean it up?

Then you remember the look on Cowles face as you signed the escrow papers. A look of satisfaction? Relief? Or devilish glee? You remember your hunch. "I *knew* I shouldn't have trusted that guy!" you explode.

More precisely, your *First Brain* knew. It was picking up signals and cues that all the New Brain logic in the world couldn't analyze. There are literally thousands of stimuli hitting your brain cells every second, and you can register but a fraction of them at the conscious level. But they do register—at *below* the conscious level. Maybe the contracted pupil signals Cowles gave off didn't match the warmth and smoothness of his smile and his words. Maybe your First Brain noted the mannerism he had of putting one finger over his lips when he lied.

There were clues. Your New Brain missed them, but your First Brain was jangling with them, trying to warn you.

"The final act of business judgment is intuitive."

ALFRED P. SLOANE, former president of General Motors

How to Test a Hunch

So how can you know if a hunch about someone is true or not?

Hunch-Tester Rule Number One: Don't trust first impressions. Don't make any commitments until you have gone back for a second look. In the case of Mr. Cowles, you could back away from the deal for a day or two, meet Mr. Cowles a second time, and see if you still feel a warning tingle in your First Brain when you meet him.

Remember, first impressions really can deceive you. As Max Gunther observes, "If you met somebody half an hour ago and have already developed a hunch about his or her honesty, goodwill, intelligence, or other character traits, dismiss the hunch as unreliable. You probably have not had time to absorb enough data. Love at first sight is fun but very, very chancy. Second sight and third sight are better. Hindsight, when it tells a story not told by first sight, can be painful."

Hunch-Tester Rule Number Two: Compare your hunch with the objective facts. In the case of Mr. Cowles, you can use a jangling hunch as a clue that your New Brain might not have covered all the bases and asked all the right questions. You might then ask yourself, "What could be wrong with this deal that I haven't thought of? Is the parcel properly zoned? Yes, we covered that. Did I ask about the taxes? Yep. What about any problems with hazardous wastes? Hmmmm." If, when you put the question to him, Mr. Cowles gulps hard, turns white, and stammers, you can be pretty sure you've found the source of your hunch. A First Brain hunch can keep your New Brain on track, checking out all the possibilities before investing trust in another person.

Hunch-Tester Rule Number Three: Never substitute hunching for doing your homework. Hunches supplement hard work and research. They don't take the place of hard work and research. If someone wants to sell you a product or an idea, check the facts, then use your First Brain as a guide in sizing up the trustworthiness of that salesperson.

Hunch-Tester Rule Number Four: Beware the wish that masquerades as a hunch! Max Gunther puts it this way: "Never confuse a hunch with a hope. If a hunch tells you something is true, and if you badly want it to be true, regard the hunch with suspicion."

Your First Brain is a good judge of people—a much better judge, in fact, than your New Brain. Your First Brain is primarily responsible for shaping your impressions of those people you like, those you dislike—and those who may pose a threat. Learn to listen to the hunches of your First Brain. Don't rely solely on hunches, but put your hunches into the mix along with all the other data. Sift it all slowly, carefully, thoroughly.

Odds are, as you learn to listen to your hunches, you'll develop a surer sense about people. Who can be trusted. Who the manipulators are. Who you should let through the Gate and who you should screen out.

The First Brain is a powerful communicating, receiving, and detecting device. To be an effective communicator, you need to learn to speak the language of the First Brain. And to avoid being manipulated by others, you need to learn to listen when your own First Brain speaks.

11

Opening the Gate

"To understand, listen to what is beneath the words."

GIVEN THE FINGER HE LENDS AN EAR

The Los Angeles police officer accelerated up the on-ramp, racing to match his speed to that of the fast-moving traffic. In the process of pulling onto the freeway, the officer misjudged the speed of the little white Toyota that was barrelling down the lane nearest the onramp, pushing seventy in a fifty-five zone. The middle-aged woman driving the Toyota had to brake and swerve to keep from hitting the patrol car.

Sure, the officer thought, the woman was speeding—but I did use bad judgment and nearly caused an accident. Feeling chagrined, the officer turned to gesture apologetically to the woman. He looked over his shoulder just in time to see her give him the finger.

Up to that point, the officer hadn't even planned to pull her over for speeding. But now! . . .

Angrily, he punched the lights and siren on. As the two cars slowed to a stop on the shoulder, the cop surprisingly recalled something the instructor had said at a recent partner/relationship training session. "There's more to being a cop than wearing a badge and catching bad guys. You're out there to solve problems. Sometimes the way to solve a problem is not to talk but to listen. You have the choice to control the outcome of the situation in a positive way."

But he didn't *want* to control the situation in a positive way. He was still teed off. He remembered that finger. He was a cop, after all. His two selves warred within him—the side that wanted to be a problem-solver and the side that wanted to throw this woman against the side of the car and show her just what kind of authority she was messing with.

"You have the choice," the instructor had said. And as he walked up alongside the white Toyota, he knew what he had to do. As the woman rolled down the window, he leaned over and said in a kind, sincere voice, "Guess you must be having a pretty awful day, ma'am."

Immediately, the woman burst into tears. She *was* having an awful day, and this policeman was the only person that day who had acknowledged her feelings, who had bothered to listen even before she had said anything. They talked for about twenty minutes by the side of the road—not as cop to offender, but as two human beings whose lives had intersected and touched, even if just for a little while.

I heard Ken Blanchard, author of the *One Minute Manager*, tell this true story to illustrate the fact that life is made up of thousands of "choice points," crossroads of decision where we have the power to make the choices that mold our destiny. One of those choices is the decision whether or not to make emotional contact with another human being, to authentically communicate. Scores of times, even hundreds of times every day, we are presented with a choice to either open the channel of genuine communication with another person, or to choke it off and isolate ourselves emotionally from others. We make these decisions in our business life, our social life, and our relationships with close friends and family members.

When we choose the open channel of human contact, when we not only talk, but authentically *listen*, something magical and mysterious takes place. Something called *communication*.

Two Kinds of Listening

Listening is a crucial ingredient in communication. The speaker who only talks and never listens is not communicating. He is simply broadcasting—sending out a message without any assurance whatsoever that his message is being received and believed. In order to make emotional contact with our listeners, in order to truly communicate, the communication channels must be open in *both* directions, not just one.

To be effective communicators we must be able not only to talk, but to listen. At first glance, communication appears to be fifty percent speaking and fifty percent listening. You talk, I listen. I talk, you listen. Fifty-fifty. But communication doesn't work that way in the real world.

In a study conducted by Decker Communications, we found that top level business executives spend about eighty percent of their time communicating, and their time spent in different types of communicating activities is:

Listening	45 percent
Speaking	30 percent
Reading	16 percent
Writing	9 percent

It's impossible to precisely measure our capacity to listen. There are so many words, visual cues, and sound nuances communicated by the sender, not to mention the screen of distractions self-created by the receiver, that optimum listening is probably only a thing of theory. Like the perfect vacuum.

With that in mind I think the studies that show we listen at only about one-fourth of our capacity might be optimistic. But even there, imagine how much more effective we could be in our careers, our relationships, and our families if we could even double our capacity— whatever that capacity is!

There are different *degrees* of listening, from a very passive, uninvolved level to a very active, intense level. More importantly, there are different *ways* to listen.

Most of us consider listening to be a process of gathering facts from someone who is speaking. If your boss gives you an assignment, you listen for the facts and details of how he wants the job done. If you turn on CNN, you listen for the facts concerning the events of the day. If you ask a stranger for directions, you listen for the facts that will enable you to get to your destination. These are all examples of what you might call *Fact Listening*.

In Fact Listening, our New Brain opens a single channel—the information channel—and, in effect, does a Jack Webb impression: "Just the facts, ma'am." This is fine for those situations where all you need to comprehend is the data. Unfortunately, many of us try to use this type of data-input gathering in *all* our listening situations. Fact Listening is the wrong method for many communication situations.

Facts Versus Feelings

Why do people talk to us? Why do they want us to listen to them? The vacuum cleaner salesman at your front door talks to you in order to separate you from a portion of your earnings. Fact Listening is the dominant mode for making a thumbs-up, thumbs-down decision on the amazing little technological wonder he wants to sell you.

But the little child tugging at your elbow talks to you in order to receive your attention and acknowledgment. If you respond to her with Fact Listening (as, unfortunately, all too many parents do) real communication will not take place. In fact, the result could be very frustrating for both you and her. You won't get any data from the child, and you'll feel she is wasting your time. She won't get the attention and acknowledgment she wants, and will feel hurt and ignored.

Feeling Listening is the form of listening we use for complete communication. It's the most important form of listening there is. Feeling Listening is active. It is multichannel, involving not just the information channel of mere words, but all the sensory input channels. Feeling Listening involves making First Brain–to–First Brain connection through eye communication. It involves being receptive to nuances and subtle emotional cues in the speaker's voice, eyes, gestures, and body language.

Feeling Listening is concerned with the facts, but it is very much concerned with getting to the feelings *behind* the facts. If we don't get to the feelings, the facts may forever remain obscure.

Perhaps the most important dimension of Feeling Listening is that it involves feedback to the speaker. We feed back acknowledgment of the speaker's importance and worth by giving steady, attentive eye communication. We feed back understanding and agreement by nodding and giving brief expressions of affirmation: "Yes. Uh-huh. Right. Amazing! No kidding? Really?" We let the speaker know and feel that he or she is being heard. We continually affirm and cement the First Brain–to–First Brain connection that takes place between two people during the act of communication.

So a good listener practices listening for feelings, not just for facts.

But what does listening have to do with speaking? If I'm the one doing the talking, why should I be concerned with listening?

It Takes Two to Make Contact

Real communication is always a two-way process. *Always.* Even if you are standing in the middle of Yankee Stadium addressing a crowd of 100,000 people. You may have been hired to speak—but you'd better be prepared to listen. An effective communicator is always sensitive to the mood, responses, and cues of his or her listeners, whether engaged in an intimate tête-à-tête or giving an address before a packed house. A speaker who doesn't listen is not really communicating. He is simply performing.

The First Brain of your listener has to be an open gate if your message is to settle on fertile soil. To keep your listener's First Brain channels of communication open, *your* First Brain must be in a receptive and listening mode, sensitive to the cues given off by your listener.

It took me some time to learn that, and I still have to really work at it. I am not naturally a good listener. I tend to be always full of my own ideas and plans for promoting those ideas. My focus has been on getting other people—clients, associates, employees, friends, and my wife and children—to listen to *me*. I didn't realize how important it was for *me* to listen to *them* even while I was trying to communicate my ideas. I didn't realize how important Feeling Listening is to the process of effective communicating and making emotional contact.

"A bore is a person who talks when you wish him to listen."

Ambrose Bierce

The irony is that in order to get people to really listen to you, you have to listen to them. And I mean *really* listen. It's not enough to just make "I hear you" noises while you think about what you're going to say when the other person finally shuts up. In the process of communicating and getting *your* point across, you have to *really* listen to the other person. Listen when they talk. Listen when they ask a question. You even have to listen when *you* are talking, because communication is a two-way process, and your listener is constantly feeding back to you via facial expressions, nodding, smiling, eye contact, gesturing, and body language.

When you practice Feeling Listening with your listeners, you not only receive data from them, you acknowledge them as human beings, you make them feel important. When they feel that affirmation from you through your attentiveness and personal interest in them, they become willing to listen to you. Trust and emotional connection are established. It's so simple, yet so profound: When you open your gate, you open your listener's gate. And real contact and communication takes place.

"Grow antennae, not horns."

JAMES BURRILL ANGELL, PRESIDENT, UNIVERSITY OF MICHIGAN

(when asked the secret of his success)

Listening with Your Eyes

Don Windham was a busy man. He sat behind a large executive desk where he kept himself busy, busy, busy, every day.

Gwen Lovejoy, Don's top manager for the eastern sales region, came in to talk to him about a personnel problem. Don—as usual—had the phone jammed in his ear, so Gwen waited patiently—as usual—for him to finish the call.

"What's up?" asked Don, setting the phone receiver down.

"Well," Gwen began, "it's about Larry Smith, the new man in the Baltimore office. He's just not working out . . ." As Gwen talked, Don tackled one of the many stacks of papers on his desk. After a few sentences, Gwen trailed off, distracted by her boss's evident lack of attention.

After a few seconds of silence, Don looked up impatiently. "Go ahead, Gwen," he said, "I'm listening." Then he went back to his papers—reading, initialing, signing, paper-clipping—all the time

Gwen was talking. To prove he was listening, he grunted a perfunctory "uh-huh" every now and then.

Gwen went on, because she was used to it. Everyone who reported directly to Don was used to it. Don often said he was listening while he did other work. Sometimes he even motioned people to talk to him while he was on the phone with someone else.

In his communication with others, Don treated Gwen and everyone else purely as sources of information—like pieces of paper that talk. He didn't have *real communication* with anybody. He didn't let anyone have *real communication* with him.

How could Gwen *really* communicate with Don? She couldn't put any emphasis or energy into her message, because who would notice it? She was not allowed to have eye communication, because Don's eyes were elsewhere. When Gwen finished talking, Don's response was, "Yeah, I'll look into it when I get a chance. Thanks for telling me." Gwen's audience with her boss was over.

Gwen left Don's office feeling typically frustrated. In her New Brain, she accepted Don's assurance that he was listening. He *said* he was listening, didn't he? But there had been no feedback, no eye contact, no acknowledgment that Gwen was a real human being reporting to her boss on a matter of genuine importance to Don and his company. In her First Brain, Gwen felt she had been ignored—and even devalued. His words said yes, his behavior said no.

Of course, Don really *was* listening. In his own mind. And he caught most of what Gwen said. He got the facts. There was some kind of problem with the new guy in Baltimore. Have to check on that.

But he didn't get around to it right away. He hadn't seen that look of urgency on Gwen's face. The matter had made no impression on his First Brain, and it was soon pushed off his agenda by the pressure of other business. Weeks passed and Gwen noticed that nothing was being done about the idiot in the Baltimore territory, even though his screwups were starting to cost the company real money. She figured she had already told Don, and she didn't want a chewing out for pestering him about the matter.

The Baltimore matter didn't come to Don's attention again until two months (and thousands of dollars) later.

An example of poor business listening—and it happens all the time. Don is a guy who deals in facts, and that's what he thinks business communication is all about: "Just the facts, ma'am." Problem is, if the only kind of listening you practice is Fact Listening, sometimes even the data doesn't get through effectively, if at all. What's more, the people around Don, like Gwen, don't feel listened to and valued. Gwen's a competent, diligent, conscientious employee—but how long

---

THREADS

by James A. Autry

Sometimes you just connect,
like that,
no big thing maybe
but something beyond the usual business stuff.
It comes and goes quickly
so you have to pay attention,
a change in the eyes
when you ask about the family,
a pain flickering behind the statistics
about a boy and a girl in school,
or about seeing them every other Sunday.
An older guy talks about his bride,
a little affectation after twenty-five years.
A hot-eyed achiever laughs before you want him to.
Someone tells about his wife's job
or why she quits working to stay home.
An old joker needs another laugh on the way
to retirement.
A woman says she spends a lot of her salary on an au pair
and a good one is hard to find
but worth it because there's nothing more important
than the baby.
Listen.
In every office
you hear the threads
of love and joy and fear and guilt,
the cries for celebration and reassurance,
and somehow you know that connecting those threads
is what you are supposed to do
and business takes care of itself.

From *For Love & Profit.*©1991 William Morrow and Company, Inc., New York.

do you think she'll continue working for a boss who makes her feel undervalued?

Even in a data-oriented enterprise like business, Fact Listening is not enough. Because a company is made up of real people, and real people need real communication. They need feedback, interaction, and attention. They need *contact*.

In family communication, social communication, and even business communication, it's not enough to listen with one ear. It's not enough to listen with both ears. We need to listen with our eyes.

A Whole-Brained Listener

It's happened to me. I'm sure it's happened to you.

You're at the morning break of an all-day conference. Or you're at a corporate cocktail party. Or a New Year's Eve dance. Or the coffee hour after church service. Whatever the setting, you are in a social situation, surrounded by a lot of people. You see someone you'd like to talk to. We'll call her Jane. She's usually a busy person—in de-mand—but there she is standing alone.

You walk up to Jane and start a conversation. While you both talk, she keeps checking the room, looking to the right, looking past your shoulder, glancing at different people in the surrounding crowd. Her eyes flit to yours every now and then to give you the semblance of eye contact. You wonder: "Is she looking for a friend? Looking for someone more interesting to talk to? Is she just bored?" Though she's not impolite, she makes you feel you're not very important.

To be a good listener is to be a whole-brained listener. You engage not only your ears and your New Brain, but all your senses and your First Brain as well. It should not come as a surprise that the most important good speaking habit is also the most important good lis-tening habit: *Eye Communication*. Without good eye contact, our com-munication is like listening to a stereo with one bad channel. There's a loose connection somewhere, and communication suffers.

Here are some tips for becoming an effective whole-brained listener:

• **Use Your Eyes.** Remember, a feeling of involvement and connec-tion between speaker and listener requires about five seconds of steady eye communication. Whether talking or listening, we convey interest and enthusiasm when we look at another person steadily for five to ten seconds before looking away.

• **Nod Your Head.** Nod in agreement! Erect posture, or even leaning slightly toward the other person, is helpful in conveying your interest and involvement.

• **Make Vocal Responses.** "Really? Hmmm. Is that right? Uh-huh. You don't say! Well, I'll be—" This stuff isn't brain surgery but

---

BREAKING THROUGH THE PAPER WALL

I've noticed a problem in most of the print media interviews I have had: There is very little eye communication because the reporter is busily taking notes. I know the reporter is listening to me, because he or she is furiously scribbling notes on everything I say. But because there is no eye communication, I feel a barrier between myself and the reporter. That notepad has become a wall of paper between me and the interviewer.

It's interesting that if the reporter were interviewing me over the phone, the notepad would not be a barrier at all. But when two people have a face-to-face conversation, something in our First Brains tells us there should be eye communication. The First Brain knows that the other participant in this conversation should not be looking down while we're talking.

But reporters have to take notes. What's the solution?

Recently I had the pleasure of being interviewed by a reporter from *Time* magazine. It was an unusual interview experience because we had a delightful talk—and the paper barrier was gone. Talking with her was not like being "interviewed." It was just like having a real conversation.

She had a notepad in front of her and she took notes—pages of notes, in fact—but she looked at *me* the whole time we talked. She wrote without looking at her notepad.

"How do you do that?" I said.

"Do what?"

"Take notes without looking at the pad."

"Oh, that. It's a skill. It took me a while to learn, but now it comes easily."

"And you can actually *read* those notes?"

"There might be a line or two I can't make out," she replied, "but that's easily worth the price. I've found it's more important to look at the person than to look at the notepad. You miss so much when you can't see a person's expression."

Well put. There's so much more to communication than the words we speak.

is important. It must be real and sincere—a demonstration of the fact that you really *are* listening—not just making a bunch of empty sounds to take the place of listening.

• **Make a Mental List.** As you listen, bullet the key points in your mind. Politely interrupt to clarify a point if necessary. When possible repeat the key points in a short summary at the end, so you can get correction if necessary. Mirroring the speaker's ideas also demonstrates that you valued the speaker, received his or her ideas, and that *real* communication has taken place.

• **Respond at the Emotional Level.** Use warmth, a smile, even a touch if appropriate. Respond with positive words that affirm the other person: "Good work." "Thanks for telling me." "I'm glad you asked me. I'll have an answer for you this afternoon." "That's great. I think we've covered everything." Bring closure to the conversation in such a way that the other person feels listened to—and important. Feel it, don't feign it.

The Gift

Dru and I were talking with our friends Ray and Betsy. Betsy was describing the experience she had the previous Sunday while visiting her father in the hospital.

"I love my Dad," she said, "but he just makes everything so hard. He's old and he's stubborn. I think this heart attack really scared him. 'You're not sending me to some old people's home to dry up and die,' he said. It was as if he thought I didn't love him. As if he thought I wanted to get rid of him."

"He'll be out of the hospital in a couple of weeks," said Ray, "but he can't go home. He can't take care of himself. He's determined to make us all miserable with his bitching and his self-pity." There was a tinge of bitterness in Ray's voice and on his face as he said this. Whereas Betsy expressed hurt and sorrow, Ray just seemed angry and resentful toward Betsy's father.

"We don't want to put him in a convalescent home," said Betsy, "but what else can we do? I must have toured twenty different homes, trying to find one that would be good for Dad. I found one in a beautiful setting, with cozy rooms and really good care. I tried to tell Dad about it but—"

"He's stubborn as an ox," Ray concluded Betsy's thought—but not with the words she would have chosen. "He kept saying, 'You can't make me go!' He wouldn't even listen when Betsy tried to tell him how nice the place was. Finally I had enough and I left."

"I stayed in the room with Dad for another hour or so," said Betsy. "I tried to get him to just look at the place, but he wouldn't listen."

There was silence for a few heartbeats.

Then Dru said, "Betsy, you worked so hard to find a good place for your father because you love him. It must really hurt that he didn't even appreciate that."

Betsy's eyes instantly filled with tears. "*Yes!*" she said—and it was like a cry of relief. Somebody had articulated her exact feelings. Somebody had understood. Somebody had finally listened. She didn't have to say anything but that one word—"*Yes!*"

Certainly Betsy's father hadn't listened. And perhaps more important, Ray had been too full of his own anger to listen to his wife's hurt.

The willingness to authentically listen is one of the greatest gifts one human being can give to another. But how many of us are really willing to give that gift to someone else? Unfortunately, most of us are too busy. Or we are too preoccupied with our own agenda. Or we are too full of our own emotions to listen to someone else's feelings. And we miss the opportunity to fully enter into that magical act that, more than anything else we do, sets us apart as *human* beings: the act of communication. Some examples of lost opportunities:

- Judy is a saleswoman. She's good at what she does. She's bright and she's aggressive. Right now she's in the office of a young man named Hal, an assistant buyer for a major department store. She's still pitching her line of products, trying to get an order, even though Hal says he has an appointment and keeps checking his watch. Judy's sure that with just a few more minutes of his time she can clinch the sale.

    If only Judy would listen for Hal's feelings and read the despairing look in his eyes—for Judy's making him late for an important meeting upstairs with the boss. Hal—who's not the most assertive person in the world—has already decided he doesn't want to deal with a "pushy" salesperson. He's determined that if he can ever get this woman out of his office, she'll never get another minute of his time.
- Mr. Burton is a senior vice president of a paper products company. He is listening to one of his subordinates, a worried-looking man named Hibbs, offer his excuses for arriving late with the budget report for his division. Hibbs has been late with several projects and

reports in recent weeks. Burton is a no-nonsense kind of guy. He believes in laying it on the line. In just a few moments, he is going to give Mr. Hibbs the chewing out of his life.

If only Mr. Burton was willing to *really* listen to his employee. If only he would take the time to read the fear in the man's eyes, the tension in his face. If only he would ask a few questions before "laying it on the line." He might find out that Hibbs is secretly fighting a desperate and lonely battle with alcohol.

- Mrs. Strickland has just landed on her daughter Cyndi like a ton of bricks. Cyndi was told to be home by eleven. She was an hour and forty-seven minutes late. Cyndi tried to explain, but Mrs. Strickland just said, "No more excuses!" She went on to say a lot more to her daughter, and when she had run out of things to say, there was a stony silence. Cyndi had looked so scared when she came in the door at twelve forty-seven. Now she just looked angry and defiant. When the silence finally became unbearable, Mrs. Strickland demanded, "Don't you have anything to say to me?"

   "Why should I?" Cyndi caustically shot back. "You never listen." Then she ran to her room. Right now, Cyndi is lying on her bed, tears spilling down her cheeks, an angry lump in her throat.

   If only Mrs. Strickland had been willing to *really* listen. Cyndi had planned to tell her mother she was late because she had a long talk with her boyfriend. She had wanted to tell her mother about the unplanned pregnancy, and how Tim was pressuring her to make a decision. She had wanted to tell her mother how confused and scared she was, and how she needed her mother to help her decide what to do. But not now. Cyndi has decided she can't tell her mother anything. She would make the decision alone.

Every day, so many opportunities to give the gift of listening. Every day, so many opportunities lost.

Listening to Acknowledge

Feeling Listening means making emotional contact with another person. It acknowledges him or her as a fellow human being. It acknowledges your respect, value and even love of the other person.

What does it mean to *acknowledge*? It means you let another person talk. You *invite* them to talk. You find ways to draw them out. You remain sensitive and aware of subtle cues to feelings that are unexpressed, either because the other person is having trouble articulating those feelings or because that person is reluctant to open up.

Listening to acknowledge is especially helpful and important when you suspect that bubbling beneath the facts are such feelings as:

Frustration, Impatience, Anger, Resentment, Disappointment, Grief, Sadness, Hurt, Regret, Fear, Doubt, Mistrust, Guilt, Jealousy, Dislike, Worry, Misgivings, or Anxiety

---

You don't argue with the other person or say he shouldn't feel that way. You don't tell her why things are really not as bad as all that. You don't try to cheer him up. You don't offer advice or try to solve her problems. You don't try to change the subject. You simply hear his feelings and acknowledge them. You may even restate those feelings and reflect them back to the person so he or she knows you really hear and really understand.

When people have painful issues going on inside, they aren't always looking for someone else to solve their problems or give them advice. Usually they just want someone to listen, to acknowledge them. That is why, for some people, the greatest benefit of psychiatric or psychological therapy they receive comes not from any medical treatment or directive counseling but from the simple fact that *somebody listened* without judging, without criticizing, but with simple acknowledgment.

That's what our friend Betsy received from Dru—a communication that said, in effect, "Betsy, your feelings are real. I hear what you are saying, and I know you must really be hurting."

After the feelings are brought out and acknowledged, *then* you can get on to the facts, if need be. And the magic of Feeling Listening is that *very often there are no facts*. Or at least none that have to be dealt with. Very often we only have to listen and acknowledge that we have heard—really heard and then "the problem" no longer looms large. I suspect that three-fourths of our personal communication problems could be solved just by listening to those to whom we normally do not listen. And by listening *only* to acknowledge. Just to be heard is often enough.

Listening to Groups

Does listening to acknowledge have a place when you are dealing with groups of people as well as in one-on-one situations? Absolutely!

Say you have been invited to give a motivational speech to a meeting of the top executives of a major financial institution. The company has been rocked by scandal, plagued by civil suits, and investigated by federal agencies. Just by walking into the room, shaking hands with a few people, making eye communication and being alert to First Brain cues, you can sense the tension, the fear, the crumbling morale. Some of these men and women will be out of work, perhaps virtually unemployable, within weeks or months. Some may be facing the destruction of their dreams.

Now that you have listened—not only with your ears but with *all* your senses—you can adjust the tone of your message. Instead of jumping onto the stage with your usual chipper, cheerful, bantering opening, you can open by honestly acknowledging the feelings in the room. You can continue responding to the eye communication and audience feedback as you proceed, adjusting the content of your talk as you go. And you can give them hope.

There are many kinds of situations where a speaker can practice Feeling Listening with a group, then acknowledge the mood of that group in order to make his or her presentation more effective and meaningful. Imagine:

- You are in a meeting of department heads of your company, presenting a plan for your department. Suddenly, the head of purchasing interrupts you and begins heatedly criticizing your proposal. He is inexplicably angry and irrational. Your first impulse is to retaliate in kind. The room is electric with emotion. You are on the spot. What will you do?
- You are speaking to a small group of literary enthusiasts about the book you have just published. You are describing a scene from the book, when a woman in the third row drops her face into her hands and begins to cry. What will you do?
- You have been invited to speak to a church that has recently suffered a public scandal and deep division. You can feel the anxiety behind the pasted-on smiles. What will you say to these people?

Groups are very much like individuals. Often groups have the same needs as individuals. A group sometimes needs to be listened to, needs its feelings acknowledged. You may never hear the group's emotions articulated in words, because the individuals in a group often lack the boldness or understanding to get up and speak for the group. There may even be group denial of the problem and the emotions. But you can sense it. You can see it in their eyes, their gestures, their body language. And you can adjust your presentation to acknowledge those unarticulated feelings.

How Listening to Acknowledge Works

Listening to acknowledge is quite simple. It is basically getting to the First Brain level of the person to whom you are listening. You get to their emotional state, or the emotions behind the problem.

Here are some tips for drawing out another person's feelings:

- Ask questions to get to why the person *feels* the way he does. Probe gently and sensitively, not intrusively.
- Respond with empathic statements. Push yourself to *understand*.
- Listen to yourself. Tap into your own First Brain. Do you feel a rising annoyance or impatience with the person you are listening to? It may be that you have a hidden emotional agenda at the preconscious level. Take care that your own feelings don't sabotage your efforts to be a good listener to others.
- Continue to ask questions and empathize until a "soothing moment" is reached. A soothing moment is completion. The person has been heard. His or her feelings have been acknowledged.

The Key to Feeling Listening

This next point is one of the ways to draw out another person's feelings, but is so important that I wanted to separate it for emphasis. The key:

- Focus on the other person from an "outside" position. Be an objective third party.

Have you ever noticed how hard it is to solve a heated conflict with another person when you're in the middle of it? And have you ever noticed how easy it is to recognize misunderstanding, misinterpretation, and miscommunication in a conflict where you are merely an observer rather than a participant? Outside objectivity brings clarity to both the feelings and the issues involved. Try to be a listener who is objective and dispassionate, with no point of view. Set your personal feelings aside. This process requires you to *not* be self-centered, defensive, competitive, or an advocate. It requires you to *think*, not feel.

And that's the hard part, isn't it? Setting your own feelings aside is not easy. Of course, you don't have to set them aside forever—just while you are listening. Later, after the person's feelings have been acknowledged, you can come back and deal with facts and circumstances—if the need to do so still exists.

This requires that the New Brain be in firm control of the First Brain. Your rational self (New Brain) must dominate the communication, even though you don't want to (First Brain). Feelings must be under the control of reason.

Remember that there is no "absolute truth" here. When you are listening to acknowledge you are listening to get at the other person's "truth." You may think this person's feelings are not valid or based in reality, but that's not the issue *while you are listening*. Get to the feelings first. Feelings are always *real*. You don't have to agree with them, just acknowledge them. As Pascal said, "The heart has its reasons which reason knows not of."

It's time-consuming, and sometimes both difficult and threatening to practice Feeling Listening. There are times—perhaps in a hostile setting, or where the circumstances are too risky, or in an aggravated negotiation situation, or when you're not willing to take the time—that you may not want to draw out another person's feelings. Only you can decide as you assess the situation if it's worth the risk. From my own experience, the great majority of the time it is.

"Listen with the eyes,
listen to the heart."

Part V

"AHA!"
FOUR TRANSFORMING
INSIGHTS

An "Aha!" is a sudden intuitive leap to meaningful understanding. It's the feeling we get when we "grok" an important truth. The Chinese call it *tun wu* and the Japanese call it *satori*, both of which mean "sudden awakening," a burst of illuminating insight. The ancient Greeks called it *heureka* (from which we get the exclamation "Eureka!"), meaning "I have found it!" In the Western Christian tradition, it is called an *epiphany*, the sudden and unexpected revelation of a deep and meaningful truth.

But I just call it "Aha!"

During the past dozen years working directly with thousands of people in communications and personal impact, I have had this "Aha!" experience again and again. In the next four chapters, I've attempted to distill some of the most important and meaningful of my "Aha!" discoveries into written form. Some of these "Aha!s" can be explained by the written word. Some just have to be experienced—so I've tried to describe how to go about experiencing the experience so you can have your own "Aha!"

Perhaps the most important feature of these four "Aha!s" is that they are practical, how-to ideas, yet they produce transcendent, break-through results. I feel there is almost a spiritual quality to these very workable concepts. Do them—and you will not only be amazed, but *transformed*.

12

Video-Cybernetics

"O wad some pow'r the giftie gie us to see oursels as ithers see us!"

Robert Burns

THE PERMANENT SCAR

One of Dr. Maxwell Maltz's early patients was an eighteen-year-old girl named Helen. She came to him with a severe scar on her left cheek, the result of an auto accident. Dr. Maltz operated on her, and when he removed the final bandages he was delighted with his work. Where the scar had been, her skin was now flawless.

Eager to see his patient's reaction, he said to her, "Helen, come and look at yourself in the mirror. What do you see?"

Helen looked. For a long time she simply looked and said nothing. Then, in a voice that was scarcely a whisper, she said, "But, Doctor, I don't see any difference."

Maltz was shocked. He went in the next room for a moment and returned with a "before" photo of the girl showing the disfiguring scar. He held the photo up alongside the mirror. "Now, Helen," he said, "do you see the difference?"

Again there was a long pause. Helen looked intently at the picture, then the mirror, then the picture again. Finally she turned to Dr.

Maltz and said, "Yes, Doctor, I see that the scar is gone, but I don't *feel* any different."

Scratching the Surface

Dr. Maxwell Maltz coined the term "psycho-cybernetics" in his best-selling self-help classic of the same name. Although *Psycho-Cybernetics* was published over a quarter century ago, the precepts that were new then hold true now. And we can even take them a step further.

Maltz was a plastic surgeon, a man who could sculpt ugly flesh into appealing form. He could take people who were born with unattractive features or who had been disfigured by injuries and reshape them into beautiful people. But after years of helping people, he made an ironic discovery: *people didn't change* even after he had "fixed" them on the outside. He had redeemed their flesh, but they still felt ugly.

Certainly you would expect that once a person's "disfigurement" was removed, he or she would be free to feel good about himself. Yet most of his clients still *felt* ugly even though they *looked* beautiful. Why? By asking questions and just scratching the surface of their psyches, he came to a profound conclusion: The poor self-image of his clients was rooted in something much deeper than a deformity of the flesh.

This discovery launched Maltz into a new profession: helping people change the way they see themselves. It became his lifelong passion and work.

Maxwell Maltz found that people with physical disfigurements undermine themselves. Thinking they are lesser than other people, they proceed to *act* that way—and it becomes a self-perpetuating cycle. Day by day, this self-sabotaging behavior digs deeper and deeper grooves into their self-image. The more people see themselves as inadequate, the more they limit themselves. The more they limit themselves, the more others see them as inadequate. It's the cruelest of all vicious cycles.

And it's not just people with physical disfigurements who undermine and limit themselves. You know it and I know it: we are *all* in the same boat. You don't have to have a scar on your face or a misshapen limb to feel unattractive and inadequate. Some of us wear our scars on the inside.

We may have come from an abusive background. We may be adult children of chemically dependent parents. Or we may have scars that were caused by psychological and emotional injuries we no longer remember. There are wounds and bruises in our self-image, even if we don't know how they got there. We all have our scars—we all feel we are less than we should be—and less than we actually are.

How tragic! Because the *actual truth is*:

We are better than we think we are!

Until we internalize this truth, carve it on our hearts, and burn it into our brains, we will continue to undermine ourselves and limit our horizons. One of the great misfortunes of the human condition is the inability of so many people to view themselves objectively, to (as Robert Burns says) "see ourselves as others see us." The power to see ourselves objectively and accurately, just as others see us, is amazing, profound—and it is freely available! *That* is the transforming truth I call:

AHA! NUMBER ONE: VIDEO-CYBERNETICS

The video camera gives you a gift no other generation in human history has ever had: *the power to see yourself as others see you!*

Plug It In, Turn It On: Cybernetics for the '90s

Today's video technology puts a power at your fingertips that no other generation has ever had! Walk into any department store, and there they are, lined up in a row, little black gizmo-studded marvels, sale-priced and ready to go! Camcorders! There may even be one pointed at you as you walk in the store, capturing your image for a security TV screen!

This technology is within the reach of virtually every middle-class family in our society—and it offers undreamed-of power. Most people will use that technology to record the baby's first words or the toddler's first steps. But you can use it to see yourself as others see you—and that means you can use it to *transform* yourself.

To be sure, previous generations could see their reflection in a mirror. And since the beginning of this century, those who could afford it could see themselves in movies.

But mirrors cannot be played back and studied. They cannot show you how the people in the last row of the theater see you. They cannot reflect your voice, so you can hear what you *really* sound like instead of how you *think* you sound.

And movie film has always been pretty expensive to use for self-improvement purposes. Plus movie film must be processed. That takes time. No instant replays. That's important in an "instant gratification" culture like ours.

But video, on the other hand, is fast, versatile, and cheap. You can buy a blank videocassette for less than five dollars *and* you can record over it again and again. What does a camcorder cost? Now it's almost down to the price of a good TV set. Like audiotape, videotape captures your *real* voice so you can hear what you *really* sound like. Best of all, you can get *instant visual* feedback from video.

NORMAN VINCENT PEALE ON VIDEO

When asked whether videotape would help a person's communicating ability, Dr. Norman Vincent Peale replied, "Yes, videotape would do that. When I see myself on a tape I immediately ask myself, how could I have done that better. I have dropped out many personal adverse habits.

"I used to do this with my nose" (as he put his right finger astride his right nostril), "not picking my nose, just sort of rubbing it. But it *looked* like I was picking my nose and I have cut that out. If my finger goes up in that direction I immediately take it down.

"I stopped a lot of nervous affectations that I didn't know I had, even after years of speaking. Yes, video feedback has definitely helped me."

From a conversation with Dr. Norman Vincent Peale

In fact, video feedback puts more self-transforming power in our hands than Maxwell Maltz ever dreamed of when he wrote *Psycho-Cybernetics*. I call this power *Video-Cybernetics*. It's the power of Psycho-Cybernetics reprogrammed for the 1990s. All we have to do is plug it in, turn it on, and *zap!* The power to radically transform our self-image and personal effectiveness lights up the phosphors of the nearest TV screen!

How can a video camera do all that? Let me tell you.

You and I already know the worst there is to know about us. We know our faults. We know our secret sins. We know things about ourselves that we pray to God nobody ever finds out. We know all about our failures and all the things we *should* be and *wish* we were but *aren't*. We all have these negative beliefs that we carry around inside us. They are all too real for us. They overshadow all the good things that we are and do and remember. Most of all, we think that everyone around us can *see* our faults and inadequacies—*but they can't*!

This is especially true when we present ourselves in a speaking capacity. We stand in front of a group of people, all eyes focused directly on us, and we feel we are being judged. We feel naked, even transparent, as if people could look inside us and see all our little secrets. *But they can't!* They only actually *see* and *hear* what we give them. But for some reason we just don't believe it.

So how can we *make* ourselves believe it? By using video feedback.

When we see our presentation played back on video, we become the audience. We have the same objective vantage point as the audience. We see ourselves as others see us.

The Pretty Ugly Duckling

Bonnie was a slender and personable lady of twenty-eight when I first met her. She was working as Patricia Fripp's administrative assistant and girl Friday. She not only ran Patricia's busy speaking schedule but also sold speeches to association and corporate meeting planners throughout the country.

She was effective and confident and attractive. But she didn't really know it.

I didn't know she didn't know it until I ran into her at a meeting we both happened to be attending. She had completed our two-day workshop that incorporates extensive video feedback. Whenever I get the chance, I always barrage new Decker graduates with such questions as, "How did you like the seminar? What could we do better? What's different in your life? Are you using what you learned?" I asked Bonnie all the usual questions. Her reply was succinct.

"I'm pretty."

That's all she said. But with that she said everything. I didn't need to ask Bonnie the details. I knew what she meant. I knew the power of video feedback. For the first time she saw herself in a different way. For the first time she saw herself as others *really* see her.

I later learned that, during her childhood, Bonnie had been merci-lessly teased by her older sisters for supposedly being skinny and unattractive. She grew up believing these cruel taunts were true. As competent and attractive as she was, she didn't know it. She didn't believe it—until she saw herself on videotape.

Bonnie is not alone. After scratching the surface of a few of my clients' psyches, I concluded that these feelings of inadequacy were rooted in painful memories of the past. For Ray, it was the fact that his nearsightedness went undiagnosed throughout most of his childhood; deeming him slow, his teachers put him in the back row where he couldn't see the blackboard. For Lisa, it was having a mother who resented and rejected her because Lisa was conceived out of wedlock and cut short her mother's promising career. For Larry, it was guilt about that incident behind the barn when he was only ten. For John, it was the fact that he never measured up to the standards of his demanding, success-oriented father. For Anne Marie, it was the incestuous rape she suffered when she was twelve.

You have scars in your own First Brain memories, and so do I. Yours may not be as severe as those I have listed—or they may be much worse. You may feel a twinge of pain or sadness as memories get stirred up. For this I apologize. This is not a textbook about psychology. It's a book about effective communicating.

But communicating *is* behavior. And our behavior is profoundly affected by how we *feel* about ourselves. So the hurts and broken memories of the past are not beside the point. To a great degree, they *are* the point. They sabotage us. They hold us down. They limit our effectiveness.

Things that happened to us ten, twenty, thirty years ago and more reach out across the years and keep us from our goals—the joys, the success, and the satisfaction that could be ours *right now*. But they don't have to. As Maxwell Maltz said, "You can make the most of what's there by gaining a true mental picture of what is there. Most of us are better, wiser, stronger, and more competent than we realize."

The irony is that almost all of our "hidden opinions" about ourselves—"I'm unworthy, I'm incompetent, I'm unattractive"—are completely invisible. Yet we act as if *everybody knows* how inadequate we are! It doesn't make sense. It's irrational. That's because it is your First Brain working.

These visual impressions of yourself are deeply imbedded in the preconscious layers of the memory-laden First Brain. Your self-image is primarily stored in your First Brain, not your New Brain. Your First Brain is visual, emotionally dominant, and unbelievably powerful—so powerful that the New Brain is not strong enough by itself to reprogram what the First Brain is convinced it "knows." You can tell yourself all day long, "I'm worthy, I'm competent, I'm attractive," but that's New Brain information. Our First Brain doesn't want to hear logic and words. It's too primal and rudimentary for that.

The First Brain must be convinced at a different level, the *visual* level. To the First Brain, a picture really *is* worth a thousand words. To the First Brain, seeing really *is* believing. That's why a visual medium like video can succeed in reprogramming the First Brain when all the words and New Brain logic in the world come up impotent.

Many people had told Bonnie she was pretty, but she remained unconvinced. Why? Words don't register where it counts: the First Brain. Bonnie's First Brain needed to see for itself. That's why the experience of our program convinced her. Again and again during the two days she saw herself on video—speaking, improvising, persuading, being herself. And she liked what she saw. Her First Brain liked what it saw. She learned to like herself.

Because of the power of Video-Cybernetics.

Building Confidence

I have trained many thousands of people in the Decker Method™. In all that time, I have not met a single person who came into the program with an accurate picture of how they come across to others. None of those thousands of people truly see themselves as others see them. And the saddest thing of all is that virtually every one of them thinks they are *less* than they truly are. Less attractive. Less capable. Less competent. Less talented. Less articulate.

"Seeing myself on video was an eye-opener," said Roger, a sales engineer with a national transportation company. "I've always been hard on myself after speaking before a group. I'd think, 'Well, I sure blew that one.' But after seeing the video playback, I realized I didn't look as foolish as I thought. In fact, I looked pretty good. That was the biggest confidence builder of the whole seminar."

Gwen, the director of children's ministries in a large California church, recalls, "I was really nervous the first day of the seminar. During my first talk, I felt shaky inside. But I watched the videotape later and I couldn't see a hint of nervousness! I took the tape home and showed it to my kids and they said, 'Mom, you look confident! Weren't you nervous?' Seeing myself on video really did a lot for my self-assurance."

Jonathan, a sales executive with a scientific instruments manufacturer, said, "The video training made me aware of a few irritating quirks in my communicating style. But even more important, it showed me some strengths I didn't know I had. That really helped my confidence."

A Professional Speaker Sees

My wife Dru Scott, who is a professional speaker, testifies to the power of video feedback. "I used to fly to the East Coast, give a presentation, then spend the entire flight back to the West Coast thinking of all the things I could have done better. I'd make a list of twenty or so things that needed to be improved.

"What's been fascinating in the past couple of years is to see my presentations on videotape. Sure, I still find twenty things that could have gone better. But I also see two hundred things I did well! That's what's useful—having that balanced and positive perspective that video gives.

"I had a session taped that I did recently in the Bay Area. The group was relatively quiet. During the talk I felt rusty and not too effective. I thought I had turned in a poor performance until I saw the tape. Then I thought, 'That's sensational! I did a *great* job!' I needed to see the two hundred things I did well in order to put the twenty rough edges into perspective. And the next week the meeting executive said, 'Absolutely on target,' so I am a real believer in video feedback."

The Unconscious Executive

In the week before our Senior Executive Program™, the lead trainer calls each executive participant. I have made many hundreds of those calls myself. Usually that executive is someone I have never met. There are two main reasons for this phone call: first, to ask the participants what their needs are, so we can tailor the seminar to meet those needs; and second, to make sure they show up. (These days, almost a hundred percent of our executive participants *do* show up. Before we started making these calls, the percentage of attendance was about sixty or seventy percent—even though they had already paid in advance. That says a lot for the importance of making a personal connection.)

When I make these calls, I always ask the executive, "What are your three greatest strengths in communicating habits? And what are your three greatest weaknesses?" I find it fascinating that not one executive in a hundred can answer those questions accurately. They don't even know where to begin.

Of course, once they have been through the program, they can answer these questions with ease. They know what their strengths and weaknesses are—because they have seen themselves on videotape.

What makes this discovery all the more dramatic is the fact that less than five percent of today's business executives have ever consciously worked at increasing their communication skills through the use of video feedback. This is absolutely incredible, given the fact that communicating is clearly *the* most important part of an executive's job—indeed, of *any* leader's job.

Why do people—especially people who should know better, people in the public eye—neglect their communication habits so completely?

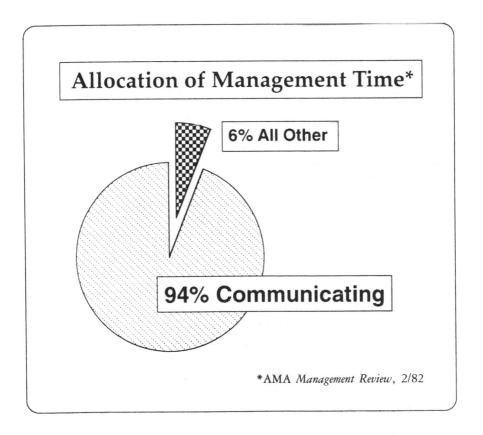

Allocation of Management Time*

6% All Other

94% Communicating

*AMA *Management Review*, 2/82

Is it because they've just given up? Is it because they believe their communication habits cannot be changed?

Most people believe you're either born with something called "charisma" or you're not. Nothing you can do about it. This is blatantly false.

The ability to communicate effectively isn't something you are born with. We're born with certain capabilities and potentials, but what we do with them is up to us. How skilled we become is up to us. Communicating is a skill we can develop. And a skill is nothing but a collection of habits coordinated together to perform a task. And how long does it take to change a habit? Twenty-one days!

Habits: Twenty-one Days to a New Life

A habit is more powerful than our conscious will. When habit says, "Do this!"—we have no choice but to obey. I can prove it to you with a simple experiment.

Fold your arms across your chest. Yes, really. Set the book down and try it. (Unless you're reading this while straphanging in the subway.) Do you have your arms crossed? Good. Now, uncross your arms and cross them again the *opposite* way. Doesn't the "wrong" way feel uncomfortable? Sure it does. Because that's not your normal habit.

Do you realize there was only *one* way for you to cross your arms? The comfortable way. The way you always do. The way you always have. You had no choice. It's your habit. If it were just as easy to fold your arms one way as another, you might have to think, "Which way shall I cross them?" But habit gives you no choice.

Does this mean we are slaves to our habits?

No. Because habits can be changed. The First Brain can be reprogrammed with new habits, good habits—habits that our thinking, reasoning New Brain desires and chooses. All you need is twenty-one days.

Why twenty-one days?

Maxwell Maltz discovered in his practice as a plastic surgeon that it took the average patient about twenty-one days to get used to his or her "new" face. In amputation cases, the phenomenon of the "phantom limb"—the sensation of the feeling and pain in the limb that is no longer there—persists for about twenty-one days.

I have found in my own experience and research that twenty-one days is a valid benchmark. You have to practice a new basketball shot or golf swing for about twenty-one days before it becomes familiar. People must live in a new home for about twenty-one days before they get used to it. It takes about three weeks of practice to make a new habit begin to feel as comfortable as the old. So for twenty-one days you would have to practice crossing your arms the "wrong" way in order for it to feel "right."

Frankly, I don't recommend it. Who cares which way you cross your arms?

But you *do* care about the habits that count—especially your communication habits.

"After getting the video feedback in the Decker training," said Janae, who works in advertising sales, "I found I suddenly had a lot of *skills* I needed to work on so that I could turn them into *habits*. Now I know there are specific things I need to do with my voice, my gestures, and my movement. My goal is to work on those communication skills until I don't have to *think* about them anymore. I'll just *do* them until they become my new, improved, natural style."

Janae's comment cuts to the essence of learning about and changing our communication habits. We all have some good habits. And some bad ones—some distracting and inhibiting ones. You can change *those* habits, but first you must know what they are.

How We Learn Anything, and Everything

There is an important framework for the process of learning, and for repatterning our habits: The Four Stages of Learning. We go through these four stages in learning *anything*. The concept is simple— and utterly profound.

Stage 1: Unconscious Incompetence

We don't know that we don't know.

Two-year-olds are wonderful people! They have such confidence! Ever watch a two-year-old try to pour himself a glass of milk? He's sure he can do it. If you try to take the milk carton away from him, he has a fit! "Me do it!" he screams. He's never poured a glass of milk before. He can barely lift the carton, much less hold it over the glass.

What is this little guy's problem? Unconscious Incompetence! He doesn't know that he doesn't know how to pour himself a glass of milk. If he gets his way, this little half-pint is going to create a half-gallon disaster!

If you've never experienced the power of video feedback, you are in that same state of Unconscious Incompetence. There's so much you don't know that you don't even know that you don't know. And what you don't know *can* hurt you, because what's at stake in your life and your career is a whole lot more important than spilled milk. You need to become aware of your communication habits—both your strengths *and* your weaknesses.

Stage 2: Conscious Incompetence

We know that we don't know.

Now we're getting someplace—the hard way. While you were putting the milk away, our little two-year-old friend grabbed the pitcher of orange juice and filled his glass. And the kitchen countertop. And a large portion of the floor. By the way, scratch one pitcher. (Next time, buy plastic.)

But there is an upside to this whole thing. The two-year-old has passed from Stage 1 to Stage 2. He now *knows* he's not competent at pouring liquids into glasses from heavy containers. He now knows that he doesn't know. You could hear it in the way he said, "Ooops!"

That's a lot like the feeling people get while watching themselves on video for the first time. They see that distracting thing they do with their hands all the time. Or they hear all those nonwords coming out of their mouths. Or they see they don't really smile at all. And sometimes they say, "Ooops!"

But there's an upside to this, too. See yourself on video and you immediately pass from Stage 1 to Stage 2. You now *know* you're not the communicator that you thought. You saw some distracting habits. But now you know what you have to work on. What's more, you saw some communicating strengths that you didn't even know you had!

Stage 3: Conscious Competence

We work at what we don't know.

In this stage, we make a *conscious* effort to learn a new skill. We practice, drill, and repeat the task.

That two-year-old boy will someday be pouring his own milk. He'll have help, at first, but he'll learn. It'll be a challenge for a while. He'll have to really concentrate on what he's doing. There'll be a few spills to mop up along the way. But he'll get it. And he'll learn other things, too.

Like throwing a ball. Or hitting one with a bat. Or roller-skating. Or riding a bike. Or driving a car. Every time he tackles a new skill, he'll have to work at it. Consciously work at it. It won't come easy. Nothing worthwhile ever does.

Learning to communicate effectively is a lot like that. It takes effort and work. It takes practice, drill, and repetition. It won't come easy, but it'll come. It just takes time and conscious effort to change your habits.

Stage 4: Unconscious Competence

We don't have to think about knowing.

The boy is ten years old. He throws a ball, swings a bat, roller-skates, rides a bike (no hands, even), and then, eureka, he's sixteen years old and driving—all without even having to think about what he's doing. It's like second nature to him. He has acquired these skills because he has acquired a set of habits. Each skill operates automatically at an unconscious level.

Learning to communicate works the same way. A speaker starts out with a distracting habit. After seeing herself on video, she learns about this habit and works hard to correct it. A few months later, she hardly remembers she ever had that distracting habit. She has become unconsciously competent as a speaker.

Stage Four is your goal. You can get there. And you can stay there.

You have the power to choose the habits that will serve you best. And you acquire those habits with the essential tool of feedback.

The Feedback Experience

Feedback is a fundamental component of any difficult and worthwhile endeavor. Picture the original Apollo rocket ship—a delivery system designed to take human beings safely to the moon. The powerful Titan booster launches the ship out of the earth's atmosphere and it's on its way. During the first few minutes, delicate sensors feed data to the guidance computer. Information on speed, attitude, altitude, aerodynamic pressure, and hundreds of other variables is updated continuously by feedback from these sensors. This feedback enables the computer to make corrections to course and speed. Without this feedback, the space capsule would never reach its destination. It wouldn't even make orbit.

Human beings, too, function on feedback. When we communicate, we need accurate information on what we are doing—both what we are doing *right* and what we are doing *wrong*—in order to function effectively, stay on course, and reach our destination. Without feedback, we are flying blind—and there's no telling where we will land.

But beware of "purpose tremor," which is caused by excessive negative feedback. When one is threading a needle or pouring a liquid their hand will often tremble because of too much concern for failure. Thus the need for balanced feedback, and sometimes *less* concern and care about our performance. As we will see in Chapter 14, it sometimes pays to put the mouth in gear and let the mind follow—to speak before you think and to act before you speak. There is a balance that can be achieved by practice—with feedback.

MALTZ ON CYBERNETICS

"The word 'Cybernetics' comes from a Greek word which means literally the 'steersman.' Servomechanisms are so constructed that they automatically 'steer' their way to a goal, target, or 'answer.' In any servomechanism, including the human mind—input comes from negative feedback, but positive modifications correct it. You cannot correct your course by standing still.

"Skilled learning of any kind is accomplished by trial and error, mentally correcting aim after an error, until a successful motion, movement or performance has been achieved. After that, further learning and continued success is accomplished by forgetting the past errors and remembering the successful responses, so that it can be 'imitated.'

"You must learn to trust your creative mechanism to do its work and not 'jam it' by becoming too concerned or too anxious as to whether it will work or not, or by attempting to force it by too much conscious effort. You must 'let it' work, rather than 'make it' work. This trust is necessary because your creative mechanism operates below the level of consciousness and you cannot 'know' what is going on beneath the surface. Moreover, its nature is to operate spontaneously according to present need. Therefore you have no guarantees in advance. It comes into operation as you act and as you place a demand upon it by your actions. You must not wait to act until you have proof—you must act as if it is there, and it will come through."

From *Psycho-Cybernetics*

The Three Types of Feedback

There are three forms of feedback: People Feedback, Audio Feedback, and Video Feedback. Each has its own advantages and disadvantages. Each has an appropriate use. You can take advantage of the power of each kind of feedback to transform your habits and improve your skills.

1. People Feedback

At every opportunity, ask for feedback. You will almost always get meaningful, cooperative responses. People always have opinions—and they love to give them to you. They'll be grateful you asked.

In formal situations, such as a high level meeting or a dinner audience of several hundred people, you might only want to ask a few trusted acquaintances. But *ask*—and use The Three-by-Three Rule (see following).

In informal situations, ask the entire audience for feedback. You'll become known among your associates and peers as someone who is open to new information, secure enough to seek criticism, and always yearning to change and grow. People will not only give you the feedback you want, they'll respect you for asking.

Ask for feedback on specific skills. Pick one of the Nine Ways to Improve Your Personal Impact from Chapters 6 and 7. If you choose Eye Communication for example, ask an acquaintance in the audience to count how many seconds you looked at him or her, how *often* you looked at him or her, whether you favored one side of the room, any distracting eye habits (such as eye dart or slo-blink), and so forth.

Take every chance you get to receive feedback, even such informal times as when you stand to address an issue in church or at a PTA meeting. Ask a trusted acquaintance how your voice sounded, how your gestures looked, whether you smiled. If you have a close friendly relationship with a client, seek feedback when you are selling to him. And use The Three-by-Three Rule.

The Three-by-Three Rule

Whenever you ask someone to give you feedback, remember the Three-by-Three Rule. And whenever you give feedback to another person, remember the Three-by-Three Rule. It's very simple. Feedback should consist of three strengths and three distractions.

So when you ask someone to give you feedback on your communicating, say, "What are three strengths I have as a communicator? And what are three distractions I have?" Don't say positives or negatives. Say strengths and distractions. This will cause the other person to focus his or her answers on the areas of your skills and habits.

If you simply say to people, "Could you give me feedback on my speaking?" you would get general comments, nice comments, empty compliments. I call this pleasant but useless form of pseudo-feedback "polite wonderfuls."

But if you follow the Three-by-Three Rule, you create a "forced choice" that has balance. You will get the objective appraisal you are looking for, because it is balanced criticism which helps you grow. Overly positive criticism doesn't give you the data you need to help you identify and change distracting habits. And overly negative criticism throttles your confidence.

Always ask for balanced feedback—and always give it.

The one criticism of our program which I hear most often is that we are not "hard" enough on our participants. This criticism comes almost exclusively from one kind of personality: the overachiever. They come into our seminars and say, "Just tell me what's wrong and I'll fix it." They don't want to "waste time" acknowledging their strengths.

At first glance, that seems like a good, businesslike, practical approach: see a problem and fix it. Why spend time eyeballing what ain't broke. The problem is that the overachievers who want to be treated this way also manage other people the same way: They see a fault, they point it out, and say, "Go fix it." They never congratulate. They never affirm. They never give a pat on the back.

Besides not being a compassionate approach to learning (or managing for that matter), this is not even an *effective* approach. In most people, a tilt toward negative feedback leads to discouragement and decreased confidence—the diametric *opposite* of the result we are trying to achieve. A hallmark of our methodology is to *always* give balanced feedback. Everybody has strengths working for them no matter how nervous or inexperienced they are. Those strengths should be reinforced while the distractions are pointed out in a firm but sensitive manner.

Three is a good number. Don't ask for a dozen positives and negatives. That's too many for people to give—and too much for you to remember. For good learning and skill development in yourself and the others around you, always remember *The Three-by-Three Rule*.

I still learn from feedback. In fact, I recently discovered a distracting

"YOUR ZIPPER WAS DOWN"

I practice the Three-by-Three Rule as much as possible in my speaking appearances. If I'm talking about feedback in my speech, it's easy enough to work it in naturally at that point. Otherwise, I simply ask for feedback at the end of my talk. You can do the same. There are circumstances where it wouldn't be appropriate, but in many situations you can create an opportunity for feedback during your presentation.

I ask people to take a blank piece of paper and write PRO and CON at the top. Under the PRO heading I ask them to list three and only three things they liked. Then—with vehemence!—I ask that they list three things I could improve. I'm always amazed at what I discover.

These are a few of the many responses I received—here in their entirety—at a speech to Ohio Edison on May 8th, 1990:

Pro	Con
Gestures	Opening
Self confidence	**Visuals could be better**
Moved around easily	
Eye contact	**Room too warm**
Visual Aids	
Valuable future info	
Political debate comments	**Too cold in the room**
High impact paper & marker	Uncomfortable chairs
Good appearance	**No bad comments**
Good eye contact	**you are a pro**
Moves well	
Some good info	**No humor**
Film clips good	**Boring**
Time for dinner	**Too many people in room**
Good speaker	**Your zipper was down**
Good gimmicks	
Good humor	

And my zipper was *not* down! You can always count on an off-the-wall response or two.

habit that I never knew I had before! I learned that I had begun to talk to the left side of the audience more than the right side. I don't know why, but I did. Now that I am aware of it, I've changed it.

The Three-by-Three rule allows you to make course corrections, like a guided missile, as you keep moving onward and upward. You continuously get feedback, you continuously update your awareness of your skills and habits, and you continuously make course corrections. That's the only way to hit the target.

2. Audio Feedback

Audio feedback is easy to obtain. Voice-recording equipment is all around us, in every home, and it's so simple to use. Record and play back your voice at every opportunity. Use a portable tape recorder or dictation-recording equipment. You can even carry a microcassette recorder in your shirt pocket or purse. Use it to record your end of telephone conversations. Or record your formal speaking opportunities. Or record your presentations at business meetings. Use your minirecorder to unobtrusively record how you communicate in stressful situations. With the touch of a button, you can learn exactly how you come across in various kinds of speaking situations, both formal and informal.

One of the newest and best tools for audio feedback is voice mail. This technology is proliferating rapidly in both business and home use. If you have it, you can use it as a learning tool as well as a communications tool. Send yourself a message. In fact, I recommend sending yourself a message at least once a day. If your problem is a monotone voice, a high-pitched voice, or too many nonwords, concentrate on changing your habits. (See the vocal exercises in Chapter 7.)

On voice mail don't just simply send yourself a "performance" message. Send yourself a *real* message. Most voice mail systems have the capability to send yourself a *copy* when you dial someone else. Just dial yourself in as well as the person you are calling, then communicate as you normally would. This way you are getting feedback on your habits in *real* situations. Do this regularly and your voice will improve dramatically.

"Observed Behavior Changes"

---

3. Video Feedback

Video technology gives us the most accurate and comprehensive feedback there is. Video enables you to see your body and hear your voice and get your content. You have the whole package. With the complete power to truly see ourselves as others see us, we can make continuous course corrections as we build new habits, shed old ones, and sharpen our communicating skills. The technology of Video-Cybernetics is all around you, right within reach. All you have to do is use it.

CHARLES SCHWAB ON GOLFING AND SPEAKING

"The video feedback was very critical to my understanding and to developing my self-confidence, to helping me see that I was OK.

"You get outside of yourself and have a real opportunity to make a real self-appraisal. And you find out that you don't look as bad as you thought you did or you don't stumble like you thought and that you were understandable, and . . . that was nice.

"With video feedback I've since moved on to another higher level in my golf. It was at Ken Blanchard's Golf University where they used videotaping extensively. I had a golf swing that I had just picked up years before. I never had a lesson but just had gone out and played. I'd been repeating a golf swing for over thirty years that was absolutely incorrect, and that I thought in my own mind was pretty darn good. But when I saw it on video, from a couple of different angles, it made me rather ill. Here I was, in my late forties, and I had to re-learn my entire swing. I practiced at it, and now my enjoyment of golf has improved a hundred percent.

"Golf is very much like public speaking. It's a confidence factor, it's a self-appraisal thing—it's an understanding and an execution. Whether speaking or golfing, the more natural you are, the better you are.

"It's the patterning. If you take an uncomfortable thing and do it in a comfortable way with repetition, you will change your pattern. My new golf swing was incredibly uncomfortable at first, but it is now comfortable. It just takes repetition. It took me a year to become reasonably comfortable. But remember, I had played golf for thirty years before that.

"People will tell you what to do, point out bad points—or even good points—and you will hear them. But they don't really register.

(*cont. on page 228*)

Until you see it, you don't understand what they are talking about. But when you see it, you get it.

"The fear of speaking was right at the highest level of stress for me. I knew that to achieve success as a person I needed to have that capability. It was sheer force of will that got me in front of an audience. I was stressed about it for days on end. Of course what has happened is that with the training, with the video feedback and the understanding that I have now, my stress level has gone down ninety-nine percent."

For optimum video feedback:

• **Buy a camcorder.** They're becoming more affordable all the time. Remember, a camcorder doesn't *cost*, it *pays*. But if you really can't afford to buy one, get access to one. Rent a camcorder for the weekend, borrow a camcorder from a friend, or arrange to use the video equipment at your place of business.

Record your rehearsals, but also record actual presentations. Mount the camera on a tripod and let it roll, or ask a friend to record your formal talks. Record informal occasions so you can see how you come across in casual conversations.

Another use for your camcorder: Record your kids. Not just birthday parties and Christmas, but in everyday situations. Talking about their friends or a vacation. Reciting a poem before the class or acting in the school play. Rehearsing a book report or a speech. Give your child the gift of an objective view of themselves. This can help safeguard their self-esteem during the years when they are especially vulnerable to the cruel remarks of their peers.

As you apply the power of Video-Cybernetics to yourself and your children, you will be able to correct distorted images of self in your own mind and in theirs. Imagine if you had been able to get objective video feedback during your own childhood and adolescence. Think of the difference it would have made to your own self-esteem. Remember, the view we receive from video feedback is almost always a better one than the image we have of ourselves.

A TEXAN AHEAD OF HIS TIME

A powerful story about the power of Video-Cybernetics fell into my hands just as I was putting this book to bed, thanks to serendipity and my wife Dru. She was on a flight from Houston to Denver, and she felt tired after giving a series of speeches. Seated next to her was a friendly, talkative Texan named Russell Fairchild, on his way to Colorado to show his prize Texas Longhorn cattle. As he began to talk, Dru quickly forgot how tired she was.

"My husband's writing a book right now," she told him, "and you should be telling this story to him!" A couple of days later, he was.

"I got to Liberty, Texas, on August 4, 1965 with eighteen dollars in my pocket. I thought that was pretty good, since I left Wisconsin with fifty dollars. Went to school at the University of Houston, and in that first year bought a dump truck and back-hoe and began cleaning out building sites." Russell Fairchild may have started in Liberty, Texas, but his real start came way before that.

"My Momma must have first begun filming me in about 1955—those first 8mm movie cameras had no sound, but we used them every bit as much as all those fancy camcorders we have now. I remember she'd come down and film every wrestling match I had, and a lot of the practices. It really taught me—you know a coach can tell you but you can't recall it all in your mind. It has always been a way of life. I think Momma recorded everything we've ever done."

And today it seems that Russ records almost everything he and *his* kids ever do. And they get results. They all show world-champion cattle, but that is only the end of the story. To get there he has videotaped every show that they are in, to see how they can do it better. "Repetition, repetition, repetition," he says. "We study it. We use it to learn. We look at what we do every show. We have videotape on the judges, so I can go back and look at a particular judge from two years before a show."

Fairchild Enterprises is big. He won't tell me what it is worth, but it is seven businesses: Starting with the back-hoe he progressed into landscaping, firewood, sawmills, chair factories, Christmas tree farms, real estate, buying land, developing land, cattle (300 head of Texas Longhorn), and now his favorite activity—showing cattle. But Russell Fairchild hasn't left his other businesses behind, and still uses video in them. "With my Christmas tree and real estate salesmen I use it a lot. We give feedback all the time, and I tell you the productivity is higher than any place that I know of. Instead of raising hell with them I just show them."

(*cont. on page 230*)

How has the power of video feedback affected his family? "The older kids were always confident. They just saw themselves over and over. My twelve-year-old Julie is really learning now. She wasn't a natural, but she is becoming one. I'm so proud of her." And as the Texas director of the International Longhorn Association he's also proud of what his whole family did last year. They showed their first world champion in 1984, and have had champions every year since. But in 1990 they won thirteen firsts at the world finals. Never been done before. And in the last eight shows, the Fairchild family has shown seventy-nine champions. Maybe will never be done again.

So be on the cutting edge. Get a camcorder. At present, over eighty percent of all homes in America have VCRs—but less than twenty percent have camcorders. A VCR is a nice enough device to own for entertainment purposes, but the real power of videotape is video feedback. If you really care about transforming your personal impact, you need a VCR with an eye that can see you, record you, and feed an objective sight-and-sound image of yourself back to your First Brain. You need a video camera. If you care about your personal impact, a camcorder is not a luxury. It's a necessity. It's an investment in *you*. (In 1985, 517,000 camcorders were sold. In 1991 3,255,000 were sold with 12.5 million in use. It's going in the right direction.)

• **Take a video feedback course.** Here you get the power of both Video-Cybernetics *and* valuable professional coaching. Naturally I recommend the Decker Program, which is available nationwide. But if not our program, there are others. Universities offer workshops and courses. Often you can find ex-newscasters, acting professionals, retired teachers, and others who conduct training with video feedback.

The first time you see yourself on video is something of a shock. The perception you get from video is very different from the perception you get from a mirror. It's as if you are looking at a different person—someone you never met before. At first, you will concentrate on all the flaws you see rather than the strengths. Video feedback is such a personal First Brain experience that in the wrong hands it can be damaging. I liken it to a scalpel—a powerful tool in the hands of a surgeon, but a potential disaster in the hands of a negative, critical "butcher." Make sure you are coached by a "surgeon" who gives you balanced feedback. In good hands, amazing things can happen.

THE MOUSTACHE GOES

Joel Whitfield is a friend who is chief operating officer of Artanis Foods International. He participated in one of our two-day programs a few years ago, and the experience had an immediate and lasting impact. Before that first day in front of the cameras he had never seen himself, and . . .

"I never really looked at myself, even though I saw my face in the mirror every morning when I shaved. But I didn't really know that until I saw myself on video that morning. My moustache didn't look good—I kind of looked like Groucho Marx—so I shaved it off that night. The group almost didn't recognize me the next day, but liked the change, and I felt much better. I really looked better. If I hadn't seen it on video there'd be a good chance I'd have it to this day.

"I also saw myself continuously put my hands in and out of my jacket pockets, like a nervous bridegroom. Looked awful, so I sewed up the pockets for a few weeks until I got out of the habit.

"Video feedback is extremely important, and I think few take the time to use it. You see yourself in real life situations, in real time. I know for a fact that I've seen myself on video playing tennis, and I have gone right out and played better. The same with speaking. But unless you see it yourself it really doesn't count."

The San Francisco State Study

In 1985, San Francisco State University sponsored a study that demonstrates the power of Video-Cybernetics. A survey was done involving 2,000 participants in an intensive two-day video feedback program. Participants placed themselves in one of the Four Stages of Speaking (discussed in Chapter 9) both before and after experiencing video feedback. The results are amazing (see next page).

In the right hands, Video-Cybernetics is a powerful tool for personal transformation. Even while it is revealing your distracting habits, video feedback *should* help you to see yourself in a positive light. Remember Bonnie's words: "I'm pretty." We are all better than we think we are. Video-Cybernetics shows us the proof.

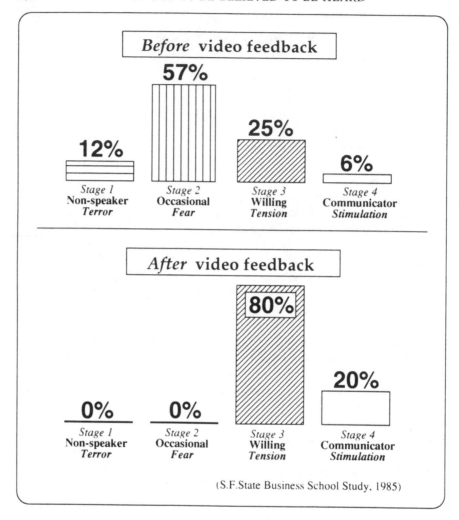

(S.F.State Business School Study, 1985)

"Sow a thought, and you reap an act,
Sow an act, and you reap a habit,
Sow a habit, and you reap a character,
Sow a character, and you reap a destiny."

SAMUEL SMILES

13

Freedom of Expression

"Nothing great was ever achieved without enthusiasm."

EMERSON

CHAINED TO A PULPIT FOR TWENTY YEARS

Dr. Ron Morris is rapidly emerging as one of the leading pastors in America. The author of eight books, he is accustomed to appearing not only before his congregation of 3,000, but also on promotional tours and in interviews on national radio and television. In many ways, he is a naturally effective communicator with an easygoing warmth and personal charisma.

But Ron had a serious problem. He had spent the last twenty years of his life chained to a pulpit.

Every Sunday morning, Ron stepped up to the pulpit and began to preach—and for the next thirty minutes or so, that's where he stayed. It was as if someone had wrapped chains around Ron and his pulpit, binding them together for the duration of his sermon. The son of a pastor, Ron had always seen his dad preach from behind a pulpit. Every other preacher Ron knew personally preached from behind a pulpit. His seminary professors taught him that the way to preach was to stand behind the pulpit. So for twenty years of ministry, Ron had dutifully preached from behind the pulpit.

Gradually, an awareness dawned on Ron Morris: That pulpit was getting in his way. It was actually a *barrier* between him and the people he wanted to reach. If only he could break free of that pulpit—but how? Not only was he bound by twenty years of habit and hundreds of years of preaching tradition, but his *notes* were in that pulpit!

So Ron—who was already one of the most accomplished public speakers in the country—came and took our seminar. We don't get many pastors in our programs—but I wish we did. If ever there was a profession that needed to make emotional contact, it's the clergy. I think seminaries do a pretty good job of teaching pastors how to organize the content of their message, but a miserable job of teaching them how to communicate with impact.

In the seminar, Ron learned most of the same concepts you have already encountered in this book. "One of the most important things I learned about in the Decker training," he recalls, "was the Mehrabian study—the one that showed that verbal content only accounts for seven percent of your believability. The rest is vocal and visual. I have a card taped to my mirror. I look at that card every Sunday morning before I preach. All it says on the card is 'Seven Percent,' a reminder that, even though I spent twenty hours preparing my sermon, it's almost like I've still only done seven percent of the task."

Ron took the things he learned back to his church and put them into practice. He found he could immediately apply all the Decker Method™ principles to his preaching—except one: Movement. He just couldn't break free of that pulpit. "It was like Linus and his blanket," he said. "I knew the pulpit and my notes were getting between me and the people. With a small wireless microphone clipped to my lapel, I literally *could* go anywhere in that sanctuary—but I couldn't let go of the pulpit and my notes."

One week, as he was preparing his message for the following Sunday, a realization came to him. "I knew *that* would be the Sunday I declared my independence from the pulpit," he remembers. "I had a story that I wanted to tell near the end of the sermon—a very moving story about how God had healed the hurts of a grieving family. I knew I wanted to come down and be with the people."

Sunday morning came, and Ron was nervous about moving away from the security of his pulpit. Though he was determined to do it, he wondered if moving away from the pulpit as he spoke would look staged and theatrical? Would it enhance this crucial story he wanted to tell—or simply be a distraction?

Throughout most of the sermon, he preached from his usual spot behind the holy barrier. But as he approached the moment to tell that crucial story, he stepped away from the pulpit, slowly crossed the platform, and descended the couple of steps until he stood at eye-level with the congregation. He was about twenty feet from his comfort zone—a tiny patch of carpet immediately behind the pulpit. Yet he continued talking warmly, conversationally, relating his poignant story not only with words, but with gestures and eye communication that were even more eloquent than words.

If you could have looked inside Ron's First Brain at that moment, you would have seen anxiety and tension. He was anxious about being separated from the comfort and security of his notes for the first time in twenty years of preaching. He felt forced and artificial as he stepped down off the platform and onto the sanctuary floor. He felt sure everyone in the congregation was thinking, "What in the world are you *doing*, Ron? Get back in the pulpit where you belong!" His gestures felt exaggerated and unreal. So did his eye communication. He felt lonely and vulnerable without the comfortable barrier of the pulpit in front of him.

But that's not what the congregation saw. They saw their pastor come down and stand among them like a friend. He told them the story as if he were having an intimate conversation with just one person. That story came alive and touched the emotions of everyone in the sanctuary. Some dabbed tears from their eyes.

"It felt risky and I was anxious about doing it," Ron recalls, "but I'm glad I did. I got as much response on that sermon as on any other sermon I've preached. The comments and letters I received were all positive, and requests for tapes just soared. My preaching hasn't been the same since.

"This has been the most significant change in my communication skills in the past twenty years. I feel the freedom to move from one end of the platform to the other, and even out into the congregation. The barrier has been removed, and it brings me closer to the people. I sense a greater attentiveness and involvement when I preach. I hold their attention more.

"The audience really *does* only get what you give them," he concludes. "Nobody knew how anxious and insecure I was, or how uncomfortable and melodramatic it felt to step down off that platform. They only saw me communicating *more naturally than I ever have before*."

The Disparity Experience

What Ron Morris is describing is one of the most profound "Aha!" discoveries in my communicating experience:

AHA! NUMBER TWO: DISPARITY

There is a *big* difference between the way we see and experience our own performance and the way others see us.

The dictionary defines *disparity* as "the condition of being dissimilar, having dissonance. A marked lack of agreement of internal feeling with external behavior." That's what always happens whenever we communicate. That's right, *always*. There is invariably a huge gap between how we feel about ourselves and our performance versus how others view us and our performance.

While trying out a new behavioral skill—movement—Ron felt anxious, uneasy, insecure, and outrageously exaggerated. But to his listeners he was confident, dynamic, warm, and inspiring. The disparity between Ron's inner feelings and the outward perception of him by the congregation was as dramatic as the disparity between fire and ice.

As long as we are ignorant of the role disparity plays in communication, we are doomed to be limited by our anxiety, insecurity, and inhibitions. But once we truly grasp disparity and the role it plays in repressing and inhibiting our communication, we can begin to turn disparity to our advantage. Armed with the knowledge that *the way we feel is not the way we come across*, we can have the confidence to inject more energy and enthusiasm into our presentations.

The Wellsprings of Inhibition

Communication rides on energy. Our confidence, enthusiasm, and emotion transmit conviction from our First Brain to the First Brain of our listeners—and it's that overwhelming sense of conviction that makes our message persuasive and memorable. When we project passion and energy, we communicate. When our energy is dampened or blocked by nervousness, people tune us out and turn us off.

As we discussed in Chapter 7, the best communicators are the little people around the age of two. The "terrible twos," they call it, but I think it's an absolutely fascinating age to behold. It is the time of the earliest flowering of the miracle of human communication—and it is there that you see real uninhibited, energetic communication taking place!

In many ways, it's too bad we have to civilize the little creatures. During the first year or so of life, before the socialization process begins, a child has absolutely no inhibitions. His eyes communicate freely as eyes were meant to. He smiles, cries, gurgles, and screams with complete abandon. A bit too much abandon.

The socialization process gets rolling at around age one—but the *real* pressure to conform begins at around age two, when he is discovering the awesome power of language. It's then that we have to teach Junior that he can't scream, screech, and scratch with complete abandon and still get along with others. A significant degree of socialization is necessary, to be sure. But when does "enough" socialization become *too much?* With the best of intentions (and for the sake of our sanity), we Big People tend to quell the exuberance of our Little People in ways that last a lifetime. At two, the child is told, "Don't shout." At eight, the message is, "Be seen but not heard." By adolescence and beyond, the message no longer comes audibly from a parent, but echoes silently in the unconscious: "Don't speak up."

The Affect-Meter

"Affect" is a term used by psychologists to describe the "feelings" side of our human makeup—our emotions, moods, and temperament. The Affect-meter is a visual representation of physical and emotional energy and enthusiasm. To have "zero percent affect" is to have no emotional energy, to be completely unexpressive, flat, monotonous, colorless, and lifeless. To have "a hundred percent affect" is to be totally buoyant, exuberant, animated, and excited. The Affect-meter swings according to how much energy we feel free to express. For some of us, unfortunately, the pointer has gotten stuck somewhere during our emotional development.

Most of us reach adulthood with certain aspects of our emotional makeup skewed out of balance by painful experiences of childhood and adolescence. We are out of balance as adults because we have not outgrown the emotional imbalances of our youth.

From birth to two years old, a human being is at full affect (maximum emotional energy). He expresses himself with virtually no inhibition at all.

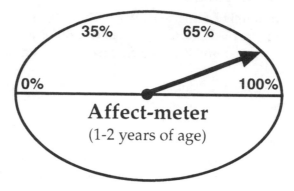

During the years from two to twelve, the momentum begins swinging to the left, toward narrow affect (minimum emotional energy). The natural exuberance of the child is gradually suppressed and deadened during the socialization process—a process which has both an upside and downside. In most people, this process gets out of balance, the meter swinging way over toward low energy/affect. The result is repression and inhibition.

During the teenage years, thirteen to nineteen, even though actual stifling has usually stopped, the meter remains down at narrow affect, resulting in the phase I call "the unexpressed years." This is the last habit pattern the child experiences, and the unrelenting forces of adolescent peer pressure reinforce this habit with a vengeance. Few teenagers escape the emotional pitfalls of the unexpressed years, and the adolescent patterns of awkwardness and shyness usually harden into inhibited adulthood.

It is the exceptional young adult who has both the strong self-image

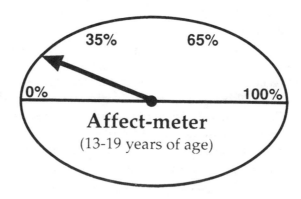

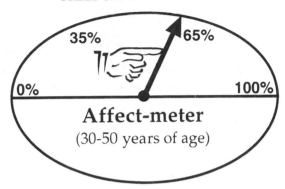

and natural energy to break through this shell of repression on their own, and our inhibiting habit patterns continue to form and harden during the years from age twenty to thirty.

It's easy to see how we got the way we are. From our earliest years on into our twenties, thirties, and beyond we have been subject to forces and pressures to conform, to fit in, to be correct. These are all inhibiting forces, pushing us deep into the pit of minimal emotional energy.

But we don't have to remain there. We *can* learn to push the meter back to where it belongs—indeed, where it has *always* belonged.

The Fully Expressive Years

The most effective communicators are those who are expressive— yet fully in control. They are alive with energy, but they know boundaries. They consciously control the Affect-meter in their own behavior. Very few of us have that kind of control. Instead, we are driven by unconscious habits laid down when we were children.

To become effective, we must *relearn* how to be fully expressive. We must *rediscover* the uninhibited state of the two-year-old, yet govern that expressiveness with the conscious control of a mature adult.

"The ability to express an idea is well nigh as important as the idea itself."

Bernard Baruch

I've worked with literally thousands of people who have passed through our programs, and I have watched them move through the stages of emotional development, adding previously undreamed of energy to their communication—and impact to their personalities. The key to transformation for these people did not lie in learning New Brain information. It does virtually no good at all to simply *tell* someone, "Release more emotional energy! It won't look exaggerated! You can smile more, project your voice more, vary your inflection more, make bigger gestures, and—you won't be judged—you'll be *effective*." Tell them all you want. They won't believe it. Because their beliefs are lodged in the First Brain.

The First Brain doesn't understand language, and cannot be persuaded by logic. Rather, the First Brain understands *visual images* and *emotional experiences*. That is why the key to transformation lies in helping people discover—*visually, emotionally* and *experientially*—that there is an enormous disparity between how they view themselves and how others view them. There is an enormous disparity between what they think is outrageously exaggerated behavior and how that behavior is objectively viewed by others.

Seeing—and Experiencing—Is Believing

First Brain belief is incredibly strong. That's why our internal disparity is so deeply rooted. In fact, I am convinced that the problem of disparity is absolutely impossible to solve without the most powerful learning tools available: *feedback*, and especially *video feedback*. Some examples:

- The morning Bill came into the training, he had a habit of making only a few diffident gestures as he spoke. After each halfhearted gesture, his hands quickly returned to the safety and security of the fig-leaf position. Even though others in the group told him he could be much larger and bolder with his gestures, he found it hard to even raise his hands above his waist while making a point. "It feels weird," he said, attempting a few larger gestures at the urging of the trainer. "I feel like a helicopter trying to take off."

  Everyone told Bill his larger gestures looked natural, while making him seem more warm and likable. Yet Bill couldn't believe what everyone was telling him. Later, when he saw the playback, a big grin of "Aha!" spread across his face—but he had to *see* it to *believe* it.

• Allison was accustomed to standing in one spot when addressing a group. She felt flagrantly exaggerated as, with the urging of her trainer, she took her first few hesitant steps while speaking. "I can't do this!" she protested, stopping dead in her tracks. "More! You looked great! Keep it up!" said the group. You could read it in her face: she didn't believe it. But she bravely tried it again, pushing for more movement as she spoke.

The video camera at the back of the room tracked her as she moved easily before the group, her eye communication carrying her from one person to another to another. Whereas her previous immobile stance had made her look stiff and intimidated, she now appeared graceful, confident, and in total control. She felt enormously uncomfortable—but after she saw the videotape she knew she looked great. But she had to *see* it and *experience* it to *believe* it.

• Josh was "uhh-dicted" to nonwords in both his formal and informal communicating. He tried pausing instead of filling the spaces between his thoughts with drawn-out *aaaaand* and *uuuuuh* sounds. But to Josh, a mere two or three seconds of silence was deafening. He practiced the Power of the Pause (see Chapter 7), pushing himself to leave three- or four-second pauses between sentences.

"How did that feel?" the trainer asked.

"Terrible," Josh answered. "I felt awkward and stupid. I felt like everybody was watching me, wondering why I had nothing to say." The trainer and the group assured him he looked great during the pauses, but Josh was disbelieving. Until he saw the playback.

Pauses that subjectively seemed to last ten or twenty seconds while he was speaking went by in a blip on the TV screen. "Hey," Josh grinned, "you edited out all my pauses!" Josh had to *see* it to *believe* it.

Disparity is constant and universal. We all have it all the time. People never truly know how they appear to other people, because our moment-to-moment experience is totally subjective. Maybe if we had eyes at the end of long stalks, like some creature out of *Star Wars*, we could get a more objective moment-to-moment view of ourselves. But being human, we are inevitably subjected to disparity.

There is no logical, rational, New Brain process for dealing with our disparity. Because disparity takes place in the First Brain. And that natural, ongoing disparity only increases when we are under pressure, such as when we speak to an audience. But even when our disparity is as wide as the ocean, it's still all contained between our ears. If we can just get in touch with this enormous dissonance between *how we feel* and *how we are*, then we can begin to break out of the shell of inhibition that has built up around us. We can move that Affect-meter in the *right* direction.

The Audience Only Gets What You Give Them

Although your First Brain might tell you otherwise, your audience does not have X-ray vision, nor does your audience have telepathic powers. They cannot look through you. They cannot hear your thoughts.

The audience only gets what you give them.

Go back and read that sentence again. I put it in a paragraph all its own because it is a profound *actuality*. In fact, it becomes a *transforming truth* once you secure it in your heart. Sure, it sounds simple. Of course, the audience only gets what you give them. Our New Brain can give simple assent to this fact, but that changes nothing.

But once our *First Brain* fully comprehends this truth, it changes *everything*.

What does it mean, in practice and under the pressure of real-life communicating situations, to know that the audience only gets what you give them? It means:

- They don't know how nervous you are.
- They don't know what your script is.
- They don't know what you are going to say next.
- They don't know how you feel.
- They don't know how many rapid-fire thoughts you have in two seconds.
- *They don't know anything—except what you give them.*

And when you actually experience this, all of these empirical truths translate into *confidence*.

Wanna Make a Bet?

One of the most valuable learning experiences in our programs is something we call The Disparity Exercise™. Here we push people to exaggerate a skill and take it far beyond their normal habits—just as Bill, Allison, and Josh did. And often I will "bet" people to encourage them to extend their energy level—to risk just a little bit more.

Tom Eisenman is a big, genial bear of a man. As an author and teacher his job requires him to speak regularly, and he's good at it. Tom is also a friend of mine, and I was delighted he was able to participate in one of our programs because I was eager for him to see how he really was—naturally effective, but with tremendous potential for growth. I knew Tom had stores of inner energy he had never tapped.

In our programs, every participant receives private coaching as well as instruction and exercises in front of and with the group. I'll never forget the private coaching session we had on the morning of the first day. I was talking to Tom about how he comes across when he speaks. "Tom, you're a big man," I said, "and you can use *all* of yourself when you communicate. You don't have to inhibit your energy. Everyone can see what a warm and open guy you are, so don't worry that you're going to intimidate people with your size. With the openness of your smile and that affable voice of yours, you can use your size and big, natural gestures as a positive force."

A CONTINUING DISPARITY

I have seen myself on video hundreds of times, yet I continue to be surprised at the level of my own disparity. "Bert," I say to myself, "you thought you showed a big, broad smile, but there you are on video again with nothing coming through but your grim grin."

Our goal is to reduce disparity to the absolute minimum that is humanly possible. We start out with an extreme disparity of perhaps a hundred percent—we feel exaggerated and energetic within, but objectively we are lifeless, motionless, and impassive. After a couple of days of exercises with video feedback, we can actually cut our disparity to about fifty percent. Not bad. With practice and continuing video feedback over the next months and years, we bring our disparity down to only ten or twenty percent. At that level, we have great awareness and confidence in our communication habits.

But we still have *some* disparity.

Disparity never goes away. Not completely. So our need for practice and video feedback never goes away either. Keeping in touch with the level of our disparity is a lifelong process.

Even for the guy who wrote the book.

"I don't know, Bert," he said skeptically. "If I put more energy in my gestures, I'll look outrageous. It'll scare people off."

"Tom," I replied, "Trust me. Don't worry about overdoing it. You can't. I guarantee it. In fact, just to show you how confident I am, I'm going to make you a bet. And if you lose, you don't pay."

"What kind of bet?"

"Same bet I've made at least a few hundred times to people just like you. And Tom, I've never lost this bet, not once. I bet you fifty dollars that you *can't* overdo it."

"What do I risk?"

"Nothing. Except making a fool of yourself. And if you do, you make fifty bucks."

"What do I do?"

"You're about to go back in with the group and do what we call The Disparity Exercise. Chris will ask you to select a skill to exaggerate. You pick gestures and movement as your area to work on. Then just do the exercise. Try to overdo it. Take it as far as you can. After the exercise, we'll let the group be the judge whether you overexaggerated or whether you looked perfectly natural. If the group says you went too far, I'll fork over the fifty bucks, right on the spot."

"You're on."

As he went back to the training room, I knew my money was safe. The next participant came in for private coaching, and for the next few minutes I didn't give any more thought to my bet with Tom Eisenman. Suddenly—

Whump! The floor and the walls shook! This was immediately followed by other loud noises, laughter, and rising above it all, a very powerful male voice. The kind of voice that could only come from a big bear of a man. Then we heard *whump* again! And once more the floor and walls shook.

"What was *that?!*" exclaimed the person I was coaching.

"That," I said, "is the sound of fifty dollars."

I didn't have to see Tom's tape to believe, but it was fun. He really *had* overdone it. From the sound of it, I thought his subject had to be "World War III." But no, he put all his energy into a story about fishing. He began by talking in his usual easygoing manner while pretending to cast a fly into an imaginary stream. Suddenly an imaginary fish took the fly. A *big* imaginary fish. It was the Moby Dick of trouts.

The fish pulled Tom off the imaginary riverbank and sent him flying across the room. Tom reeled and fought and struggled with that fish while narrating the whole experience with excitement, energy, and confidence. Loud, loud confidence. It was an epic struggle. It was thrilling. In fact, I genuinely got my fifty bucks' worth.

Why am I telling you this story? Because Tom Eisenman is one in a million. He's the exception that proves the rule. I continue to make that fifty-dollar bet, and I've never had to pay anyone but Tom.

THE STANFORD STUDY

What do you need for success in your career? That's the question explored by Professor Thomas W. Harrell of the Stanford Graduate School of Business during a twenty-year longitudinal study. Harrell concluded that while there are "no certain passports to success," there are three qualities that consistently appear to have a positive influence on the professional careers of those studied:

1. An outgoing, ascendant personality.
2. A desire to persuade, to talk, and work with people.
3. A need for power.

Although the ability to communicate effectively does not necessarily intersect with the need for power, it *does* have a crucial bearing on the first two qualities: an outgoing personality and the desire to speak and interact persuasively with people.

How to Be Free

Our goal is total "Freedom of Expression"—the free and uninhibited release of our full communicative energy. And you *can* be free to achieve all the most important goals in your life and career. You *can* be free to communicate with visual impact and dynamic energy.

First, free yourself from bondage to a lectern. Remember how Ron Morris spent twenty years chained to a pulpit? Don't *you* become chained to a lectern. Just as the pulpit tradition no longer works in churches, the lectern tradition no longer works in business and social speaking situations.

PLEASE REMOVE THIS

"Elizabeth Dole brings to her new position the media savvy she gained in half a dozen federal jobs. At last March's annual meeting of the Labor Policy Association, Mrs. Dole, the featured speaker, insisted that the employer group furnish her a lectern. When speech time arrived, she walked up to the lectern—and asked her hosts to remove it so she could talk to the gathering more personally."

From *The Wall Street Journal*, November 23, 1990

Almost every formal speaking situation will have a lectern. In fact, a lectern fairly *proclaims* formality! In the old days of the orator and speech-reader, this worked fine. It could hold heavy manuscripts. It was something safe and sturdy to lean on and even hide behind. But all a lectern is good for these days is manufacturing boredom.

A LECTERN BY ANY OTHER NAME . . .

. . . is not a lectern.

There's a lot of confusion out there about what you call those big hulking objects that people tend to stand behind when they read speeches. Some people call a lectern a podium.

But a lectern is not a podium is not a platform. So beware of using the wrong terminology. As professional speaker Patricia Fripp says, "A podium is what one stands *on*. A lectern is what one stands *behind* or *beside*."

The actual dictionary definitions for lectern, podium, platform, and dais are:

Lectern (lec'tern) n. Any stand that serves as a support for the notes or books of a speaker.

Podium (po'de-em) n., pl. -dia (-de-e) or -ums. An elevated platform for an orchestra, conductor, lecturer or the like; dais.

Platform (plat'form) n. abbr. plat. Any floor or horizontal surface raised above the level of the adjacent area, such as a stage for public speaking; podium.

Dais (da'is) n., pl. -ises (i-siz). A raised platform as in a lecture hall or dining hall upon which honored guests or speakers sit or stand.

Interchange podium with platform or dais, if you like, but let the lectern stand alone.

Your goal, in formal speaking situations, is to make formal situations *informal*. Make them real, human, and involving. To do this, you have to get out from behind the lectern. Sure, you can put your notes on the lectern. And I mean *notes*—not a scripted speech. Your notes should be a set of trigger words and cues, not a word-for-word manuscript to be read. Keep the notes on the lectern as an available reference, check them now and then when you need to, but *get away from that lectern*, use the full platform or stage as your playing field, and *move*.

What if you need to refer to your notes, but you are way out to the side of the lectern, or even out in front of it? No problem. Just pause. Walk over and refer to your notes. Then step out and continue. You will be perceived as confident and in control—because you are.

If possible, use a lavalier microphone, the kind that attaches to your lapel or collar. All hotels with conference and meeting rooms have them—but you may have to ask for them. The hotel hospitality staff is probably not used to speakers using lavalier mikes *and* a lectern. But just think of the confidence you will demonstrate as you step out from behind the lectern, defy decades and decades of deadly speaking tradition, and break down the barrier between yourself and the audience.

The Physicality Exercise

There's another exercise we do in our training that frees up the energy of expression. It's called The Physicality Exercise™. We get three or four people in front of the group and they each do a winger, each on a different subject—*all at the same time*. The goal of each participant is to get the audience to listen to *them*. How? With *energy*! The have to move, use eye communication, use big gestures, put energy into their voices—*anything* to get attention. If you just stand motionless and drone on, you don't stand a chance.

It's a fun exercise. And it's powerful.

Most important of all, there's a big surprise when it's all over. The surprise is this: People see themselves on videotape and discover that they have an enormous capacity for expression they never knew they had. All they are doing is trying to get people's attention, but in the process they are unleashing real communicative energy. Perhaps it's the fact that there's safety in numbers, or perhaps the exercise just brings out the competitive spirit in people. Perhaps they don't worry about being judged anymore, because everybody's talking at the same time.

But in those moments during that exercise a wonderful release of inhibitions takes place. The participants become highly energized. They become completely themselves—expressing fully and freely. And they are effective.

"The Physicality Exercise was really good for me," recalls Roger, a sales engineer. "When I speak, I tend to project very little energy. My voice is very level, I don't move, I don't gesture. All of a sudden I was in a situation where two other people were drowning me out with noise and energy—and I had to get the attention of an audience. Pretty soon I was standing on chairs, shouting like a revival preacher, or gesturing to the ceiling. I needed to see that it was possible to loosen up, to exaggerate, to have fun while I'm communicating. Once I realized it is more fun and more effective to put more energy into my speaking, it became easier to do."

Janae said, "My voice can be very small, even babyish. But I'm in a job where I'm trying to sell people and convince them of my competence. So I've had to work on my voice to make it more full-sounding and authoritative. I always feel like I'm overdoing it when I exaggerate my voice that way. I mean, sometimes I really feel like a goofball. But when I hear my 'exaggerated' voice on video or on voice-mail messages, it doesn't sound forced or goofy. It sounds great."

Unless you make your living as a carny barker, there aren't too many situations where you are called to compete with other communicators for the attention of a crowd. But you *do* have to communicate all the time, and you *do* have to compete for the attention of your listener. Even if you are alone with your listener, having a one-on-one conversation in nice quiet surroundings, you have to reach that person's First Brain and make emotional contact. And the set of behavioral skills that work in The Physicality Exercise are *exactly the same* as those you use in any other communicating opportunity: visual behavior and energetic behavior.

A Tale of Two CEOs

If only there was an Energy Pill.

Unfortunately, there is no such thing. If there were a pill that would unleash dormant communicative energy, I would have prescribed it many times to many people—including some of the most prominent senior executives in American business. Let me tell you about one top executive who would have gladly paid any price for an Energy Pill.

If you read the business journals you probably would recognize his name. He's not in the Fortune 500, but is the CEO of a prominent multimillion-dollar retail company. I'll just call him Ken.

It was a brisk fall morning when Ken arrived at our San Francisco headquarters for an all-day session. As is my custom we started with a brief chat about communicating—how he felt about speaking, what his goals were, where his perceived strengths and weaknesses lay. It didn't take me long to figure out Ken's real problem. Heck, I knew it within the first minute.

Ken demonstrated virtually *no* energy or enthusiasm. His Affectmeter had swung all the way over to narrow affect—and stuck there.

Sometimes you wonder how a guy who appears chemically free of enthusiasm and gusto can rise to the top spot in a highly competitive field. Sure, Ken was articulate. He was intelligent. He was well-educated. But he was also a crashing bore.

If there *was* such a thing as an Energy Pill, I would have poured out a handful and fed them to him like M&Ms. Lacking that, all I could do was try to show him the value of energy in communicating. And it was a struggle.

At the end of the day, he understood intellectually what I was talking about. His New Brain had absorbed the data. He couldn't argue with what the videotape showed him many times over. And now he really *wants* to be more enthusiastic. But the habits are hard to break. He's made progress, but still so far to go. Since Ken is already smart, savvy, and successful, maybe with his reborn enthusiasm he can take his company *into* the Fortune 500.

By contrast, one man who is there, and leading his company even higher, is David Johnson, CEO of the Campbell Soup Company. Johnson is an Australian-born, fifty-eight-year-old powerhouse of communicative energy. A front-page story in *USA Today* describes his animated communicating style as "oratorical magic." Johnson doesn't walk into a room, he "charges" in using "showmanship to rattle complacency." His "enthusiasm" and "flare for the outrageous" have proved to be "a potent recipe for changing a moribund corporate culture."

According to writer Mindy Fetterman, a typical Johnson speech is filled with rich metaphors, stirring quotations, a dynamic vocal range, and above all, *energy*. "He starts out quietly in a measured tone," she writes. "His voice rises in a preacher's cadence . . . He flings his arm out to point to the horizon, Daniel Boonelike, as his argument hits its pinnacle." You can just *feel* Johnson's highly charged emotions tingling in that description.

Has Johnson's communicating style had an effect on the fortunes of Campbell Soup? As Fetterman says, "Since Johnson became CEO on Jan. 1, 1990, the turnaround in Campbell's earnings, stock price and focus has been dramatic. . . . In just 14 months, Johnson has brought two consecutive quarters of record earnings and a record high stock price of $72 ⅜ on March 4 [1991], versus a 1990 low of $42 ¾ on Sept. 24. . . . Second-quarter earnings rose 29 percent from the previous year to $135 million."

The story of David Johnson and Campbell Soup is just one of hundreds of stories in which the fortunes of an entire company were lifted by the enthusiasm and personal energy of one individual. A lot of people would say that Johnson has the "gift" of personal energy— meaning that "some of us got it and some of us don't." And it may be true that Johnson feels free to exhibit so much energy because he happily escaped or overcame the sort of influences that squeezed the energy out of the CEO whom I call Ken.

The fact is, we *all* have a similar kind of energy inside us that David Johnson exhibits. Most of us just haven't used it.

Don't let discomfort be your guide. Exaggerate. Risk. Let your energy get *out*. My experience with thousands of business and professional people—and even a clergyman or two—tells me that the results are well worth the effort.

"Nothing is so contagious as enthusiasm.
It moves stones. It charms brutes.
Enthusiasm is the genius of sincerity, and
truth accomplishes no victories without it."

EDWARD GEORGE EARLE BULWER-LYTTON

14

Think on Your Feet

"Men grind and grind in the mill of a truism, and nothing comes out but what was put in. But the moment they desert the tradition for a spontaneous thought, then poetry, wit, hope, virtue, learning and anecdote, all flock to their aid."

EMERSON

Literary Ethics, 1838

YOUR DIVINE CIRCUITS

Jill Barad paused in the middle of her presentation, looking out over the faces of the top executives and managers of Mattel, Inc. Barad, the woman who made Barbie even more famous, had just been made president of Mattel USA, and was now widely acknowledged as one of the top women executives in the country. She was addressing her first annual Mattel International Management meeting. Her pause had riveted everyone's attention. All eyes were on her, fixing her with a collective expression of anticipation. What would she say next?

At that precise moment in time, even *she* didn't know. But she wasn't worried. She was confident that the next word she spoke would be exactly the right word.

She didn't pause because she ran out of ideas, but because of a

251

superabundance of ideas. There was a story she could tell that would tie right in with the point she just made, giving it extra emphasis. At the same time, she remembered a quotation she had read in a newsletter that morning and mentally filed away. Should she tell the story? Use the quotation? Both? Neither?

"The ideas were bouncing in my head like Ping-Pong balls," Barad recalls. "Before, I would have been flustered. Since learning about how to *use* my mind creatively—for the first time it was exhilarating. Stimulating. At that moment I realized the power you have when you're open to choose your direction as you speak. I realized I could go anywhere I wanted with my talk, and the audience would follow right along with me. They didn't know what was going on in my head. They didn't know if I was sticking to my 'script' or not. And I knew I could easily have held that pause even longer while I sorted out my options."

Within milliseconds, Barad had settled on her course. She told the story. And the quote. Along the way, an absolutely inspired transition came to her that brought her back to her prepared conclusion. The applause was enthusiastic.

In a workshop a few months earlier, Jill Barad had discovered:

AHA! NUMBER THREE: MENTAL AGILITY

You have the ability to be spontaneous,
to speak as well as you think,
and to think as you speak.
All you need is knowledge and confidence.

Mental agility means *thinking on your feet*. (Or, if you do a lot of your speaking while sitting down, *thinking on your seat*.) Mental agility is a *learnable skill*. The ability to speak spontaneously is not something you're born with, it's something you can master. In the next few pages, you're going to discover ways to tap reserves of spontaneous communicating power you never knew you had.

Maybe you don't agree with the saying, "Put your mouth in gear, the mind will follow." After all, it goes against the way we have been taught. Seems to go against conventional wisdom. Aha! That is why we have the *"Aha!s"* in this book—a new way to look at the truth behind the appearance of things. My experience with thousands of people has shown that this new concept is *true* (except in courtroom testimony and the like.) And after you walk with me through this chapter I think you might agree. I *know* you will agree if you take the notions here and try them out in your own life.

Spontaneity is grounded in *confidence* and *knowledge*—confidence in the astounding potential of the human mind and knowledge of how your mind works. In his "Essay on Spiritual Laws" Emerson said, "Let us get our bloated nothingness out of the path of the divine circuits." That's all that keeps you from being the spontaneous, inspiring communicator you really want to be—the "bloated nothingness" of self-imposed limitations.

Precision versus Impression

One way we limit ourselves and bottle up our spontaneity is that we often insist on being *precise* when we speak. Precision, of course, is very important in contracts, reports, books—written documents that are labored over, footnoted, and referred to for data and information. But speaking serves a completely different purpose from writing.

Speaking is the medium of *impression*. Impressions are powerful, but they are imprecise. Impressions are the stuff of the First Brain. Precision is the focus of the New Brain. The more you concentrate on precision in your speaking, the more you sacrifice power and spontaneity.

"When we encounter a natural style we are always surprised and delighted, for we thought to see an author and found a man."

PASCAL

If you are an avid Academy Awards watcher, you know how boring and forgettable most acceptance speeches are. Most are precisely memorized lists of people the Oscar-winner wants to thank. But then who could ever forget the memorable words of Sally Field: "You really do love me!" That was way back in the 1980 Academy Awards after she won her Oscar for her 1979 performance in *Norma Rae*. And it probably was the only thing most people remember from that show—and it was spontaneous.

One television critic, Jack Matthews of the *Los Angeles Times*, understood the importance of spontaneity to the Academy Awards show when he wrote, "Do not be so adamant about nominees having prepared acceptance speeches. Falling apart at the podium provides just about the only spontaneity on the show." And it is just that spontaneity that provides the "human touch" we so sorely thirst for in the formal circumstance.

The Audience Only Gets What You Give Them

Remember, the audience only gets what you give them. This is a powerful concept for both behavior (they don't know how you feel—unless you tell them or show them) *and content*. The listener does not have your script. When you speak, you can take the listener's mind in any of a dozen different directions—and you can decide *which* direction *right on the spot* in a flash of inspirational insight—

If you trust the power of your mind.
If you are aware of the principles of how the mind works.
If you know how to use those principles.
And if you have the confidence to implement those principles.

Graduates of our program report that the statement, "The audience only gets what you give them," is one of the most transforming truths of the entire seminar.

"I was giving a talk in front of the workshop," recalls David, a small-business owner. "I had the outline of the talk in my mind and I rarely had to refer to my notes—which was incredible, since I always used to *read* speeches from a script. During my talk, I accidentally skipped a point. Without realizing it, I hooked right into my next point and kept on going. Not only did the audience not notice, but I didn't even notice myself until afterward. It was a breakthrough to realize I didn't have to say to the audience, 'Oops, I forget something!' I was able to look competent and confident because no one knew that something had dropped out of my script but me."

"The audience only gets what you give them. That's a big revelation for me," says Gwen, who speaks regularly as teacher and administrator. "When I gave my prepared talk before the group, I did the whole thing without any notes. I had rehearsed it the night before, and by the next morning I just didn't need my notes anymore. During the talk, one thing happened that I *didn't* rehearse: I accidentally switched two stories. I put Story A with Concept B and vice versa. The amazing thing was nobody noticed. The stories made their intended impact even in the 'wrong' place. I got the concepts across and the whole group told me I communicated my ideas well."

My wife, Dru Scott, is not only in demand as a public speaker but has also authored five books, including the best-selling *How to Put More Time in Your Life*. So Dru is no slouch when it comes to knowing how to communicate effectively both in person and in print—and she knows that they are two completely different ways of communicating.

"When you write," she says, "you organize your content very precisely. You edit. You make sure you have smooth transitions and your argument flows logically, step by step.

"But when you speak, spontaneity and impact are more important than the precise organization of your content. You can't edit. You have your content and you have stories that illustrate the truths of your content. So you tell your stories, then you build bridges from your stories to your content. By watching the responses of your audience, you can tell if you need to build a few more bridges in order to make your point.

"In writing if you don't have a very clear structure, it falls apart. But in speaking, it's much more important to have good stories than good structure. You can take a bushel basket full of stories, dump them all out, and make connections to your content. If you do that, you'll probably be very effective—you'll be a hit. Yet a printed transcript of the same talk might look hopelessly unstructured and jumbled.

"The audience only gets what you give them. That's such a big truth, really important. You never go back and say, 'Oh, I should have told you this.' Usually, they won't even miss it."

New Brain in Control

Ironically, although spontaneity and openness allow a strong connection at the fundamental First Brain level, it is the New Brain that actually controls the thought processes that get you there. Up to now, we have been talking primarily about how the First Brain—the primitive, unreasoning part of our mind—relates to the communicating process. Now we move from the First Brain to the powerful New

Brain; the logical, creative left and right cerebral hemispheres of our brain—the most recently developed part of our brains—that part which makes us *human*. It is in the cerebral cortex that mental agility takes place. Informality, spontaneity, and wit are the dominion of the New Brain.

Most of us have two great fears when it comes to speaking. We fear becoming either a Rambler or a Blocker. We are afraid that once our mouth is in gear, it will ramble on and on ahead of our brains, never getting to the point, making no sense, and making us look like fools. Or we are afraid that, once the spotlight comes on, we will develop a total mental block. No words, no thoughts, no ideas, no nothing! Again, we will look like fools.

These are real fears—but they are easily surmountable when you know what to do.

No longer do we have to fear the disastrous derailment of our train of thought that would turn us into a Rambler or a Blocker! Now we are free to fuse all the fantastic capability of our total brainpower— First Brain and New Brain working effortlessly and automatically together to make you an effective and spontaneous communicator.

In the next few pages, you're going to learn how to unleash the power of your New Brain to become more relaxed, confident and informal in your communicating—and more effective at persuasively reaching the First Brain of your listeners.

Principles of Mind

The most amazing wonder in the universe is situated right between your ears. As astronomer Robert Jastrow observes in *The Enchanted Loom*, "The human brain is more complicated than the astronomer's universe; it is the most complicated object science has ever tried to understand."

Your brain contains about 10 billion nerve cells (called "neurons"). Each neuron is connected to surrounding cells by a network of fibers called axons and dendrites, and may have as many as ten thousand fibers leading into it from other cells. Because of the intricate complexity of your brain's circuitry, the number of possible interconnections between the cells of your brain is many orders of magnitude greater than the number of atoms in the entire universe. Memory and learning expert Tony Buzan demonstrates this truth by visually picturing, first, the number of atoms in the universe:

10,000,000,000,000,000,000,000,000,000,000,000,000,
000,000,000,000,000,000,000,000,000,000,000,000,000,
000,000,000,000,000,000,000,000

That number is 1 followed by a hundred zeros. But the number of different patterns or interconnections possible in the human brain is vastly larger; 1 followed by over eight hundred zeros:

10,000,000,000,000,000,000,000,000,000,000,000,000,
000,000,000,000,000,000,000,000,000,000,000,000,000,
000,000,000,000,000,000,000,000,000,000,000,000,000,
000,000,000,000,000,000,000,000,000,000,000,000,000,
000,000,000,000,000,000,000,000,000,000,000,000,000,
000,000,000,000,000,000,000,000,000,000,000,000,000,
000,000,000,000,000,000,000,000,000,000,000,000,000,
000,000,000,000,000,000,000,000,000,000,000,000,000,
000,000,000,000,000,000,000,000,000,000,000,000,000,
000,000,000,000,000,000,000,000,000,000,000,000,000,
000,000,000,000,000,000,000,000,000,000,000,000,000,
000,000,000,000,000,000,000,000,000,000,000,000,000,
000,000,000,000,000,000,000,000,000,000,000,000,000,
000,000,000,000,000,000,000,000,000,000,000,000,000,
000,000,000,000,000,000,000,000,000,000,000,000,000,
000,000,000,000,000,000,000,000,000,000,000,000,000,
000,000,000,000,000,000,000,000,000,000,000,000,000,
000,000,000,000,000,000,000,000,000,000,000,000,000,
000,000,000,000,000,000,000,000,000,000,000,000,000,
000,000,000,000,000,000,000,000,000,000,000,000,000,
000,000,000,000,000,000,000

The vast, elaborate circuitry of the human brain gives it a subtlety and speed that even a hundred Cray supercomputers working in sync could never hope to match. Mind researchers believe that the human brain is capable of weighing up to 10,000 separate factors at once—

at a level almost entirely beyond our consciousness—when making decisions.

Every time you get on an airplane, you trust your physical existence to an air traffic control computer that is little more than a glorified abacus compared to the wonderful supercomputer you carry on your own shoulders. You trust your life to something as primitive as a mass of wires and silicon chips. Are you willing to start trusting your personal and business communicating to your own amazing brain? Are you ready to rely on the divine and virtually limitless circuitry of your biological thinking machine to carry you through your communicating situations with skill, with style, and with impact?

"But I *can't* be spontaneous!" you may protest. "My mind just goes blank!" Wrong. The problem is not that our minds go blank under pressure. The problem is that we internally censor the multitude of things we could have said. Or we are afraid. Our emotions flood our electro-chemically driven brain machinery, and it becomes turbid, if not immobilized. Just because we haven't learned to trust our own minds.

How do we break through the fear and find the freedom we desire?

It just takes a few concepts, a shift in perspective, and . . . practice! Practice, drill, and repetition. Practice gives us experience. Drill gives us skill. Repetition builds our confidence.

Why Do It

When Jill Barad had to decide whether she would tell that story or not, she was able to make a conscious choice. She had the ability to use new thoughts, pertinent thoughts, relevant thoughts—at that moment. The key to your mental agility is staying "in the moment." That is a term that comes from the world of improvisation, which says no *precise* rigid script. Plan, but be ready to adapt. Don't think too far ahead. You have the freedom to go *off plan if you choose*. (Note that I do not say not to be prepared. Only preparation gives you the *ability* to go off plan.)

*"The man who can think
and does not know how to express what he thinks
is at the level of him who cannot think."*

PERICLES

A speaker who thinks on his feet is *open* to new thoughts and new situations. That stray idea, that pertinent story, that funny aside that occurs on the spur of the moment can be incorporated into your presentation. If you are stuck in a rigid, formal text, you have no flexibility, no capacity to tailor your message to the dynamics of the moment.

It *is* risky sometimes to trust our minds. It can be scary. It is easier and much more comfortable to read a script—to perhaps even parrot the words of a speechwriter. But the result you will get by exposing your mind is definitely worth the risk.

FAST THINKING

In the Bush-Dukakis Presidential debates, one of the most memorable moments came when Bernard Shaw asked Michael Dukakis the embarrassing question, "If Kitty Dukakis were raped and murdered, would you favor an irrevocable death penalty for the killer?"

Dukakis did not respond as a husband might, with outrage at the question, but answered in a rote and memorized way; "No I don't, Bernard, I think you know that I opposed the death penalty all my life, and I don't think it's a deterrent . . ." It was as if he had only one answer to the "death penalty" question. He had no flexibility, and suffered for it.

But Shaw wasn't done yet with his rude questions. He next asked George Bush, "If you are elected and die before inauguration day, . . ." but he didn't get to finish it. Bush interrupted with an immediate smile, a cock of the head, and a wry scolding tone in his voice as he retorted, "Bernie . . ." The tense edge to the question was drowned in the audience's laughter. And Bush was seen as clever, warm, and responsive. A marked contrast.

George Bush *had* to think on his feet, and trust his instantaneous response. The time from Shaw's words "die . . ." to Bush's response of "Bernie . . ." was less than a second.

Remember, our minds work at an incredibly fast speed, and can unearth a treasure trove of ideas and stories *right on the spot*—if we are open to it.

A speaker who thinks on his feet can also adjust to new situations and changing time frames. Suppose you are slated to speak at the company sales meeting. You're on just ahead of the chairman and the president—and right before lunch. You were supposed to speak for half an hour, immediately after the "brief remarks" of the big guys. But the big guys took fifty-five of their alotted thirty minutes—leaving you just five minutes to say it all.

The average speaker would look at his neatly typed stack of note cards and begin to panic. But not you! You can think on your feet. You can adapt. You get up to speak, serene in the knowledge that you can hit most of the highlights of your talk, include some of the best stories and anecdotes while skipping some surplus detail—and wrap the whole thing up with a big finish at straight-up twelve o'clock. Because you were open and flexible, you can adapt on the spot. Because you have mental agility. Because you can think on your feet.

Handling Distractions

You know of Murphy's Law: "If anything can go wrong, it will." Then consider O'Toole's Law: "Murphy was an optimist." There are always distractions.

Once you've mastered the skill of thinking on your feet, you can handle anything—even the most outrageous distractions—with ease and with impact. I witnessed the following scene, incredible as it seems.

Wayne was a tall, lanky, thin-faced engineer, one of a procession of boring speakers at the National Fire Sprinkler Association annual convention. Like the other speakers before him, Wayne read his speech from a script. He had brought lots of slides to show, but the projector quit working partway through his presentation. He continued droning on though, describing pictures no one could see, just as if the projector was still clicking away. Meanwhile, five people stood in a hallway at the front of the room, trying to figure out the fuse box.

On top of that, through an open door in that same hallway, people pushed food carts with squeaky wheels, serving a banquet in the room next door. And there was banging and hammering coming from the room on the other side as someone was setting up an exhibit for that night.

Amid all these distractions, Wayne just droned on, either not knowing what was going on, or more likely helpless to know what to do. This wasn't in his script! I looked around the room. Some of Wayne's "listeners" were dazedly studying the ceiling tiles or the backs of their eyelids. Some were reading newspapers. Some just got up and left.

A speaker who thinks on his feet knows how to handle distractions, and even turn them to his advantage. Distractions happen when you are having an informal chat, a job interview, a meeting, or a formal speech. If you are well prepared, if you know your stuff, and if you are confident in your ability to weave the unexpected into your communication, you become invincible. Nothing can throw you off or derail your train of thought.

How to Do It

1. Be—In the Moment

"In the moment" is a concept that comes from the world of improvisation. I first learned it from Sue Walden's Improvisation Workshop. This was a great experience where, among other things, I learned to "be" a washing machine. I actually acted out the physical essence of a washing machine, and thereby lost some of my physical inhibition in front of people. And you cannot "be" a washing machine without being spontaneous. Sue gave a definition that is the key:

> "Being in the moment is the experience of being totally focused on, and absorbed in, what's going on *as it's happening—in present time.*"

It can best be visualized by the picture of how Jonathan Winters "is." Can you easily picture Jonathan Winters as living his life "in the moment"? Robin Williams is the same—a protégé of Winters, he is about as manic as they come. And as funny.

Why is the spontaneity from the world of improvisation so often so funny? And so much fun? Because it is intensely human. Because it is real. Because it shows the "poetry, wit, and hope" that Emerson spoke of earlier. It is genuine—and it connects.

In contrast, take another theatrical event we visited earlier. In 1991 the Academy Awards once again were a classic in scripted formality. Cue-card heaven. And, as is becoming the norm, the show did not leave a great impression on its viewers. As one observer put it, "Watching the Oscar telecast last night was like opening a bottle of flat seltzer. Everything seemed to be in the proper place, but there wasn't any fizz. What was once the year's glitziest TV show has become a reliably rigid entertainment about on a par with one of Perry Como's old Christmas specials."

The Academy Awards are parallel to our formal speaking—albeit our audiences might be a bit smaller. We feel there is so much on the line with a large group that we can't risk anything "going wrong." So we "can" our presentations and ourselves, reading speeches and giving preprogrammed responses. We don't play it "in the moment," relying on our minds and our ability—we play it safe. Playing it safe was efficient in announcing winners for the Academy Awards, but it missed the boat in involvement. *It was mechanical.* It did not effectively engage the First Brain of the millions of people who were watching. We tuned out. Because it was not in the moment.

Being in the moment is an attitude that can become a mind-set. You can best gain this attitude from participating in an improvisation workshop. Not to be "funny" but to free your mental (and physical) inhibitions. But you don't have to go that far—you can practice being in the moment on your own. Work on being "ready" for what comes, to not preplan as much as anticipate. It does not mean to *not* prepare plans (see below), but prepare for changes to your plans. It is to welcome change as a challenge to your communication abilities— always learning and striving to choose the best response. It is practicing being in the moment every moment. It is the essence of mental agility.

"The number one characteristic of students who later become heads of companies is the ability to withstand uncertainty."

DAVID A. THOMAS, dean, Cornell Business School

---

2. Pause

Trust the power of your mind! Let those divine circuits sizzle! If you find yourself at a momentary loss, use the Power of the Pause. You won't ramble. You won't block. You'll be effective and spontaneous. In fact, you will watch in amazement as your train of thoughts goes barreling down the tracks, powerful and unstoppable.

See again the exercises to gain the Power of the Pause in Chapter 7. If nothing else, this tool is essential to grasp and master. Here it will gain you very valuable thinking time to *use* your mental agility. And this is on top of the already discussed benefits of using the pause to rid yourself of nonwords and add dramatic impact to your communications.

3. Prepare

The key to being spontaneous when you speak is to be well prepared. Does that sound contradictory? Isn't spontaneity the *opposite* of being prepared? Not at all. There's nothing haphazard, disorganized, or sloppy about spontaneity. In fact, the better prepared you are and the more thoroughly you know your stuff, the easier and more comfortable it will be for you to take off in new directions at a moment's notice. You will have a deep pool of ideas, information, facts, stories, analogies, case histories, and details from which to draw. Even more important, you will have the *confidence* that comes from being well prepared.

Those who use their planning skills to prepare their subject, and who also use their thinking skills and adaptability to adjust their message to the given situation have *the best of both worlds*—strong substance and maximum impact.

Always have a focused *Point of View (POV)*. The mind is like a magnet, and when an attitude of positive advocacy—that is, a powerful idea, an opinion, a sense of direction—is at the center of your mind, your mind will naturally attract concepts, stories, and analogies that make a strong, persuasive impression on your listeners. If your mind suddenly and unexpectedly lands on a good concept or story while you are speaking, don't censor yourself. *Go with it.* You have a good mind. Use it as an ally to make your speaking more spontaneous and powerful.

"Even pudding needs a theme."

WINSTON CHURCHILL

---

4. Exercise

Mental agility is a skill. Like any other skill, your mental spontaneity and agility can be stretched, enhanced, and strengthened by repetition. As your experience grows, so will your confidence.

Here are two simple yet powerful exercises you can easily do on your own. They will help you to speak as effectively and spontaneously as you can think:

- **Free Association**

    We associate freely all the time—in informal settings. When you get a phone call, you get a stimulus—the "hello, how are you"—and you respond. You have a hundred or so different responses you can make. When you get a question from someone in a meeting, or when you are in a conversation at lunch, or on the golf course, or answering the front door—you get a stimulus, and you make a response. You are making an associative connection in a casual and easy manner.

    Wouldn't it be great if you were under pressure and you had a stimulus and you could *choose a response* just as easily? For example, a question on a TV panel show, or when you lose your way in a speech. You can *choose a response* that is appropriate to the situation if you just don't panic. If you are practiced at making associative connections in your mind. If you are comfortable with the habit of pausing and thinking and speaking.

    You bring that natural associative connection that you have in the informal situation to the formal by practicing *free* association. This is purely an exercise that gets you comfortable with roaming around in your mind, picking and choosing the connections you will make.

    To free associate, just take a couple of minutes to do the exercise right at the end of the next four paragraphs. I'll explain first. You will look up from this book, and take the first thing you see as your first "subject." You will then say a sentence about that subject, and immediately connect that sentence/thought to another sentence/thought on a different subject. Make sure to make a rational, but immediate, connection. (Don't think about it—be in the moment.) And then continue on in that manner so that after a minute or so you have "free associated" on a few dozen subjects. I'll give you a sample (although it will look pretty silly in print) . . .

    "I like digital clocks because they are easy to read. It gives me time to read books, which I like to do. The last book that I read was a self-help book, since I am writing a book right now. I love Og Mandino's works because they are truly inspirational. The last time

I was inspired was watching Michael Jordan play basketball. What a skill. I really like basketball—and it gives me a great activity to do with my son Ben. And with Sam too, though he's away at college. I wish Ben would practice a little harder at the game—he might play more. It would serve him in his training for life skills too. It is important to work hard early in life to reap the benefits later. That was one of Freud's principles—delayed gratification. That might be a good concept to preach and teach to the younger generation. Patience is tough to learn though, particularly when doing exercises like this one. Et cetera, et cetera."

It helps to do the exercise out loud (assuming that no one is around) and to have fun with it. Relax, and don't worry about how you sound—no one is listening. And realize that you will get better and better at it—and that it is *just an exercise*.

Okay. Go ahead and do the Free Association exercise.

(Pause)

And if you are now reading this paragraph without having tried it, go back three spaces. For you will have missed an important experience in gaining natural mental agility.

And you will want to practice it, for you will get better and better. Realize that practicing free association is just exercising your "brain muscle." There is nothing you can do with free association except strengthen your brain muscle. It is like Michael Jordan lifting weights. The exercise won't help the accuracy of his jump shot, but it sure will help his strength and dexterity when it comes time to shoot.

• The Winger

This is the next step up the ladder of mental agility. This is just as it sounds—your job is to "wing it" for a full minute. Have a friend spring a subject on you—any subject at all. Car repair. Hot-air balloons. Mushroom farming. The solar chromosphere. Samarkand rugs. Anything at all. Without any preparation, talk for one minute about that subject. You are the expert. Fill that minute with talk. Don't worry about actually *being* the expert—this is an exercise. Just "wing it."

The two rules of wingers are that you must "fill" a minute with your talk. And you don't have to tell the truth. The reason for the first rule is it forces you to just do it, without thinking whether you are saying the "right" or "best" thing. The reason for the second rule is that it will free up your mind to make *free* associative connections. You don't have to worry about accuracy in this exercise of the mind muscle. Although you are bringing more *focus* into your associative connections than in the free association exercise, you are still roaming freely.

Record yourself, and you will find several things. First, you did it. A lot of people think they can't manage it—they will block. (And it is a basic mental exercise. It may seem just a bit fearful only because you haven't ever done anything like it before.) Second, you are better than you think you are. You will find you make a lot more sense than you think.

Every person who goes through the Decker Program does a winger within the first few hours after they walk through the door. There's pressure. There's tension. There's anxiety. But of the more than 50,000 people who have gone through the training, *not one* has failed. Every person who tries it is amazed at the communicating skill they never knew they had. You will find the same.

Summary of Steps to Mental Agility

1. Don't read a speech. You don't need to. Use your mind.

2. Have a strong POV. Let it work like a magnet.

3. Trust your mind. Put your mouth in gear; the mind will follow. Let your ideas come freely.

4. Be in the moment. Pause. Prepare to change.

5. Don't worry about transitions. Each transition will fall into place like the ball on a roulette wheel. Let your transitions come naturally.

6. Be confident! The inner game of communications is one where the mind flows freely. You don't have to think about it—just *do* it.

When you discover the freedom of mental agility and spontaneity, you'll discover anew what Henry Ford was talking about:

---

*"Whether you think you can, or you think you can't,
you're probably right."*

15

Mastery

MASTERY IS CONFIDENCE

It happened last night, during the writing of this book, so the picture is still very fresh in my mind. I was so nervous that you'd have thought I was the one in the middle of the basketball game. But no, I was just a nervous dad sitting in the bleachers, watching my sixteen-year-old son Ben getting ready to take his two foul shots.

The confident, proud father in me was sure Ben could sink both shots. Another part of me, the part that identifies with Ben, the part that remembers being sixteen and standing on that hardwood court, stomach knotted, all eyes on me, poised to shoot—that part was not so sure. *It may not go in!* that part of me screamed. Something inside me writhed and tensed.

Ben bounced the ball twice—he took aim—and the ball sailed in a perfect parabolic arc.

It might not go in! that doubting part of me screamed again as I came to my feet.

But it did. Swish. One down.

One more shot. A few more seconds of suspense. When I was Ben's age, I was pretty good at basketball. But I never felt the kind of mastery to put free throws in a hundred percent of the time. Come to think of it . . .

Ben put the ball in the air. It looked every bit as true and straight as the first shot—for a long second and a half or so. It hit the backboard, the rim, then bounced off to the side.

Finishing my thought, I really only felt confident enough to sink my foul shots about half the time. Like Ben did last night.

I know why I was nervous. It came from my own feeling of not having had total mastery of the game. I projected my own anxiety about my own half-mastery of the game on Ben. I was nervous about Ben's performance that night because I could remember how anxious I used to be thirty-some-odd years earlier when I was in Ben's shoes. I remembered what it felt like playing a game I hadn't mastered a hundred percent. All of which brings us to the capstone Aha!:

AHA! NUMBER FOUR: CONFIDENCE = MASTERY

Mastery begets confidence.
And confidence begets mastery.
One, and the other, comes with doing it over and over.

Like the serpent that consumes its own tail, our ability to perform is linked in a closed circle to our confidence in our own ability—and vice versa.

I now can sit serenely in the right-hand seat of a car while Ben is driving. Many months ago, when I was teaching him how to drive— well, that was a different story. Ben was nervous, and I was anxious, with visions of accidents and liability suits dancing in my head. But today Ben has thousands of miles of driving experience, which has given me confidence in his mastery of the task. Ben is confident, too, and for the same reason: his *experience* behind the wheel has given *him* a sense of mastery.

"Do the act and the attitude follows."

WILLIAM JAMES

Have you ever observed someone attempting a task for the very first time—a task over which they feel absolutely no sense of mastery whatsoever? Remember your child's first awkward steps? Or remember your own childhood when you first picked up one of those fat green first grade pencils and tried to write your name? Remember the time your dad put you on a bicycle and sent you wobbling down the sidewalk for your very first two-wheel solo?

Mastery does not come from someone holding your hand. Mastery does not come from training wheels. Mastery comes from *doing*, pure and simple. Nothing in the world can take the place of simply tumbling out of the nest, flapping your wings, and doing what needs to be done to stay aloft. As you do, you learn. As you learn, you gain mastery. As you gain mastery, your confidence increases. As you become more confident, you do more, learn more, gain more mastery, and life becomes an upward spiral.

Confidence is the capstone of all your communicating skills. People talk about speakers who have a "magnetic personality," yet a great deal of that "magnetism" comes from confidence. Confidence attracts trust like a magnet. Your own confidence communicates powerfully and directly with the First Brain of your listener. When you trust yourself and your own communicating skills, others will naturally trust you as well.

THE MASTER Of CONFIDENCE

"As a youngster in various small midwestern towns, I had some pretty negative self-images, only I didn't call them that. I'm not sure the term 'inferiority complex' had been invented yet, but if an inferiority complex means a whole nest of inadequacy feelings, that is what I had.

"Where did they come from? I'm not at all sure. My father and mother were both unusually able, strong-minded, outspoken individuals. Maybe somehow I felt that I'd never quite measure up to them, or to their ambitions for me. Or maybe it had something to do with my physique, which was slender and lightweight. I was almost frail compared to my younger brother Bob, who was a rough, tough football player.

"Perhaps I equated being skinny with being inadequate in other ways. Anyway, it bothered me a great deal, and no matter how hard I tried to gain weight, nothing seemed to help.

". . . when I got to college and had to get up occasionally in class and give answers, I acted like what I was: the possessor of a huge inferiority complex. This self-image of inadequacy might have gone on indefinitely had it not been for something a professor—Ben Arnesson was his name—said to me during my sophomore year. One day after I had made a miserable showing, he told me to wait after class. Then,

(*cont. on page 270*)

when we were alone, he said some things that were tough and to the point.

"He said that I had a reasonably good mind, but that I was not making adequate use of it by being so hesitant and bashful. 'How long are you going to be like this,' he demanded, 'a scared rabbit afraid of the sound of your own voice? You probably excuse yourself by thinking that you're just naturally shy. Well, you'd better change the way you think about yourself, Peale, and you'd better do it now, before it's too late.' "

As they say—the rest is history. In his book *Positive Imaging*, Norman Vincent Peale describes how he changed his vision of himself and mastered the art of public speaking. With his newfound confidence he became a minister, and then a world leader, bringing hope and a positive view of life to millions of people.

The First Steps

It was a blustery spring day in New York City when I first met Dr. Peale. I visited him in his charming office across from the Museum of Modern Art on Fifth Avenue. He had all the vim and vigor you would expect, and here he was a month shy of his ninety-third birthday— traveling to Toronto the next day to give a speech before thousands. In our meeting he expanded on how he personally gained confidence.

"I was an anomaly," Dr. Peale recalled. "I had no confidence at all, and I was shy to extreme pain. I was what they call bashful.

"Oh, I'll never forget Ben Arnesson. After he talked to me I went down the stairs from the classroom and I stopped on the fourth step from the bottom. It's still there on that campus, and I set up my kind of a prayer meeting. I said, 'Dear Lord, you can take a drunk and make him sober, you can take a thief and make him honest—can't you also take a mixed-up young fellow like I am and make me normal. I believe you will do it. Thank you very much. Amen.'

"Then I expected a miracle to happen, and a miracle did happen over time. At that moment I felt strangely peaceful and sort of happy. I believed that he was going to do this for me and change me. Then the next day a professor of English, my major, called me into the office and said, 'Peale, what do you know about Emerson?' I said, 'Not much, Professor.' 'Well,' he said, 'I am giving you this book to read and I want you to observe that what Emerson teaches is the sovereignty of the human mind when it is working.'

"Then later I discovered on my own a book by William James, who was the father of American psychology. He said that the greatest discovery of this generation is that the human being can alter his life by altering his attitudes of mind.

"I took myself by the nape of the neck and I said, 'Get with it.' I've stood outside the wings of many a hall when I was being introduced and I talked myself into going out there with extreme confidence and talking about confidence and I *made* myself confident. By talking about it and then acting."

"The skill to do comes from the doing."

CICERO

The Natural Self

The key to getting what you want out of your life, your career, and your relationships is being able to communicate effectively and persuasively. And the key to effective communication is mastery of your natural self.

Your natural self is that combination of your unique personality, mind, opinions, and behaviors. When we freely express that natural self, we are effective. We communicate with excitement, enthusiasm, and confidence—and reach the First Brain of our listeners, naturally. The problem is that under pressure we rarely are natural.

To have mastery over your natural self means to be aware of both your *natural strengths* as well as weaknesses as a communicator. Too many just see the weaknesses—and the balance is off. Remember the Three-by-Three rule. Acknowledge the strengths, and build upon them. Use them confidently and effectively. Then recognize and practice to transform the weaknesses into strengths.

The process of achieving mastery over your natural self never ends. It's a continuing journey of self-discovery and self-improvement. The process grows more and more rewarding as you go on because the rewards get bigger and more gratifying.

In Decker Communications' training programs, we teach that the

Natural Self is a behavioral skill—the finishing touch on all the behavioral skills you work on as a communicator—because the Natural Self is more than a concept. It's an *attitude* you put into practice.

Every other skill you are building as a communicator is ultimately a subset of the overall process of mastering your Natural Self. The goal of communicating is to become relaxed, authentic, confident, and persuasive. Every other skill you are building is focused on that single goal.

The Natural Self is there inside you. It has been all along. The problem is that, somewhere along the line as you were growing up, the perfectly natural function of getting up in front of people and communicating with them has been turned into a chore, an ordeal, a struggle. So you choke, you freeze, you bottle up the Natural Self that yearns to break free.

Did you worry about what others were thinking about you the last time you stood around the water cooler with your buddies, talking about Joe Montana's game-saving pass in the 49ers game? Of course not! Your Natural Self was in control!

The last time you were on the phone with your college roommate, talking over old times, old flames, old movies, and golden oldies, did you feel naked without a stack of notecards and a lectern to stand behind? Of course not! It was just you—your Natural Self—talking to an old friend. You were confident and relaxed—and you were communicating effectively.

Remember that dinner party last week? Were you stiff and stammering while you told your friends about your latest business triumph or real estate deal? Heck, no! Those were your friends, and you were at your best—just being your Natural Self.

The other night, when you talked to your kids about what it was like to live in the good old days before CDs and VCRs—didn't you have passion and energy and enthusiasm in your voice? Of course you did! Those kids are your own flesh and blood, and what could be more natural than being your Natural Self around your own family?

Is there any rational reason why you should behave any differently, why you should be any less natural when you get up to speak to a group of ten people—or a hundred or a thousand? There is not.

Remember the two-year-old, that uniquely unsocialized, uncivilized *master* of natural communication? He gestures freely! He communicates with his eyes! He uses wide variation in his vocal range! He has energy! And he's not afraid to use it! It's impossible to say with certainty, but

I have a hunch that at least fifty percent of the two-year-old mind operates on a purely First Brain level. His cerebral cortex has only had twenty-four to thirty-six months to be imprinted. He operates on the basis of wants and needs and total immediacy. His First Brain knows what he wants, and he knows how to get right to your First Brain.

Keep the model of that two-year-old natural communicator in front of you. That natural communicator is still inside you. It's been there all along—chained down, perhaps, by the rigid control of your New Brain. It's time for your Natural Self and your New Brain to get back to a comfortable, respectful, right relationship with each other. Your New Brain—the part of you that has been socialized and civilized—needs to learn to let your Natural Self go free, so that *you* will be free to express yourself with feeling and energy, so that *you* will be free to make emotional contact with your listener.

By now, you probably know what your three greatest strengths are as a communicator. Perhaps you have good posture when you speak, high energy in your gestures, and a reliable command of language. Great! These are the areas where you already have a high degree of mastery. These skills should be a source of confidence and encouragement to you. You've taken an inventory of your communicating skills and found that you are better than you thought you were!

Now, do you know what your three weakest areas are as a communicator? Poor eye contact? Too many nonwords? Monotone voice? Good! Now you know where to concentrate your efforts and sharpen your skills. Work on *one* skill at a time. Practice. Grow. Master each skill in turn.

Soon you will be feeling confident and transformed in each of these areas. You'll start to feel at ease in speaking situations, whether one-to-one or one-to-a-thousand. You'll be confident, because you won't be "giving a speech," you won't be "performing," you'll just be *you*, communicating naturally and effectively.

And when you've achieved a comfortable degree of mastery over your Natural Self, you will be free to connect with the First Brain of your listener. You will be *naturally* persuasive. You will be heard, because you will be believed. You will be playing the communicating game as it was meant to be played, because communicating is a *contact sport*.

And that's what it's all about: making *emotional contact* with your listener.

How to Do It

Knowing how to build your confidence is easy. All you have to do is *risk*. Trouble is, most of us don't like to take risks. We prefer the security of a sure thing. But the fact is that the highest rewards *always* go with the highest risks. The only thing sure about a sure thing is that the rewards will never be very great.

To get what you really want out of life you have to put a piece of yourself on the line. When you take that risk of putting yourself forward and communicating something of yourself to other people, the odds are *overwhelming* that you will succeed—as we've seen in Chapter 8, about ninety-five percent of the time. And the result will be greater confidence. Success breeds success. Particularly when it comes to expressing your natural self.

"I was scared to death," said Roger, a sales engineer. "I'm one of those people who's terrified of getting up in front of a group. I didn't want to be there, knowing I'd have to speak in front of people and in front of a video camera. But I figured I had to take this opportunity for self-improvement. By the end of the seminar I was clearly much more confident. The fear of speaking never completely goes away, but now I have a handle on how to channel that fear and make it work for me."

"I didn't have confidence going in," said Tricia, a manager for marketing support. "The confidence came after I learned what my habits were—how to strengthen the good ones, how to replace the bad ones. The confidence came from doing. In everything we did, we saw results. I saw change and growth in myself and in the others in the group. I walked in scared, but I walked out with a smile, feeling really confident for the first time in my life."

Tom, a teacher and administrator, echoes Roger's and Tricia's experience. "Going in I was surprisingly fearful!" he recalls. "But as I did my first couple of impromptu speeches, as I saw myself on video and got feedback from the group and from the trainers, it wasn't intimidating anymore. Coming out, I felt I had the tools and the confidence not only to be a better speaker but a better leader. I do a lot of communicating in meetings, small groups, and team settings as well as in front of large groups, and the things I learned have made me more effective and confident in *all* those settings."

"*He who risks nothing need hope for nothing.*"

FRIEDRICH SCHILLER, from his play *Don Carlos.*

Too many live lives of "quiet desperation," continually waiting and hoping for something good to happen to them, while at the same time being too timid, too bound to their cozy comfort zones to move out and take a *risk*. The sad thing is they will receive nothing for their efforts—for they have made no effort.

Clearly, the risk is worth it. The rewards are great.

My goal in this book has been to challenge you. To affect you. To encourage the effort. To change your outlook on what communications is really all about, and show you how to use the First Brain to transform your own personal communications. Transform is a big word, but I know you can do exactly that, because I did.

About fifteen years ago I reached a nadir of my own. I had my own film company, but some of our hoped-for triumphs had dissipated into disappointing box office, and contracts for documentaries were slim. I had to face the fact that I wasn't successful, and I had to regroup and reconsider. It wasn't the first time that things were gloomy, but it was the first time that I set some goals. Real goals—goals that I wrote down. And the first time that I decided to take some risks. Real risks. Personal risks.

One of the goals was "to be able to get up anytime and speak with confidence." It was almost too much to hope for—to be able to get up at the spur of the moment and be able to talk in any situation and do it fairly well without fearing it worse than death. But that was my goal. And I made that goal, but only by committing to *do it. By risking.*

I spoke at every opportunity. I joined speaking clubs. I did courses. I worked on *my own behavior*. For the first time I stopped hiding behind the camera—I had always directed others on how act in front of the camera, under pressure—now it was time to learn it myself. And *eureka*! It worked. And in the process I began to learn much of what led to this book.

And with that speaking commitment my other goals were met too. On the professional side I reached my *written down goal* of a certain level of income. In one year. And on the personal side I reached my goal of honoring a renewed commitment to my family. Immediately.

The amazing thing is that none of this really took more work. Just the commitment to do it. Just the willingness to risk.

Conscious Steps for Growth

I have made that transformation. And so can you. Here are eight steps that transformed my communications. Do these eight things and within one year you will be amazed at the changes in *your* personal impact. And in your life.

1. Think First Brain! Absorb the First Brain concept, even if you find it hard to accept initially. It is the lens through which you should look at all your communicating opportunities. It works. It's true. It will transform the way you communicate.

2. Know Your Strengths and Weaknesses. Watch yourself on video, then grade yourself in each of the skill areas. Or have a friend observe you and assess you in those areas. Acknowledge strengths, and then give special attention to the weakest areas in your behavioral skills.

3. Focus on One Skill at a Time. Don't try to completely make yourself over all at once. Be like the juggler, who starts learning with one ball at a time. He then adds another, and another—until he can juggle four or five at once. You add singly to your many-faceted repertoire of skills.

4. Speak at Every Opportunity. At meetings, at social engagements, at every encounter with people, formal and informal. Determine your POV and state it. Practice. Gain mastery and you will gain confidence.

5. Get Feedback every chance you get. Have a friend or colleague critique you with the Three-by-Three rule. In fact, enter into a mutual agreement with that friend or colleague that you will both work on the principles in this book, critique each other, and support each other as you learn and grow.

6. See Yourself on Videotape as often as possible. This is essential for objective feedback. It is a new age for personal impact in our communications because of the breakthroughs in videotape technology. This is no longer home movies. Its portability and immediate access provide for the first time the ability to see ourselves as others see us. That is a profound experience.

7. Take Risks. Live the adventure of human growth, of reaching for the farthest limits of your potential.

8. Just Do It!

Let me leave you with one final thought. It's a truth I discovered at my low point fifteen years ago when I first set my goals about speaking. I've used this thought and said it so much that it's become an adage with which we close every Decker Communications workshop. It seems only fitting to close this book in the same manner:

"Each time we ask more of ourselves than we think we are able to give, and then manage to give it, we grow."

For more information on Bert Decker and Decker products, seminars, and speaking availability, call toll free:

800–547–0050

Or contact your local Decker office in:

Chicago	New York
Los Angeles	Newport Beach
New Jersey	San Francisco
	Sunnyvale

Corporate Headquarters:

Decker Communications, Inc.
44 Montgomery Street
San Francisco, CA 94104

415–391–5544

Endnotes

Introduction

Page xv: Quotes and sales figures on General Schwarzkopf are from *U.S. News & World Report*, 5/27/91, *USA Today*, 6/24/91, and *Time*, 7/8/91.

Chapter 1

Page 4: Quotes on Bush and Dukakis are from *Time*, 11/21/88, p. 27, and *Time*, 2/29/88, pp. 44–45.

Page 5: Quotes in sidebar "The Man Who Seals off Emotion" from *Newsweek*, 7/25/88, p. 25, and *Time*, 2/29/88, pp. 44–45.

Page 9: Michael Jordan heads the list, but close behind at #4 is Magic Johnson. This is the first time that two basketball players have been at the top of the endorsement dollar, and largely because they are both attractive, articulate, and First Brain friendly. Source is *Sports Marketing Letter*, 6/25/91 in *USA Today*, 6/25/91.

Page 9: From *The Washington Post*, 8/22/87.

Page 12: Quotes used in the sidebar "A Combustible Character in the Coolest of Mediums" are from *Time*, 2/8/88, pp. 16–17, 24–26.

Chapter 2

Page 17: The best definition I've found of the preconscious comes from *Webster's Ninth New Collegiate Dictionary*.

Page 20: John Kennedy's quote and some of the source material on the debates are from Theodore White, *The Making of the President 1960* (NY: Atheneum Press, 1961), p. 294.

Page 22: This information on Nixon's attention to detail, and the quotes in the following sidebar "Dissecting the Nixon Debacle," are from Fawn M. Brodie; *Richard Nixon: The Shaping of His Character* (NY: W. W. Norton & Co., 1981) pp. 421 and 427.

Chapter 3

Page 38: From *Business Week*, 5/20/91.

Page 40–42: The quote here and the information in the following sidebar "The New

Communicator as Corporate Pitch Man" are from Maynard M. Gordon, *The Iacocca Management Technique* (NY: Dodd, Mead & Co., 1985), pp. 76, 115, 134–135.

Chapter 4

Page 47: Details and quotes on Katie Couric's rapid rise to prominence came from stories in *People*, 4/22/91, and *USA Today*, 4/5/91.

Page 48: Detailed discussion of the brain causes some people to go "brain dead," so I chose to put just the basic explanation of the First Brain in the text. Yet I feel this concept is so important that it needs more detailed attention here, and actually much greater amplification and study even beyond its application to communications.

After reading hundreds of books and papers on brain research, I conclude that in the last twenty-five years there has been perhaps a ten-fold increase in the knowledge of the brain. And we *do* know a lot about the anatomy of the brain.

Yet it is evident we are still in our infancy in knowing the *behavior* of how this phenomenal mechanism actually works. No one has actually seen the neuronal network operate as a man or woman thinks. Even more so, no one has seen the interweavings of the immensely complex *parts* of the different brain systems. We don't know exactly how it works—we just know that it *does* work.

But we have good guesses and improving theories. Brain researchers agree that human beings have a basic "triune" brain, consisting of:

1. The brain stem and reticular activating system (reptilian brain).
2. The limbic system (mammalian brain).
3. The cerebral cortex.

I have placed the first two "brains," the most primitive ones, into a single category that I call First Brain. The reason is simple—they are complementary in dealing with emotion and reaction to emotion. Scientists and researchers generally agree that they both work similarly, and very powerfully, in directing our behavior at an unconscious level. They are also neglected by the general public and have been traditionally deemed unworthy. That is changing. "Scientists were preoccupied with thinking, not emotion. Rational thought, after all, was the faculty deemed by the English philosopher Francis Bacon 'the last creature of God.' " (*U.S.News and World Report*, 6/24/91 issue featuring "Where Emotions Come From.") To join these emotion related systems together brings their importance into focus.

The New Brain then is the cerebral cortex—the most sophisticated part of our brain, and it is conscious where the other two are not. It is also the most well-known and emphasized, and yet it *is* only one part of our whole brain makeup.

Today scientists "are rejecting the notion of a human being as simply a 'thinking machine,' seeing human beings instead as biological organisms whose survival depends upon constant interaction with the environment. Emotions, far from being 'trivial,' contain, as one expert put it, 'the wisdom of the ages'—warning us of danger, guiding us toward what is good and satisfying, signaling our intentions and our reactions to others. Emotions are the most familiar—and the most intimate—aspect of human experience, and they are gradually yielding their secrets.

"It was only in the late 1950s that researchers were identifying specific brain regions that seemed to play a central role in emotion. But only in the last few years have high-tech brain scanners, new methods of staining cells, powerful computers and other developments allowed scientists to begin systematically mapping the highways and traffic patterns of the emotional brain." (*U.S. News & World Report*, 6/24/91)

Page 49: Some additional details on the physical makeup of the First Brain:

THE BRAIN WITHIN A BRAIN

Your First Brain is a kind of "brain within a brain." In fact, it actually is two brains within a brain. The components of your First Brain include:

- The brainstem—often called the "reptilian brain," because it looks and functions roughly like the entire brain of a reptile. Your brainstem is embedded deeply in the base and core of your brain. It's main purpose is keeping you alive—regulating your heart, lungs, and other vital organs, as well as your sleep cycle. It contains the Reticular Activating System (RAS) that is responsible for alertness, and consists of a network of cells designed for the rapid spread of excitation throughout the whole brain. The RAS is critical to the "fight or flight" response discussed in Chapter 8. It's the oldest and most primitive part of you, having developed more than half a billion years ago.
- The limbic system—often called the "old mammalian brain," because it is nonexistent in reptiles, and was first seen in mammals between 200 and 300 million years ago. This region in the center of the brain is the seat of human emotion. Drawing on studies of both animals and humans, researchers have succeeded in mapping specific control centers for emotions. They have even learned to stimulate pleasure, sexual desire, anger, aggression, elation, depression, and fear in animal subjects by surgically probing these centers. These emotions were originally part of the hard-wired survival programs of reptile and early mammal brains. These survival programs, which are common to all mammals, including you and me, are hunger, thirst, danger ("fight or flight response"), sex, and parental care.

Then comes the cerebrum—with its thin sheath of cerebral cortex, topping and surrounding the brainstem and limbic system. It is this thin layer of cerebral cortex—the New Brain—that has produced our civilization, science, technology, industry, art, music, literature, and economy—in short, everything from the propeller beanie to the space shuttle.

But it is the animal-like First Brain that produces our passions, that fuels our drives toward pleasure and survival, and that shapes our communication.

"Flared like a wishbone, the limbic system wraps around
the top of the brainstem. From its many structures arise
memory, pleasure, pain and the brain's ability to balance
the extremes of emotion."

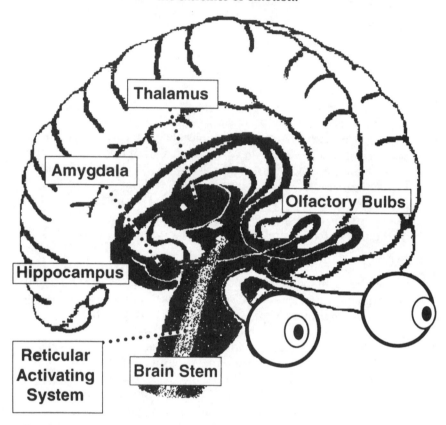

"Gatekeeper to consciousness, spark of the mind,
the reticular activating system connects with
major nerves in the spinal column and brain. It
sorts the 100 million impulses that assault the
brain each second, deflecting the trivial, letting
the vital through to alert the mind. "

From *THE BRAIN: Mystery of Matter and Mind*

HOW THE FIRST BRAIN PROCESSES INFORMATION

Your First Brain is loaded with an array of mechanisms that filter, modify, and channel incoming information. They work closely together, something like an unconscious team of the emotions. Although their intimate interweaving makes it difficult to see how each of them operate, scientists have thrown the bright light of research on the brain in recent years so we can begin to get an understanding of their separate functions.

The most basic mechanism is found in the core of the brain stem. It's called the reticular activating system (RAS), and it works something like a telephone bell, signaling the New Brain that sensory input is on its way. When an unexpected sound or a flutter of motion suddenly attracts your attention, it's because this system in your brain stem has fired a signal (the nonverbal equivalent of "Hey!") to your New Brain. When you, as a speaker, use surprise, sound, motion, or energy to get and keep your listener's attention, you are ringing this "telephone bell" in your listener's head. You are reaching the First Brain.

The main information processing system within the First Brain is the limbic system, a collection of structures located deep in the center of the brain. The limbic system encompasses sensory input. One example: Have you ever had an immediate and strong emotional response when you first caught the smell of the forest floor, or of baking bread or cookies, or the salt spray of the ocean, or a fragrant perfume? Although your New Brain will later figure out *where* the feeling comes from (often housed deep within your memory), it was the olfactory bulbs of the limbic system that gave you that emotional reaction even before you became conscious of *why* you felt it. (Smell and the sound of music both appear to be another language of the First Brain, often triggering immediate emotional response.) Scientists now believe that the limbic area is not only the center of emotional stimulus, but is the main switching station for all sensory input. It determines what sensory input is passed on to the New Brain for analysis and decision-making— and what input is filtered out and ignored. All the signals you give off when you speak (including your mannerisms, gestures, eye contact, inflection, and other nonverbal cues) pass through the limbic system for processing.

If these nonverbal cues convince the listener's limbic system you are friendly, your message gets a clear channel to the decision-making processes in your listener's New Brain. But if those cues suggest that you are an uncomfortable or threatening presence, the limbic system will alter or block your message.

(*cont. on page 284*)

Part of the limbic system is a structure called the thalamus, a kind of exchange where most of the major nerve pathways of the brain meet and mingle. Here, messages destined for different processing centers of the New Brain are routed, shunted, or blocked altogether. Just as all roads once led to Rome, nearly all nerve pathways in the brain lead to the thalamus. In many ways, the thalamus is like a central switchboard which ties all the far-flung reaches of the brain together into a single network.

Very recent research shows that the fingernail-size amygdala may play a greater role than previously thought. This almond shaped organ of the limbic system, housed deep in the temporal lobe, communicates directly with the thalamus and cortex, and works closely with the thalamus as a kind of "emotion central." New York University neuroscientist Joseph LeDoux found that the amygdala may make the first, crude judgment of an event's emotional significance, and then serve as a relay between the hippocampus and the cortex.

Another First Brain mechanism that is critically important to the communication process is the hippocampus, a tiny nub within the limbic system that makes memory vivid. Some scientists have likened the hippocampus to the "record" button on a VCR. Your brain receives many hundreds of sensory impressions every second. Most of these impressions are fleeting and quickly forgotten. But during a time of joy, triumph, tragedy, or danger, the hippocampus detects our elevated emotions and (figuratively) presses the "record" button, causing all incoming impressions to be recorded in the long-term storage centers of the New Brain.

A recent article in *The New York Times* (September 24, 1991) announced even newer research that shows the hippocampus also plays a role as the gatekeeper, linking various memory components in the cortex. This research also states that the amygdala works with the hippocampus in bringing emotion to memory. (Obviously brain research is moving fast, and we may not be certain of the exact links between thalamus, amygdala, and hippocampus, but we are certain that they all work in concert in the limbic system to control our memory and emotions.)

Because of the "record" function of the hippocampus, a highly emotional scene from a movie can stay with us for years; we can easily recall details from our wedding day, the birth of a child, or the death of a loved one. Even if we can't remember what we had for lunch last week, we can remember exactly where we were the day President Kennedy was shot or the day the space shuttle *Challenger* exploded.

Clearly, emotion is the key to making communication memorable. That's why, if you really want to get your message across and persuade

people, you have to make emotional contact with the listener. You
have to reach the First Brain. You have to press that "record" button
inside your listener's preconscious mind.

Chapter 5

Page 66: This quote is from *Fortune*, 6/3/91.

Chapter 6

Page 81: Although the visual research information came from many of the references listed
in the bibliography, one of the most valuable sources of this data was David Wolper's PBS
documentary *The Incredible Machine*.

Page 82: From research quoted in Zig Ziglar, *See You at the Top* (Gretna, LA: Pelican
Publishing Co., 1975), p. 85.

Page 83: There has been extensive research on the use of visual aids—providing overwhelmingly the impact of using visuals in all communication settings, particularly business presentations. In addition to Professor Albert Mehrabian's work, the data has been taken from studies
done at the University of Wisconsin, Wharton School of Business at the University of
Pennsylvania, University of Minnesota, 3M, and Harvard.

Page 84: Professor Albert Mehrabian is probably one of the most important communication
researchers working today. His study referenced here from his book *Silent Messages* is a
landmark study. Often misinterpreted, it does *not* mean that content is only worth seven
percent of a message, but that in an *inconsistent* message, content will only be believed seven
percent of the time when compared to the other vocal and visual signals. When there is
no inconsistency—when a communicator is excited, enthused, and confident—there is no
inconsistent message, and then this research is not applicable. The communicator and his
message are one.

Page 105–106: The quotes on Bill Parcells are from *USA Today*, 1/29/91 and 7/19/91.

Page 110: Here's an interesting aside on the smile and facial expression:

" 'YOUR FACE, MY THANE,

. . . is a book where men may read strange matters,' Lady Macbeth
warns her husband in Shakespeare's great tragedy, knowing that a
furrowed brow or a curled lip can be a revealing barometer of emotional
life. But it remained for psychologists, inspired by Silvan Tomkins, to
develop systematic ways to measure and compare the precisely tuned
movements of more than thirty facial muscles, and to link the language
of sneers, smiles, and grimaces to other aspects of emotion.

"The person who communicates his feelings is, of course, only half
the equation. In a complex social world, we are readers of emotion,
too. Using ever more sophisticated tools, researchers are beginning to
find out how the brain detects and analyzes emotional signals. Working

(*cont. on page 286*)

with monkeys, for example, neuroscientist Edmund Rolls and his colleagues at Oxford University have isolated a group of nerve cells, located in part of the brain's temporal lobe that processes visual information, that responds exclusively to faces and appears capable of recognizing individual faces as well. A second set of neurons, about two millimeters away, apparently helps determine which emotion a face displays. Together, Rolls says, the two sets of cells allow monkeys—and probably humans as well—to determine who and what they are dealing with in the environment.

"Neuroscientist Nancy Etcoff of MIT studied a brain injured patient who *could not* recognize faces, but who held a job and had no trouble conversing. Etcoff concluded, 'People who can't recognize facial emotions feel like they can't read between the lines, and there's a tremendous awkwardness in relating to other people.' "

(*U.S. News & World Report*, 6/24/91)

Chapter 7

Page 131: The opinions about Mario Cuomo were heard on "The Rush Limbaugh Show," March 18, 1991.

Page 131: From Robert S. McElvaine, *Mario Cuomo, A Biography* (NY: Charles Scribner's Sons, 1988), p. 350.

Page 145: Note also the relevance of this remark by Jonathan Winters to "paint word pictures" in the section of Chapter 8 on use of language (Skill #6). These quotes are from an article in *USA Today*, 2/26/91.

Chapter 8

Page 155: This oft-quoted list of fears can be found in *The Book of Lists*, ed. David Wallechinsky, et al. (NY: William Morrow, 1977), but the research was originally conducted and published by the Sunday *Times* of London, 10/7/73.

Chapter 9

Page 174–175: The story of Major James Nesmeth is paraphrased from *See You at the Top* by Zig Ziglar.

Chapter 10

Page 184: Pupil cues are only one of many fascinating behaviors that Desmond Morris explores in his excellent book, *Manwatching* (p. 169). This is a coffee table book that is worth having.

Page 186: The research by Max Gunther was done before he knew of the concept of the First Brain, yet they are very complementary. His ideas are used extensively in this discussion of intuition. His rational explanation of how "luck" works in *The Luck Factor* is quoted here (p. 125), and in the next several pages (pp. 133 and 136). This is a little gem of a book that is little known, and unfortunately now out of print.

Chapter 11

Page 204: I have drawn heavily on the methods of both Harville Hendrix (*Getting the Love You Want*) and Ellyn Bader and Pete Pearson (*In Quest of the Mythical Mate*), for some of the tips and techniques used in Feeling Listening.

Chapter 12

Page 217: My estimate of only five percent of executives/managers having had video feedback experience is based on all of the video feedback training programs available. I think it is actually much less than this, when you count the number of executives and managers in this country and count the number of people who have been trained. I have often stated verbally that it is about one percent, but for publication purposes did not want to be accused of exaggerating. Yet even if it is as much as five percent, it still is a very small figure.

Page 219–221: The Four Stages of Learning is now a common trainer's tool, but the origination has been attributed to the great psychologist Abraham Maslow.

Page 230: From Electronic Industries Association research, 1991, and *Entertainment Weekly*, 9/20/91.

Chapter 13

Page 245: From the Stanford University Graduate School of Business Study: Harrell & Alpert, March 1986.

Page 249–250: From a story on CEO David Johnson, *USA Today*, 3/13/91.

Chapter 14

Page 256: From that insightful and beautiful book by Robert Jastrow, *The Enchanted Loom* (NY: Simon & Schuster, 1981), p. 64.

Page 256: Tony Buzan has done extensive research and innovative application of how the mind works. His best book is *Use Both Sides of Your Brain*. The memorable analogy cited here is one of several on the fantastic capacity of the human brain.

Page 262: From John Carman's column in the *San Francisco Chronicle*, 3/26/91.

Chapter 15

Page 270: The original quote in the sidebar is from Dr. Norman Vincent Peale's book, *Positive Imaging* (NY: Fawcett Crest, 1985), p. 12.

The several other references I have made to Dr. Peale are from an interview we had at his New York offices on April 11, 1991.

Bibliography

Adams, James L. *Conceptual Blockbusting, Third Edition* (Menlo Park: Addison Wesley, 1986).

Ailes, Roger. *You Are the Message* (New York: Doubleday, 1988).

Albrecht, Karl. *Brain Power* (Englewood Cliffs, NJ: Prentice-Hall, Inc., 1980).

Arnheim, Rudolf. *Visual Thinking* (Berkeley, CA: University of California Press, 1969).

Autry, James. *Love & Profit* (New York: William Morrow, 1990).

Bader, Ellyn and Peter T. Pearson. *In Quest of the Mythical Mate* (New York: Brunner/Mazel, 1988).

Beier, Ernst and Evans Valens. *People-Reading* (New York: Stein and Day, 1975).

Birdwhistell, Ray. *Kinesics and Context* (Philadelphia, PA: University of Pennsylvania Press, 1970).

Buzan, Tony. *Make the Most of Your Mind* (New York: Linden Press/ Simon & Schuster, 1984).

——. *Use Both Sides of Your Brain* (New York: E. P. Dutton, 1974).

—— and Terence Dixon. *The Evolving Brain* (New York: Holt, Rinehart & Winston, 1978).

Calvin, William H. *The Cerebral Symphony* (New York: Bantam Books, 1990).

——. *The River that Flows Uphill: A Journey from the Big Bang to the Big Brain* (San Francisco: Sierra Club Books, 1986).

Covey, Stephen R. *Seven Habits of Highly Effective People* (New York: Simon & Schuster, 1989).

Davis, Flora. *Inside Intuition* (New York: McGraw-Hill, 1971).

Diagram Group. *The Brain* (New York: G. P. Putnam, 1982).

Edwards, Betty. *Drawing on the Right Side of the Brain* (Los Angeles, CA: Tarcher, 1979).

Ekman, Paul and Wallace Friesen. *Unmasking the Face* (Englewood Cliffs, NJ: Prentice-Hall, 1975).

Fast, Julius. *Body Language* (New York: Simon & Schuster, 1970).

Fincher, Jack. *The Brain: Mystery of Matter and Mind* (Washington, DC: U.S. News Books, 1981).

Gordon, Maynard M. *The Iacocca Management Technique* (New York: Dodd, Mead & Co., 1985).

Gregory, R. L. *Eye and Brain* (New York: McGraw-Hill, 1966).

——. *The Intelligent Eye* (New York: McGraw-Hill, 1970).

Gunther, Max. *The Luck Factor* (New York: Macmillan, 1977).

Hall, Edward T. *The Silent Language* (Greenwich, CT: Fawcett, 1959).

Hart, Leslie A. *How the Brain Works* (New York: Basic Books, Inc., Publishers, 1975).

Heinlein, Robert A. *Stranger in a Strange land* (New York: G. P. Putnam's Sons, 1961).
Hendrix, Harville. *Getting the Love You Want* (New York: Harper & Row, 1990).
Hilton, Jack. *On Television* (New York: Amacom, 1980).
Hodgson, John and Ernest Richards. *Improvisation* (New York: Grove Press, 1979).
Horney, Karen. *Neurosis and Human Growth: The Struggle Toward Self-Realization* (New York: W. W. Norton & Co., 1970).
————. *Our Inner Conflicts* (New York: W. W. Norton & Co., 1966).
Iacocca, Lee and William Novak. *Iacocca: An Autobiography* (New York: Bantam Books, 1984).
Jastrow, Robert. *The Enchanted Loom* (New York: Simon & Schuster, 1981).
Maltz, Maxwell. *Psycho-Cybernetics* (Englewood Cliffs, NJ: Prentice-Hall, 1960).
Mar, Timothy. *Face Reading* (New York: Dodd, Mead & Co., 1974).
Marsh, Peter. *Eye to Eye* (Topsfield, MA: Salem House, 1988).
Maslow, Abraham H. *Toward a Psychology of Being* (New York: Van Nostrand, 1968).
McKim, Robert. *Experiences in Visual Thinking* (Monterey, CA: Brooks/Cole Publishing, 1972).
Mehrabian, Albert. *Silent Messages* (Belmont, CA: Wadsworth Publishing Co., 1981).
Minsky, Marvin. *The Society of Mind* (New York: Simon & Schuster, 1988).
Molloy, John T. *Dress for Success* (New York: Warner, 1975).
Morris, Desmond. *Bodywatching* (New York: Crown Publishers, 1985).
————. *Manwatching* (New York: Harry N. Abrams, 1977).
Ornstein, Robert and Richard Thompson. *The Amazing Brain* (Boston, MA: Houghton Mifflin Company, 1986).
Peale, Norman Vincent. *Positive Imaging* (New York: Fawcett Crest, 1985).
Restak, Richard. *The Brain: The Last Frontier* (New York: Doubleday, 1979).
Rico, Gabriele Lusser. *Writing the Natural Way* (Los Angeles, CA: Tarcher, 1983).
Russell, Peter. *The Brain Book* (New York: E. P. Dutton, 1979).
Sagan, Carl. *The Dragons of Eden: Speculations on the Evolution of Human Intelligence* (New York: Random House, 1977).
Samuels, Mike and Nancy Samuels. *Seeing with the Mind's Eye* (New York: Random House, 1975).
Satir, Virginia. *Your Many Faces* (Millbrae, CA: Celestial Arts, 1978).
Schrank, Jeffrey. *Deception Detection* (Boston, MA: Beacon Press, 1975).
Segalowitz, Sidney J. *Two Sides of the Brain* (New York: Prentice Hall, 1983).
Spolin, Viola. *Improvisation for the Theater* (Evanston, IL: Northwestern University Press, 1983).
Springer, Sally and Georg Deutsch. *Left Brain, Right Brain* (San Francisco, CA: W. H. Freeman & Co., 1947).
Tannen, Deborah. *You Just Don't Understand* (New York: William Morrow, 1990).
von Oech, Roger. *A Whack on the Side of the Head* (New York: Warner Books, 1983).
Whiteside, Robert L. *Face Language* (New York: Simon & Schuster, 1974).
Willingham, Ron. *Integrity Selling* (New York: Doubleday & Company, Inc., 1987).
Wonder, Jacquelyn and Priscilla Donovan. *Whole Brain Thinking* (New York: William Morrow, 1984).
Ziglar, Zig. *See You at the Top* (Gretna, LA: Pelican Publishing, 1975).
Zimbardo, Philip. *Shyness* (Reading, MA: Addison Wesley, 1977).

Index